# First World War
## and Army of Occupation
# War Diary
## France, Belgium and Germany

### 16 DIVISION
Headquarters, Branches and Services
Royal Army Ordnance Corps
Deputy Assistant Director Ordnance Services
21 January 1916 - 28 February 1919

WO95/1961/2

The Naval & Military Press Ltd
www.nmarchive.com
**Published in association with The National Archives**

Published by

## The Naval & Military Press Ltd

Unit 10 Ridgewood Industrial Park,

Uckfield, East Sussex,

TN22 5QE England

Tel: +44 (0) 1825 749494

www.naval-military-press.com

www.nmarchive.com

*This diary has been reprinted in facsimile from the original. Any imperfections are inevitably reproduced and the quality may fall short of modern type and cartographic standards.*

© **Crown Copyright**
**Images reproduced by permission of The National Archives, London, England, 2015.**

# Contents

| Document type | Place/Title | Date From | Date To |
|---|---|---|---|
| Heading | WO95/1961. 16 Division Headquarters Branches & Services Dec 1915-Feb 1919 Deputy Assistant Director Ordnance Services | | |
| Heading | 16th Division D.A.D.O.S. Dec 1915-Feb 1919 | | |
| Heading | 16th Div. Vol I | | |
| War Diary | Amettes | 21/01/1916 | 01/02/1916 |
| War Diary | Busnes | 29/02/1916 | 29/02/1916 |
| War Diary | Nouex-Les-Mines | 02/04/1916 | 30/06/1916 |
| Heading | War Diary DADOS North Division 1st. July to 31st. July 1916. Volume No. 8 | | |
| War Diary | Nouex-Les-Mines | 01/07/1916 | 31/07/1916 |
| Heading | War Diary. DADOS 16th Division Month of August, 1916. Volume 9 | | |
| War Diary | Nouex-Les-Mines | 04/08/1916 | 25/08/1916 |
| War Diary | Raimbert | 26/08/1916 | 31/08/1916 |
| Heading | War Diary D.A.D.O.S. 16th Division For Month of September, 1916. Volume 10 | | |
| War Diary | Forked Tree | 01/09/1916 | 09/09/1916 |
| War Diary | Treux | 10/09/1916 | 10/09/1916 |
| War Diary | Corbie | 11/09/1916 | 21/09/1916 |
| War Diary | Westoutre | 22/09/1916 | 30/09/1916 |
| Heading | War Diary Month of October, 1916. Volume 11 Dados 16th Division. | | |
| War Diary | Westoutre | 01/10/1916 | 31/10/1916 |
| Heading | War Diary For Month Of November, 1916. Volume 12 D.A.D.O.S. 16th Division | | |
| War Diary | Westoutre | 01/11/1916 | 30/11/1916 |
| Heading | War Diary For Month Of December, 1916. Volume 13 D.A.D.O.S. 16th Division | | |
| War Diary | Westoutre | 01/12/1916 | 31/12/1916 |
| Heading | War Diary for month of January, 1917. Volume 14 DADOS 16th Division | | |
| War Diary | Westoutre | 01/01/1917 | 31/01/1917 |
| Heading | War Diary For Month of February, 1917. Volume 15 D.A.D.O.S. 16th Division | | |
| War Diary | Westoutre | 01/02/1917 | 28/02/1917 |
| Heading | War Diary For Month Of March, 1917. Volume 16 Unit. D.A.D.O.S. 16th Division. | | |
| War Diary | Westoutre | 01/03/1917 | 30/03/1917 |
| War Diary | Westoutre Locre | 31/03/1917 | 31/03/1917 |
| Heading | War Diary For Month of April, 1917. Volume 17 Unit. D.A.D.O.S. 16th Division. | | |
| War Diary | Locre | 01/04/1917 | 30/04/1917 |
| Heading | War Diary Volume 18 For Month Of May, 1917. Unit. D.A.D.O.S. 16th Division. | | |
| War Diary | Locre | 01/05/1917 | 31/05/1917 |
| Heading | War Diary For Month of June, 1917. Volume 19 Unit. D.A.D.O.S. 16th Division. | | |
| War Diary | Locre | 01/06/1917 | 12/06/1917 |
| War Diary | Locre Merris | 13/06/1917 | 19/06/1917 |

| | | | |
|---|---|---|---|
| War Diary | Godewaersvelde | 20/06/1917 | 22/06/1917 |
| War Diary | Zeggers Cappel | 23/06/1917 | 30/06/1917 |
| Heading | War Diary For Month of July, 1917. Volume 20 Unit. D.A.D.O.S. 16th Division. | | |
| War Diary | Zeggers Cappel | 01/07/1917 | 23/07/1917 |
| War Diary | Poperinghe | 24/07/1917 | 31/07/1917 |
| Heading | War Diary. For Month of August, 1917. Volume 21 Unit. D.A.D.O.S. 16th Division. | | |
| War Diary | Poperinghe | 01/08/1917 | 03/08/1917 |
| War Diary | Vlamertinge | 04/08/1917 | 17/08/1917 |
| War Diary | Watou | 18/08/1917 | 21/08/1917 |
| War Diary | Achiet Le Petit | 22/08/1917 | 27/08/1917 |
| War Diary | Boisleux au Mont | 28/08/1917 | 31/08/1917 |
| Heading | War Diary For Month of September, 1917. Volume 22 Unit. D.A.D.O.S. 16th Division. | | |
| War Diary | Boisleux au Mont | 01/09/1917 | 30/09/1917 |
| Heading | War Diary For Month of October, 1917. Unit. D.A.D.O.S. 16th Division. Volume Number 23 | | |
| War Diary | Boisleux-au-Mont | 01/10/1917 | 29/10/1917 |
| Heading | War Diary For Month Of November, 1917. Volume 24 Unit. D.A.D.O.S. 16th Division | | |
| War Diary | Boisleux-Au-Mont | 01/11/1917 | 19/11/1917 |
| War Diary | Ervillers | 20/11/1917 | 30/11/1917 |
| Heading | War Diary. For Month of December, 1917 Volume 25 Unit. D.A.D.O.S. 16th Division | | |
| War Diary | Ervillers | 01/12/1917 | 02/12/1917 |
| War Diary | Ytres | 03/12/1917 | 04/12/1917 |
| War Diary | Flamicourt | 05/12/1917 | 06/12/1917 |
| War Diary | Villers Faucon | 07/12/1917 | 31/12/1917 |
| Heading | War Diary For Month of January, 1918. Volume. 26 Unit. D.A.O.D.S. 16th Division | | |
| War Diary | Villers Faucon | 01/01/1918 | 31/01/1918 |
| Heading | War Diary For Month of February, 1918. Volume. 27 Unit. D.A.D.O.S. 16th Division | | |
| War Diary | Villers Faucon | 01/02/1918 | 21/03/1918 |
| War Diary | Perronne | 22/02/1918 | 22/02/1918 |
| War Diary | Cappy | 23/02/1918 | 25/02/1918 |
| War Diary | Lamotte En Santerre | 26/03/1918 | 26/03/1918 |
| War Diary | Hamel | 27/03/1918 | 27/03/1918 |
| War Diary | Fouilloy | 28/03/1918 | 03/04/1918 |
| War Diary | Saleux | 04/04/1918 | 04/04/1918 |
| War Diary | Cerisy | 05/04/1918 | 08/04/1918 |
| War Diary | Fauquembergues | 09/04/1918 | 09/04/1918 |
| War Diary | Wismes | 10/04/1918 | 10/04/1918 |
| War Diary | Vaudringhem | 11/04/1918 | 14/04/1918 |
| War Diary | Aire | 15/04/1918 | 30/04/1918 |
| War Diary | Aire-Sur-Lys | 01/05/1918 | 16/05/1918 |
| War Diary | Samer | 17/05/1918 | 18/06/1918 |
| War Diary | Aldershot | 18/06/1918 | 31/07/1918 |
| War Diary | Samer | 01/08/1918 | 18/08/1918 |
| War Diary | Monchy Cayeau | 19/08/1918 | 22/08/1918 |
| War Diary | Barlin | 23/08/1918 | 23/09/1918 |
| War Diary | Houchin | 24/09/1918 | 10/10/1918 |
| War Diary | Sailly Labourse | 11/10/1918 | 18/10/1918 |
| War Diary | Billy | 19/10/1918 | 19/10/1918 |
| War Diary | Phalempin | 20/10/1918 | 20/10/1918 |

| | | | |
|---|---|---|---|
| War Diary | Templeuve | 21/10/1913 | 09/11/1918 |
| War Diary | Taintignies | 10/11/1913 | 15/11/1918 |
| War Diary | Martinsart | 16/11/1913 | 29/11/1918 |
| War Diary | Avelin | 30/11/1918 | 28/02/1919 |

WO 95/1961
16 Division
Headquarters Branches & Services

Dec 1915 - Feb 1919

DEPUTY ASSISTANT DIRECTOR
ORDNANCE SERVICES

# 16TH DIVISION

D.A.D.O.S.
DEC 1915-FEB 1919

Stapo. 16⅔ Str:
_____
Bd. I

14.12.15 —
st. 7.16
i. 2.16

Dec '15
Feb '19

Army Form C. 2118

# WAR DIARY
## or
## INTELLIGENCE SUMMARY
(Erase heading not required.)

| Place | Date | Hour | Summary of Events and Information | Remarks and references to Appendices |
|---|---|---|---|---|
| AMETTES. | 21.12.16 | 4.30p. | Left BLACKDOWN (ALDERSHOT) on 14.12.15 at 7.30 a.m. and proceeded by motor car to FOLKESTONE in the company of the A.A.A. & Q.M.G. 16th Division & the Staff Captains of 47th & 48th Infantry Brigades. Embarked at FOLKESTONE about 2 p.m. reaching BOULOGNE between 4 & 5 p.m. Stopped at BOULOGNE for the night.<br><br>Left BOULOGNE at 10.10 a.m. and proceeded by road to IV Corps Hdqrs. via DRURES: THEROUANNE: AIRE: NORRENT FONTES: LILLERS: CHOQUES: and BETHUNE; and from IV Corps Hdqrs. to CHATEAU DE DROUVAIN, where Divisional Hdqrs. were to be.<br><br>The following days were spent in endeavouring to find a place suitable for the purposes of an Ordnance Office and Store. Sundry minor local purchases were made.<br><br>Great difficulty was experienced in finding a place suitable for a store with command of traffic on account of the congested state of the district arising from the transfer of troops billeted here. There was no building available as near refilling point as was desirable until No. 4. A.O.D. Travelling Workshop moved from GOSNAY. These premises were occupied on 28.12.15 for 1st Division Ordnance Services. | |

# WAR DIARY
## or
## INTELLIGENCE SUMMARY

Army Form C. 2118

| Place | Date | Hour | Summary of Events and Information | Remarks and references to Appendices |
|---|---|---|---|---|
| | 31.1.16 | | The Capt. Adjnt. ordered the evacuation of these premises & Divisional HdQrs. moved from BOMY to AMETTES but one compartment at 90 S NAY has been reserved for Reserve of hypo-pellets helmets. Store is now established at REL Y near refilling point but office remains at AMETTES. | |
| | 1.2.16 | | Work has been seriously handicapped throughout by (1) the distance of railhead (FOUQUEREUIL) from stores (2) scattered position of units; (3) distance of office from stores. The first difficulty remains. The second has been got over as far as possible by sending out convoys but the heavy loss of time and practically of the services of a warrant officer for 2 days. | |

T.S. Omond
Lieut.
for ADC 16ᵗʰ Division

# WAR DIARY
## INTELLIGENCE SUMMARY
*(Erase heading not required.)*

| Place | Date | Hour | Summary of Events and Information | Remarks and references to Appendices |
|---|---|---|---|---|
| BUSNES | 19.2.16 | 6 p.m. | Office too small for AHETTES to RELY. This made Ordnance and Canteen Stores accumulate very bad – in barns not thatched – they are cleared as far as possible. The Division moved home – at 1st Corps Recon. Area on 28th and Stores & Office has found its way at BUSNES. The best case and office we have found near 38 A.P.26a. The 49 bttalks Brigade and Divisional clothing has been issued. The demands for boots have not been so heavy owing to last halt. Initially, became habitual for to repair of boots has been regularly in advance to demands. It has had another to establish a divisional barriers' depot. As soon as the Division has settled down in a locality where proper facilities is the way of a building can be obtained.<br>J.S. Carter<br>DADOS 16th Division |  |

**Army Form C. 2118**

# WAR DIARY of I.D.A.D.O.S 16th (Mid.) Division
## or
## INTELLIGENCE SUMMARY
*(Erase heading not required.)*

| Place | Date | Hour | Summary of Events and Information | Remarks and references to Appendices |
|---|---|---|---|---|
| NOUEX-LES-<br>MINES | 24/4/16 | 6 p.m. | Offices & stores were moved from BUSNES to LILLERS on 10.3.16. D.I. were re-opened here in RUE D'AIRE. The Division remained in LILLERS until 27.3.16, when it moved to the 1st Corps Conle. Area — Head Quarters being accomm. at NOEUX LES MINES.<br><br>The Divisional Armourer Staff is now in working order — the following work has been carried out — 160 rifles have been overhauled & put into fuller order; 4 Penn. light M.G. equipped with 16 ground sighting sights each; 10 bicycles have been stored & issued; 2 Very pistols, 1 Lewis Gun & 1 Vic. rifle repld. Office has been opened. Report books ready for issue. Gun accessories & 1 Trench Mortar cleaned & overhauled. The 2nd 5th Lewis Guns Accessories & 1 Trench Mortar cleaned & overhauled. The 2nd & 5th have been carried out since 15.3.16. when Shops were opened.<br><br>Horse box arrived from HAVRE to CALAIS on 24.3.16. 1st horse box arrived from HAVRE to CALAIS on Night of 24.3.15. to CALAIS on Night of 24.3.15.<br><br>Stores have been coming to hand readily and no S.A.A. bullets have recent in his issue. Units are now in a position S.A.A. daily will be supplied by Divisional Rly. I than convoys are sent to Brand.<br><br>4 Lewis Machine Guns have been delivered by heirs & Crewing this care to Division Hand on the 27.3.15. These have been difficulty Gyn. Race in 48 hours. No 14 keviosfes are coming stand very slow — they are | |

1875 Wt. W 593/826 1,000,000 4/15 J.B.C. & A. A.D.S.S./Forms/C. 2118.

Army Form C. 2118

# WAR DIARY
## or
## INTELLIGENCE SUMMARY
*(Erase heading not required.)*

| Place | Date | Hour | Summary of Events and Information | Remarks and references to Appendices |
|---|---|---|---|---|
| 2/5 | | | Constantly knocked by hurts in to front line as they pefer his life of knowledge to any other but has been supplied. | |
| | 2.4.16. | | | |

J.C. Orrow
Captain
D.A.D.S. 16th Division

# WAR DIARY
## INTELLIGENCE SUMMARY
*(Erase heading not required.)*

Army Form C. 2118

DADOS 16A

Vol 4

| Place | Date | Hour | Summary of Events and Information | Remarks and references to Appendices |
|---|---|---|---|---|
| NOEUX-LES-MINES. | 3.5.15 | 6 p.m. | The Division remains in the line and during the greater part of the month of April demands for stores have considerably decreased. The Divisional Artillery has taken its place in the line and draws for stores Technical Artillery stores have come to hand very well. Convoy work has ceased entirely for the first line since the Division came out to the Country, and it is now concentrated as it has not been since it left BLACKDOWN. Trench mortars are in a constant need of repair. This is done whenever possible in the Divisional Armourers' Shop but serious damage to barrels necessitates despatch to No. 24. Ordnance Workshop at LA BEUVRIÈRE. The Armourers' Shop has been concentrated at the kiln carried on in April by the Divisional Commander. On 27th & 29th of last month the Germans made two gas attacks on the front line. Here too an immediate call for large numbers of gas helmets – 4000 have sent | |

| Place | Date | Hour | Summary of Events and Information | Remarks and references to Appendices |
|---|---|---|---|---|
| | | | Infantry
To each Brigade Headquarters on 27th – to meet emergencies. 10,000 Division Reserve of similar helmets P.H. helmet all remainder and to have supplied came up till practically no delay. No return, until Other Commanders have taken return & further hardenate new practically all returned before 15.4.16.

3.5.16

T. Owen
Capt.
A.D.D.S. 16E Division | |

Army Form C. 2118

D.A.D.O.S
16 D 23
Vol 5

# WAR DIARY
## or
## INTELLIGENCE SUMMARY
(Erase heading not required.)

| Place | Date | Hour | Summary of Events and Information | Remarks and references to Appendices |
|---|---|---|---|---|
| NOUEX-LES-MINES. | 3.6.16. | 3 p.m. | The Division remains in the line belonging to 1st CORPS LOOS SALIENT. There has been no recurrence of gas attacks since 27th & 29th April, and demands for anti-gas helmets have severely diminished. Demands for VERMOREL SPRAYERS continue - Many have been repaired in the Divisional Armourers' Shop. Whistles have been overhauled and are in the course of last month, and all Stokes still due or indents passed to 20th April have been hastened. The second batch of carrying anti-gas helmets has now been issued. It is of an improved type, large enough to carry on over anti- Frost helmet and goggles with ease. 8. 3" STOKES MORTARS have been supplied to the Division in May. Considerable difficulty was previously experienced in obtaining supplies of these Mortars but supply is now improving daily. During the first half 2 Lewis Guns have been destroyed by damaged by enemy Shell fire. The complete gun is kept available at the Base and demands are promptly met but there remains a certain amount of difficulty in regard to the | |

# WAR DIARY
## or
## INTELLIGENCE SUMMARY

Army Form C. 2118

| Place | Date | Hour | Summary of Events and Information | Remarks and references to Appendices |
|---|---|---|---|---|
| NOEUX-LES-MINES | 3.6.16 | 3pm continued. | Spare parts. Lewis Guns now for 96 R. Irish Fusiliers & 6th Connaught Rangers. One 18pr. gun had the reflector for C/182 Bde R.F.A. This is the first replacement of = the Ordnance that has had the made. the gun only was required. The following are some of the principal items of work carried out in the Divisional Armourers' Staff :— <br><br>Rifles repaired etc. 3872 <br>Cycles " 110 <br>Stretchers " 70 <br>Vermorel Sprayers " 15. <br>Lewis Guns " 13. <br><br>On 21st May 2 shells fell outside the Office — one burst underneath the other smashed all the windows — but did no other damage. <br><br>/S. Omond <br>Captain <br>D.A.D.O.S. 16th Division <br><br>※ 3-6-16. | |

# WAR DIARY

## INTELLIGENCE SUMMARY

Army Form C. 2118

DADOS 16 of 3
Vol 6

| Place | Date | Hour | Summary of Events and Information | Remarks and references to Appendices |
|---|---|---|---|---|
| NOEUX-LES-MINES. | 6.6.16 | 4.15pm | 8th MUNSTER FUSILIERS reported one Lewis Gun entrayed on 2nd inst, and 8th R. Irish Fusiliers one on 3rd inst. R.S.R. of the Rest Guns in replacement were received on 5th inst. | |
| | | | 2 3" STOKES TRENCH MORTARS have been received on 5.6.15. and Nos 6-47/2 & 49/1 - These have brought the total number of 3" STOKES in possession of the Division up to Sixteen, 15 are in Action while one is kept with the Role. in reserve for instructional purposes. The Division also has 14 3.7" Trench Mortars. | |
| | 8.6.16 | 3pm | Division completed this day with New Respirators. An Original Frame. | |
| | | | D.A.D.O.S. 1st Army inspected the Office etc. 6 days accompanied by R.A.D.O.S. 1st Corps. | |
| | 10.6.16 | 9.15pm | C.O.O. CALAIS BASE and D.A.D.O.S. 1st Army visited Office, store, workshop and Divisional Ordnance Staff today. | |
| | 13.6.16 | 10pm | A Battery 77th Bde R.F.A. and A Bty 180 Bde R.F.A. each had one gun condemned today. | |

# WAR DIARY
## INTELLIGENCE SUMMARY
(Erase heading not required.)

Army Form C. 2118

Instructions regarding War Diaries and Intelligence Summaries are contained in F.S. Regs., Part II. and the Staff Manual respectively. Title Pages will be prepared in manuscript.

| Place | Date | Hour | Summary of Events and Information | Remarks and references to Appendices |
|---|---|---|---|---|
| NOEUX-LES-MINES | 15.6.16 | 2 p.m. | J.O.M. conferred re 4.5" Howitzers in charge of 2 Bty. 77 Brigade R.F.A. | |
| | 17.6.16 | 2 p.m. | 8 3-inch STOKES Trench Mortars received to-day. Issue of Box Respirators: | |
| | | | K helmets P.H.G. Carfleters:- | |
| | | | Infantry Bns – 52 – each   R.A. H.Q. – 50. each | |
| | | | " Bde. H.Q. – 10  "         R.A. Bde. – 10.  " | |
| | | | Bde. M.G. Coys. – 150. "   T.M. Bty. – 25.  " | |
| | | | Divl. Signal Coy. – 210. "  F.A.'s – 10  " | |
| | 18.6.16 | 2 p.m. | Distribution of 8 3" STOKES received yesterday:- 476 Bde. 3. 485 – 1. 486 4. | |
| | 20.6.16 | 2 p.m. | 1 Lewis Gun belonging to the Indian Frontier Force beyond repair in Divisional Armourers shop. | |
| | 22.6.16 | 2 p.m. | 4 two-inch Trench Mortars received from Ordnance Officer, 1st Corps Traffic, for X/16 Trench Mortar Battery. Thus completes the Divisional Medium Batteries in 2-inch. | |
| | | | New Lewis Gun issued to 9th Batn. Fusiliers. | |
| | | | Divisional Gas Officer commenced an examination of 12,000 Divisional Reserve of anti-gas helmets. | |

# WAR DIARY
## or
## INTELLIGENCE SUMMARY

*(Erase heading not required.)*

Army Form C. 2118

| Place | Date | Hour | Summary of Events and Information | Remarks and references to Appendices |
|---|---|---|---|---|
| NOEUX LES MINES | 23.6.16 | 2 pm | 2 Watt STOKES received from O.O. 1st Corps. Troops on trams and returned to 47th Rly. ie. Right Rte - in the LOOS SECTOR. | |
| | 27.6.16 | 6.30 pm | The intervening days have been quiet & nothing of note has occurred. 7th LEINSTERS reported loss of one LEWIS GUN. | |
| | | 10 pm | Authority received to demand 26 new LEWIS GUNS from HAVRE BASE & complete Bns. to 16 per. Bn. Box respirators issued P.A.G. Helmets also removable from CALAIS to scale for Bns. viz 6 hearts Gas 12 4 C. Lieut. Rodd injured. Arrival Returnees Coff | |
| | 28.6.16 | 6.24 pm | 2 3" STOKES received this morning to complete Division to 24 3" STOKES MORTARS. | |
| | | | 9 LEWIS GUNS & 9 F.R. Dismantling Trainers front Bergent Affair, and a list Gun demanded | |
| | 29.6.16 | 11 am | Lewis Guns for 7th Leinsters received - 5 15th T.M. handed over to 1st Army Stores. 9 Frank Mortars, ST. VENANT. 9 LEWIS GUNS received from 7th R. Irish Fusiliers | |

1875 Wt. W593/826 1,000,000 4/15 J.B.C. & A. A.D.S.S./Forms/C.2118.

# WAR DIARY
## INTELLIGENCE SUMMARY
*(Erase heading not required.)*

Army Form C. 2118

| Place | Date | Hour | Summary of Events and Information | Remarks and references to Appendices |
|---|---|---|---|---|
| NOEUX-LES-MINES. | 29.4.16 | cont'd | It is presumably a gun which was reported lost during gas attack of 27th and 29th April. The gun is in good condition. It has been issued to the R. Munster Fusiliers in exchange for one which is reported the working badly. The latter gun will be sent to Armourer's Shop to-morrow. Heavy Siegecraft issued for Guns which have been affirmed by 9.R.D. & A.R.O.S. but not issued in Stocks have not been received in this country. It would appear the issue of 9.R.D. etc. are littlest until there are a definite prospect of an issue being made. This, of course, applies to stores for which provision can be made of the issue in bulk. | |
| | 30.4.16 | 9 am. | News gun for 8th Dinwiddies Fusiliers received this morning. There is a tendency to their Divisional Ordnance Staff into a sort of organisation instead of passers only. Knife Shall remain the seat of the Railhead Ordnance Staff. He is particularly interested in connection with the return of Pat clothing and has excelled in the hopping of muncle recoils & practically helpers and in the last before last over 100 letter had the written - and O.C. etc. in the French troubled with correspondence. Moreover to take up a considerable about of the staff's time which would be better employed on looking after the arms clothing equipments of the troops. Police have leading will | |

Army Form C. 2118

# WAR DIARY
## INTELLIGENCE SUMMARY
*(Erase heading not required.)*

Instructions regarding War Diaries and Intelligence Summaries are contained in F.S. Regs., Part II. and the Staff Manual respectively. Title Pages will be prepared in manuscript.

| Place | Date | Hour | Summary of Events and Information | Remarks and references to Appendices |
|---|---|---|---|---|
| NOEUX-LES-MINES | 30.6.16 | 9 a.m. | Order which troops are flying the 2nd of July. | |

2/6.

J.S. Moore
Captain
D.A.D.O.S. 16th Division

WAR DIARY

DADOS

16th Division

1st. July to 31st. July 1916.

VOLUME No. 8

Army Form C. 2118

# WAR DIARY
## INTELLIGENCE SUMMARY
*(Erase heading not required.)*

Instructions regarding War Diaries and Intelligence Summaries are contained in F.S. Regs., Part II. and the Staff Manual respectively. Title Pages will be prepared in manuscript.

| Place | Date | Hour | Summary of Events and Information | Remarks and references to Appendices |
|---|---|---|---|---|
| NOEUX-LES-MINES | 1.7.16 | 6pm | The following expenditure of trench mortar ammunition of Bn. Counted out in Divisional Ammunition Dump during the Month of June:— Grizzlies — expended & redrawn — 113. Rifles — inspected & repaired (where necessary) 2968. Trench mortars — repaired — 19. Vermorel Sprayers — " — 57. Picks — " — 67. Trench Levers — Cleaned, taken down & overhauled — 38. Periscopes — — 29. Petrol tins for carrying water filled — 428. 2 two inch Trench Mortars were discharged by Rest fire to-day. Two will be drawn from Reserve in charge of O.D. I Coy Troops — and 2 have been arranged from the Base. | |
| | 2.7.16 | 10pm | 26 Lewis Guns received to complete the Division to six per Bn. | |
| | 3.7.16 | 5pm | 3" STOKES Mortar demanded from BASE for 176 Bde. T.M. Bty. — It replaces one condemned — | |

1375 Wt. W393/825 1,000,000 4/15 J.B.C. & A. A.D.S.S./Forms/C. 2118.

Army Form C. 2118

# WAR DIARY
## or
## INTELLIGENCE SUMMARY
(Erase heading not required.)

Instructions regarding War Diaries and Intelligence Summaries are contained in F. S. Regs., Part II. and the Staff Manual respectively. Title Pages will be prepared in manuscript.

| Place | Date | Hour | Summary of Events and Information | Remarks and references to Appendices |
|---|---|---|---|---|
| | 7/9/16 | 10 am | New 3" STOKES MORTAR dismounted on 5.7.16 received M'bag and issued to 47 T.M.B. | |
| | 8/9/16 | 6 pm | Magazines received to complete 2 new LEWIS GUNS per Bn. & a scale of 64 per LEWIS GUN. | |
| | 11.7.16 | 6 pm | R.A. units to receive the following together:- R.A.H.Q. 2 - R.A. Bde Hq. - 2 and 2 per Bty - a total of 42 Engcbos - Harris & Saddlery to withdraw & Saddlery sent to the R.A.C.F. | |
| | 12.7.16 | 6 pm | # 1 Ordnance Q.F. 18 pr. enclosures by I.O.M. Spollin cedah Belaying & R.Hy. 182 Bde. R.F.A. for damage caused by a puncture - New pan received from to R.A.O.F. | |
| | 15.7.16 | 6 pm | # Ordnance Q.F. 18 pr. Received on 12 hr. for R/182 Bde. received and sent to No 24 Ordnance Workshop, LA BEUVRIÈRE. Two # Ordnance complete with Carriages, Ammunition Limbers etc. Received and issued to A & R. Btys. 182 Bde R.F.A. | |

# WAR DIARY or INTELLIGENCE SUMMARY

Army Form C. 2118

(Erase heading not required.)

| Place | Date | Hour | Summary of Events and Information | Remarks and references to Appendices |
|---|---|---|---|---|
| NOUEX-LES-MINES | Contd. 15-7-16 | | The C.I.S.A. and A.D.O.S. 1st Army inspected Armourers' Shops today. | |
| | 18.7.16 | 5pm | One Lewis Gun demanded for 7/R Innskilling Fusiliers to replace one reported destroyed by enemy fire. | |
| | 20.7.16 | 6pm | Lewis Gun demanded on 18.7.16 - received and issued | |
| | 25.7.16 | 5.45pm | One Lewis Gun for 85 Inniskilling Fusiliers and one for 6B CONNAUGHT RANGERS demanded. One 2nd Trench Mortar belonging 5/RB Contexments & D.A.H. No.24 Ordnance workshop - a new one drawn from O.O. I Corps Troops. In this case found only required. | |
| | 27.7.16 | 10am | Lewis Guns demanded on 25.7. last received and issued | |
| | 29.7.16 | 4pm | A Lewis Gun belonging to 7/R LEINSTER REGT. found beyond repair in the Armourers' Shops and a new one subsequently demanded. | |

**Army Form C. 2118**

# WAR DIARY
## or
## INTELLIGENCE SUMMARY

(Erase heading not required.)

Instructions regarding War Diaries and Intelligence Summaries are contained in F.S. Regs., Part II. and the Staff Manual respectively. Title Pages will be prepared in manuscript.

| Place | Date | Hour | Summary of Events and Information | Remarks and references to Appendices |
|---|---|---|---|---|
| NOEUX-LES-MINES | 30/7/16 | 5 pm | Base wire that no LEWIS GUN is available for issue to 7th LEINSTER REGT. Applied accordingly to D.H.Q. 47th Infantry Brigade will carry on without any further action being taken. | |
| | 31.7.16 | 10 pm | There is nothing to note for to-day. Local purchase has been less this month — it is presumably because many of the demands of units have been met down to certain extraneous things like trousers suit for clerk entries and so on. This should be increasingly so especially as supplies from the BASE coming up with practically unfailing regularity. Approximately 145 to 150 tons of stores are obtained & issued to units from the BASE | |

J.S. Dunne
Captain
D.A.D.O.S. 16th Division.

Vol 8

WAR DIARY.

D.A.D.O.S. 16th Division

MONTH OF AUGUST, 1916.

VOLUME:- 9.

# WAR DIARY

## INTELLIGENCE SUMMARY

Army Form C. 2118

Instructions regarding War Diaries and Intelligence Summaries are contained in F. S. Regs., Part II. and Staff Manual respectively. Title Pages will be prepared in manuscript.

| Place | Date | Hour | Summary of Events and Information | Remarks and references to Appendices |
|---|---|---|---|---|
| NOEUX-LES-MINES | 4-8-16 | 6pm | The LEWIS GUN demanded on 29th July from 7th LEINSTER REGT. was received to-day. This gun has been the longest than any other gun ever demanded. There has apparently a shortage at the Base. Altho' moment of putting there are 4 2inch Trench Mortars out of action. One has been condemned by the I.O.M. and 3 are under repair at his workshop. The principal source of weakness is in the Breech mechanism. | |
|  | 5-8-16 | 9.15pm | Another LEWIS GUN for 7th R. Innis. killing Facilities demanded to replace one destroyed by enemy fire. | |
|  | 7-8-16 | 10.30am | LEWIS GUN demanded on 5th received this morning. | |
|  | 9-8-16 | 3pm | A.D.O.S. I Corps inspected the fuel line transport of 9 H Q 47 & and 48th Infantry Brigades. The principal point brought to notice was the |  |

# WAR DIARY / INTELLIGENCE SUMMARY

Army Form C. 2118

| Place | Date | Hour | Summary of Events and Information | Remarks and references to Appendices |
|---|---|---|---|---|
| | 9/8/16 | Contd. | want of proper breaking-up of sheds — also the completion of the fixing of strengthened hangers for hooks of G.S. limbers wagons and certain minor alterations to the Travelling Kitchens. | |
| | 10-8-16 | 16.30 p.m. | A tentative hear scheme for dealing with Salvage Stores circulated from Corps H.Q. It is laid down that the ADOS of a Division is to be responsible for looking after A.S.C., Medical and Veterinary Salvage Stores — and to account for them. It is again part of the tendency referred to in War Diary for 30-6-16 — viz. to make the Divisional Ordnance Officer responsible for receipt back and not the actual requirements of the troops. It will be necessary for the ADO.S. in the matter. | |
| | 11-8-16 | noon | A.H.Q. agreed to modification of the Corps Salvage Scheme so far as the Division is concerned — the D.A.D.O.S. is only to deal with Ordnance stores and to leave other supplies alone. | |

# WAR DIARY
## or
## INTELLIGENCE SUMMARY
(Erase heading not required.)

Army Form C. 2118

Instructions regarding War Diaries and Intelligence Summaries are contained in F.S. Regs., Part II. and the Staff Manual respectively. Title Pages will be prepared in manuscript.

| Place | Date | Hour | Summary of Events and Information | Remarks and references to Appendices |
|---|---|---|---|---|
| NOEUX-LES-MINES | 14/2/16 | 2pm | A.D.C. I Corps inspected the transport of 49th Infantry Brigade and No 5, 112th & 113th Field Ambulances. | |
| | 18/2/16 | 3.30p | D.O.R. Southern Section. I Army concerned one Ordnance Q.F. 18pr. (gun subs) belonging to B/182 Bde. R.F.A. for premature. | |
| | 19/2/16 | noon | Inspection of Train Wagons attached to R.A. units by D.O.R. No. 24 Workshop. | |
| | 20/2/16 | 10am | D.Q.T. 10pr recovered on 17-2-16 received today and issued to D.A.T. No. 24 Workshop. Copy of letter received from A.D.O.S I Corps stating that A.D.C. A.S.C. & D.D.V.S. between Armies taking place. No arrangements or information given as to how Ordnance in a Division are to much Returns. A letter sent to A.D.O.S I Corps raising the question of transport of office effects, reserve of gun helmets etc. | |

# WAR DIARY
## INTELLIGENCE SUMMARY

*(Erase heading not required.)*

Army Form C. 2118

| Place | Date | Hour | Summary of Events and Information | Remarks and references to Appendices |
|---|---|---|---|---|
| NOOEK-LES-MINES | 22/8/16 | 9.30pm | Fire intended by a trove Gun by A.A. & g.M.G. Unsuccessfully at 7.30pm to-night. No other details available. | |
| | 23/8/16 | 5.45pm | 1 Vickers Gun for 49th D.9. Coy. and 1 LEWIS GUN for the Middlesex Faciers demanded. The VICKERS could have been spared if it had not been necessary to close down the Divisional Armourers Shop in consequence of the move. | |
| | 24/8/16 | 10pm | Approximately 2 tons of stores returned to Railhead on closing down. | |
| | 25/8/16 | 11am | Armourers returned from Bus. this afternoon. | |
| RAIMBERT | 26/8/16 | 5pm | D.H.Q. moved this day to RAIMBERT. One LEWIS GUN and one VICKERS received and issued. | |
| | 27/8/16 | noon | Saw A.D.O.S. 1st Army, at LILLERS. He said that from a Departmental point of view he was quite satisfied with him but say his Ordnance could not then have ever had been carried out. | |

Army Form C. 2118

# WAR DIARY
## or
## INTELLIGENCE SUMMARY
*(Erase heading not required.)*

Instructions regarding War Diaries and Intelligence Summaries are contained in F.S. Regs., Part II. and the Staff Manual respectively. Title Pages will be prepared in manuscript.

| Place | Date | Hour | Summary of Events and Information | Remarks and references to Appendices |
|---|---|---|---|---|
| | 27.8.16 | contd. | Transport arrangements concluded. Divisional Reserve of 9 in. Helmets to proceed S. road for NOEUX starting at 8 am in 4 lorries from the A.S.P. Unit certain details of A.O.C. to be in charge — the 20CC to proceed by train in Off. g. train from CHOCQUES on 29th inst. | |
| | 28.8.16 | 9 pm | Authority received to demand 2 more Lewis guns per Bn. Bringing scale up to 8 per Bn: also 12 hand carts per Bn - for LEWIS GUNS. Demanded these from HAVRE BASE. | |
| | 30.8.16 | noon | Entrained yesterday at CHOCQUES at 4.12 pm and detrained at LONGEAU for CORBIE at 2 am — Got men out and men into billets at 4.15 am. Visited A.D.O.S. XIV Corps in the afternoon. | |
| | 31.8.16 | 6 pm | Moved to Forbal Tree Camp on the MÉAULTE-BRAY-sur-SOMME road. Office and stores contained only rail covers. | |

V.E. Amos Captain
Ad. D.O.S. 16th Division

WAR DIARY

D.A.D.O.S 16th Division

FOR MONTH OF SEPTEMBER, 1916.

VOLUME 10

Army Form C. 2118

# WAR DIARY
## INTELLIGENCE SUMMARY
*(Erase heading not required.)*

Instructions regarding War Diaries and Intelligence Summaries are contained in F.S. Regs, Part II. and the Staff Manual respectively. Title Pages will be prepared in manuscript.

| Place | Date | Hour | Summary of Events and Information | Remarks and references to Appendices |
|---|---|---|---|---|
| FORKED TREE. | 1.9.16. | 6p.m. | Visited AMIENS to local purchase of calico for signals to aircraft. | |
| " | 2.9.16. | 6.30p.m. | Visited for 1 Lewis Gun complete for 7th R. Irish Fusiliers - 1000 sheets from Field Cashier XIV Corps - also visited Ordnance Workshops at MORLANCOURT and RIBEMONT - Railhead at HÉRICOURT, where 50 feet blanks and six revolvers were drawn. | |
| " | 3.9.16. | 5.30p.m. | 8th R. Irish Fusiliers demanded a LEWIS GUN - which was also wired for - Rescue & gas helmets brought up from CORBIE. | |
| " | 4.9.16. | 6p.m. | LEWIS GUN for 7th R.I. Fusiliers received - also a consignment of rest blanks | |
| " | 5.9.16. | 7p.m. | A.H.Q moved from Forked Tree to the CITADEL CAMP - Ordnance Dumps to remain at FORKED TREE. | |
| " | 6.9.16. | 7p.m. | Railhead moved to GROVETOWN - which was visited - temporary siding - very little Ordnance returned seen - Received LEWIS GUN for 8th R. Irish Fusiliers received and issued. | |

Army Form C. 2118

2

# WAR DIARY
## INTELLIGENCE SUMMARY
(Erase heading not required.)

Instructions regarding War Diaries and Intelligence Summaries are contained in F.S. Regs., Part II. and the Staff Manual respectively. Title Pages will be prepared in manuscript.

| Place | Date | Hour | Summary of Events and Information | Remarks and references to Appendices |
|---|---|---|---|---|
| FORKED TREE | 7.9.16 | 6.30pm | 2 LEWIS GUNS complete handed over for 85 CONNAUGHT RANGERS and 2 also for 85 INNISKILLING FUSILIERS. A.D.O.S. XIV Corps visited dump to-day. | |
| " | 8.9.16 | 6.30pm | 2 LEWIS GUNS handed over for both 7th LEINSTER REGT. and 85 INNISKILLING FUSILIERS. Visited Advanced D.H.Q. at MINDEN POST. | |
| " | 9.9.16 | 6.30pm | Orders received to exchange dumps etc. with A.A.D.O.S. Guards Division. | |
| TREUX | 10.9.16 | 6pm | Moved this day from FORKED TREE to TREUX. A.H.Q. remained at the CITADEL CAMP. - Advanced H.Q. coming in from MINDEN POST. | |
| CORBIE | 11.9.16 | 6.30pm | Moved from TREUX to CORBIE. A.A.D.O.S. 20th Division had not moved from his dump at CORBIE - He took charge of the dump at 7pm & moved in to 16 GA PLACE - CORBIE. | |
| " | 12.9.16 | 6pm | Visited all units in 3 Infantry Brigade and urged early supply of indents for all items - Very full lists boots, clothing etc. in order to re-equip men | |

1375. Wt. W593/826 1,000,000 4/15 J.B.C. & A. A.D.S.S./Forms/C. 2118.

# WAR DIARY
## INTELLIGENCE SUMMARY
*(Erase heading not required.)*

Army Form C. 2118

| Place | Date | Hour | Summary of Events and Information | Remarks and references to Appendices |
|---|---|---|---|---|
| CORBIE | 12.4.16 | contd | units of the Division to refill as possible. | |
| " | 13.4.16 | 6pm | HEILLY RE. sailed from Amiens — Visited HEILLY. | |
| " | 14.4.16 | 10 am | Railhead altered from HEILLY to CORBIE in consequence of the night's visit. R.O.s CORBIE. | |
| " | 15.4.16 | 6.30 pm | To AMIENS on local purchase. | |
| " | 16.4.16 | 6.30 pm | Ordered to move for CORBIE to HALLENCOURT. | |
| " | 17.4.16 | 7 pm | R.A. units T.M. Bde (Medium & Heavy) & No 1 Cy. Train transferred to Ordnance grande Division. | |
| " | 18.4.16 | 7 pm | Move to HALLENCOURT. | |
| " | 19.4.16 | — | Rickets at HALLENCOURT. | |
| " | 20.4.16 | — | Orders to move to FLETRE. | |
| " | 21.4.16 | — | Moved to FLETRE with O.C. Signals — on arrival here found that A.T.Q. had been moved to WESTOUTRE. Ordnance staff travelled by train reaching BAILLEUL & then WESTOUTRE about 9.15 pm | |

Army Form C. 2118

# WAR DIARY
## INTELLIGENCE SUMMARY
*(Erase heading not required.)*

Instructions regarding War Diaries and Intelligence Summaries are contained in F.S. Regs., Part II. and the Staff Manual respectively. Title Pages will be prepared in manuscript.

| Place | Date | Hour | Summary of Events and Information | Remarks and references to Appendices |
|---|---|---|---|---|
| WESTOUTRE | 22/9/16 | 10 pm | T.O.R. was from A.D.M.S. 4th Canadian Division - Notified A.D.S. 2nd Army & A.D.O.S. IV Corps of arrival. Visited A.D.O.S. | |
| " | 23/9/16 | 6 pm | Visited Salvage Dump at CANADA CORNER - Railhead at HAZEBROUCK - Workshops at HAZEBROUCK (heavy potte) and at BAILLEUL (Light Mobile). Instructions as to returns and demands for near past. Box requisition received from A.D.S. | |
| " | 24/9/16 | 6 pm | Visited C.R.A. 3rd Can. D.A. & with Staff Captain 85, 95 & 105 Bde. C.F.A. A.D.O.S. called in the afternoon - said new stores must be built. IV Corps bank of clothes because of delay. To BAILLEUL on local business - also visited Salvage Dump. | |
| " | 25/9/16 | 6 pm | To BAILLEUL on local business. | |
| " | 26/9/16 | 6 pm | Affiliation Armourer Staff Sergeants. | |
| " | 27/9/16 | 5.30 pm | Visited 118th F.A. 1st Can. C.C.S. 2nd & 3rd C.C.S. for Establishments. Collected about 120 Scales of kinder aft aft footwear. | |

1875  Wt. W393/326  1,000,000  4/15  J.B.C. & A.  A.D.S.S./Forms/C. 2118.

# WAR DIARY
## INTELLIGENCE SUMMARY
*(Erase heading not required.)*

Army Form C. 2118

| Place | Date | Hour | Summary of Events and Information | Remarks and references to Appendices |
|---|---|---|---|---|
| WESTOUTRE | 28/9/16 | 9am | Stone work nearly completed on B.H.E. has sent up standards for D.A. at present attached to French Div. Instructions & drill gun bolts received:- 600 to each Bde. - 200 to each Field Coy. 200 to Pioneer Bn. | |
| " | 29/9/16 | 7pm | United Salvage Dump & collected various stores - A.D.O.S. 3rd Cav Army visited here afternoon. Notified orderlies & hour of 3rd Cav. D.C. & about 1/16 D.A. received. A.D.O.S. inspector - No one able to give any information as to when 3rd Cav. Da. is going - ie R.Horse Division. Inst. Bellows attached for inflation. | |
|  |  |  | V.S. Ormond Captain  A.D.V.S. 16th Division - | |
| " | 30/9/16 | 9pm | P.S. 22 LEWIS GUNS required by Division while in 45 Army - # 3" STOKES MORTARS # 3 Vickers Guns | |

1875. W1. W593/326 1,000,000 4/15 J.B.C. & A. A.D.S.S./Forms/C. 2118.

WAR DIARY

MONTH OF OCTOBER, 1916.

VOLUME 11

D.A.D.O.S. 16th Division

Army Form C. 2118

# WAR DIARY
## INTELLIGENCE SUMMARY
*(Erase heading not required.)*

| Place | Date | Hour | Summary of Events and Information | Remarks and references to Appendices |
|---|---|---|---|---|
| WESTOUTRE | 1.10.16 | 6pm | To Bailleul on local purchase. Also visited Salvage Dump. 116 Field Ambulance and 6th Connaught Rangers. Issue of box respirators of new pattern to 3rd Canadian Divisional Artillery completed. | |
| " | 2.10.16 | 10.30 am | D.A.D.O.S. Canadian Division wrote to say that 16th Div Artillery were going to establish depot on the Ordnance representative left behind to assist in Canadian administration of Ordnance for 16th D.A. Reply sent to the effect that the representative had always and his to do when properly supervised. | |
| " | | 6.30pm | Notification received that 2nd R. Irish Regiment would form to Division on 2/1 H.A.C. joining 7th Division. On arrival of 2nd R. Irish Regt. 7/8 R. Irish Fusiliers would be amalgamated into 7/8 R. Irish Fusiliers. Programme to be absorption of others to follow. Visited Salvage Dump Kemmel. | |
| " | 3.10.16 | 4.30pm | Notification to transfer 3rd Canadian Divisional Artillery to Ordnance 4th Canadian Division received. This done tonight. | |

Army Form C. 2118

# WAR DIARY
## INTELLIGENCE SUMMARY
*(Erase heading not required.)*

Instructions regarding War Diaries and Intelligence Summaries are contained in F. S. Regs., Part II. and the Staff Manual respectively. Title Pages will be prepared in manuscript.

| Place | Date | Hour | Summary of Events and Information | Remarks and references to Appendices |
|---|---|---|---|---|
| WESTOUTRE | 3.10.16 | 7pm | Moved Office to hut near Divisional H.Q. and Signals. Fuller Stores collected from SALVAGE. 7th Inniskilling Fusiliers brought into 2 German machine guns which they had carried off with them from the Army Area. Informed them that they must take them to the Railhead themselves. No motor lry after some of their own equipment on the Somme to make room for the guns. | |
| " | 4.10.16 | 4.45 | Went to HAZEBROUCK and BAILLEUL to enquire about balance of 5th Green Satchels — 11 francs per tote — further enquiries are to be made by the local dealer. Also visited Train H.Q. this morning in regard to account for 15 Carpenters for protection of Reserve rations from 51st Supply Column. Returned to BAILLEUL early this afternoon and brought 2 acetylene lamps for Divisional Bomb Store. Lake visited Salvage Dump with A.A.Q.M.G. | |
| " | 5.10.16 | 3pm | 15,000 pairs of socks received and handed over to Divisional Laundry. Visited Railhead, Rawdry and Folks for instruction of Kent Rathbone. | |
| " | 6.10.16 | 6.35pm | Quiet morning in the Office. But 19 cases of clothes received at Railhead. They stores were compendiously many, but is far too great a quantity of stores | |

# WAR DIARY
## INTELLIGENCE SUMMARY
(Erase heading not required.)

Army Form C. 2118

| Place | Date | Hour | Summary of Events and Information | Remarks and references to Appendices |
|---|---|---|---|---|
| WESTOUTRE | 6/10/16 | cont. | RE consciously handled in the small accommodation at present available. Has seen D.A.D.O.S.ec carried on it's impossible task. Went to METEREN with D.A.D.H.Q. to see R.A.K.Q. — missed Staff Captain but saw D.T.M.O. who informed him that the Medium T.M.Bs have no guns and no handcarts - advised him to report difficulty - Small local purchase. Thence to BAILLEUL for | |
| " | 7/10/16 | 12.30pm | Visited Mrs Salvage Dump at WESTOUTRE. | |
| | 9.30pm | Received letter from D.A.O.S. 2nd Army asking for opinion as to "holding" demands for machine gun parts. Replied to the effect that it was inadvisable to ask D.O.S. to undertake extra work of this sort. | |
| " | 8/10/16 | 8pm. | One LEWIS GUN demanded for 7th R. Irish Fusiliers to replace one beyond local repair - indented unit to hand the condemned one in. No tire has reached Railhead K1487. | |
| " | 9/10/16 | 3.15pm | Fire No 14 principles received. This completes 165 Divisional Artillery and one for Division H.Q. The 3 kinks T.M.Bs. and V/16 are not yet completed 49th Bde also has one due to replace one found beyond local repair before his Division went to 4th Army | |

1875. Wt. W593/826 1,000,000 4/15 J.B.C. & A. A.D.S.S./Forms/C.2118.

# WAR DIARY
## INTELLIGENCE SUMMARY
*(Erase heading not required.)*

Army Form C. 2118

| Place | Date | Hour | Summary of Events and Information | Remarks and references to Appendices |
|---|---|---|---|---|
| HECTOUVRE | 9/10/16 | Cont. | To BAILLEUL to arrange issue/purchase of Cocoa, rifle, long" | |
| | | 7.15 pm | D.H.Q. reported that the 3 Medium Batteries were without any 2" Trench Mortars - Intent, Ceasefire, visit the RAEC to replace & like number. Handed over in 1st Corps Area. | |
| " | 10/10/16 | 3pm | Visited No.4 Supply Column and Cabbage Dump. Reserve of P.H. Helmets. The unit draws from 10,000 to 2,500 P.H. Helmets plus 2000 Box Respirators (new pattern). Proportion of 1600 ordinary 400 of both small & large. The balance of P.H. Helmets to be returned to Base. No reserve of P.H. Helmets & Box Respirators in the reserve of anti-gas appliances held by each Division both equipped with new pattern Box Respirators. A.D.O.S. informed me on the Telephone that the Canadian Division had asked for 380 sets of each below when in this area and that it was proposed to send them over to us. Agreed to take them and arranged for a D.R.O. to be put in calling for units so that detail[s] could be arranged prior to their arrival. Also sent Colours at Railhead. | |
| " | 11/10/16 | Noon | The LEWIS GUN demanded on 8/K for 75 R. Irish Rifles - received - also to P. 2" Trench Mortars demanded on 9" inst. Visited D.O.M. IX Corps and | |

Army Form C. 2118

# WAR DIARY
## INTELLIGENCE SUMMARY
(Erase heading not required.)

Instructions regarding War Diaries and Intelligence Summaries are contained in F. S. Regs., Part II. and the Staff Manual respectively. Title Pages will be prepared in manuscript.

| Place | Date | Hour | Summary of Events and Information | Remarks and references to Appendices |
|---|---|---|---|---|
| WESTOUTRE | 11/10/16 | cont'd | O.O. IX Cafe Troops and arranged to other 9.45 T.M. Also 1000 of 2000 copies machinated which are being issued the Division. Also visited Salvage Dump and Town Major, house. | |
| " | | 5pm | R.E. Stables should has shut the day. Also visited 113 F.C. | |
| | | | 4. 2nd T.M. & 1. 9.45 T.M. | |
| | | | Visited to D.T.M.O. this afternoon | |
| " | 12/10/16. | 6.30pm | No more 2nd T.Ms are coming from RASE to complete demand for 12 as 1st Army are sending 8 of these handed over by this Division before leaving 1st Corps. 2nd R. Irish Regt. Join the Division in Calcular - 14.5 wet. Visited Kemmel Shelt. Greengate - Young Shelt and Via Jellia. Finished this afternoon - Report Shelt, Greengate - Young Shelt and Via Jellia. | |
| | | | | |
| " | 13/10/16 | 11.30am | 8 2nd T.M.s and 11 handcarts were received from Division in 1st Army late last night and handed over at 6A Cdy TTE to D.T.M.O 3 reinforcements arrived to replace Cpl'nal Stanley, Pte Payne and Thomas. | |
| | | 9.30pm | To Neuville this afternoon to arrange local purchase of racks for corks. They will be ready on Tuesday. One or two that small local purchase made at 8pm went to 85 Dublin Fusiliers transport line with an air cylinder for STRAHOS HORN | |

D.A.D.O.S.
16TH (IRISH) DIV.

1375 W. W593/826 1,000,000 4/15 J.B.C. & A. A.D.S.S./Forms/C. 2118.

**Army Form C. 2118**

# WAR DIARY
## INTELLIGENCE SUMMARY
*(Erase heading not required.)*

Instructions regarding War Diaries and Intelligence Summaries are contained in F. S. Regs., Part II. and the Staff Manual respectively. Title Pages will be prepared in manuscript.

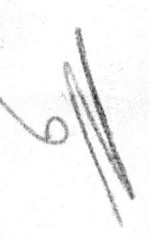

| Place | Date | Hour | Summary of Events and Information | Remarks and references to Appendices |
|---|---|---|---|---|
| WESTOUTRE | 14 to 16 | 6 p.m. | A quiet day. Relieved that 13 handcarts could be drawn at 2nd Army Workshops – not heavy vehicles as Kno practice in 1st Army. Visited H/Q to Brigade H.Q. Seekm 1/1/6 F.A. at SCHERPENBERG, & to Hastings Farm Coy and Quicksand Cpr at HQRE. Arranged for particulars of A.R.O. regulating to drawing of stores – units to draw by Bde Groups – R.A. in another group and also Divisional Troops. Issues to start at 8.30 a.m. and finish at | |
|  |  | 12.15 p.m. |  | |
|  | " | 10 p.m. | 13 handcarts obtained from 2nd Army Workshops and delivered to A.T.M.O. This makes the Medium Batteries complete. | |
|  | 15/16 | noon | Visited 49th Brigade H.Q. with D.A.Q.M.G., to arrange for the disposal of 17 Sanitary Section & re amalgamation of 7th & 8th R. Irish Fusiliers. | |
|  | " | 4 p.m. | D.A.Q.M.G. signed letter to 49th Bde. Returning 7/8 R. Irish Fusiliers to hand over Anaflame stores to D.A.D.O.S. | |
|  | " | 7 p.m. | C.R.A. and O.C. 177 Bde. R.F.A. same in about clothing for 177 Bde. Wrote letter obtaining location and visited to R.A.C.E. to send supply of small parcels and of woollen | |

# WAR DIARY
## INTELLIGENCE SUMMARY
*(Erase heading not required.)*

Army Form C. 2118

Instructions regarding War Diaries and Intelligence Summaries are contained in F.S. Regs., Part II. and the Staff Manual respectively. Title Pages will be prepared in manuscript.

| Place | Date | Hour | Summary of Events and Information | Remarks and references to Appendices |
|---|---|---|---|---|
| WESTOUTRE | 16.10.16 | 10 a.m. | 5 Armourers reported for duty in Divisional Armourers Shop. | |
| | | 1 p.m. | Test gas alarm today. Message received at 12.40 p.m. All craft wore Box respirators for 10 minutes - the others were covered by military police. | |
| | | 4 p.m. | Otherwise there has been a quiet day. Wrote order in regard to having SAA come into free the morning - Apparently rebel cracks and not. | |
| | | 11.20 p.m. | 380 sets of Gun Fittings advised from No. 11. Ordnance Dept - to arrive at Railhead tomorrow morning. Arranged through Q. for 6 extra lorries from Divisional Park and a fatigue party B.24. | |
| " | 17.10.16 | 7 p.m. | K. 15t. ANZAC CORPS from 18t inst. 180 Rds R.F.A. & No. 3 section D.A.C. less S.A.A. and Grenade portion to be attached 19 lorry loads of Gun Fittings arrived from Railhead today. The balance will be moved as soon as possible. Wrote to D.A.D.O.S. 2nd Army to suggest not to send Gun Fittings which will not be sent at once. Lieut Balkin on attested certain stores from 7/8 R. Irish Fusiliers - One practically no technical stores such as Cordexin Fuzzeten or Automatic telescopic sight. Asked D.A.A. & G.9 who asked for an explanation. | |

D.A.D.O.S.
16TH (IRISH) DIV.
No.
Date

# WAR DIARY
# INTELLIGENCE SUMMARY

*(Erase heading not required.)*

Army Form C. 2118

Instructions regarding War Diaries and Intelligence Summaries are contained in F.S. Regs, Part II. and the Staff Manual respectively. Title Pages will be prepared in manuscript.

| Place | Date | Hour | Summary of Events and Information | Remarks and references to Appendices |
|---|---|---|---|---|
| WESTOUTRE | 18/9/16 | 6.30pm | To BETHUNE & MERVILLE with D.A.Q.M.G. a local furniture and outstanding affairs of R.I. 165 Fld Laundry at BETHUNE. 9 new Grain bags & tent bottoms received from Railhead to-day. Balance will be brought up to-morrow in 6 lorries from R.C.P. and Fatigue party from 48th Brigade to-morrow. | |
| " | 19/10/16 | 6pm | D.A.Q.M.G. visited Armourers' Shop - Issued 1900 boots to Laundry - Tent Bottoms cleaned - There is nothing. | |
| " | 20/9/16 | 6.45pm | G.O.C. and D.A. & Q.M.G. inspected Armourers' Shop and Ens to-day. Also re loading of socks for men in trenches at the HOSPICE, LOCRE. He states that everyone in the trenches is to get a wash & clean pair of socks every night - Very cold day - the temperature falling rapidly after 6.30pm. | |
| " | 21/9/16 | 9.30pm | No tactics to-day - a quiet day. | |
| " | 22/9/16 | 6pm | First consignment of horse-rugs and bullet proof jackets received. Six truck of stores at Railhead which was visited. One air cylinder for 4th Bde changed at HAZEBROUCK. Commenced going over vehicle with a view to received Called out this morning at 2.30 am - a/c alarm - 8 air cylinders collected from O.D. IX Corps Troops. | |

1875 W.- W593/826 1,000,000 4/15 J.B.C. & A. A.D.S.S./Forms/C. 2118.

# WAR DIARY
## INTELLIGENCE SUMMARY
*(Erase heading not required.)*

Army Form C. 2118

| Place | Date | Hour | Summary of Events and Information | Remarks and references to Appendices |
|---|---|---|---|---|
| WESTOUTRE | 23/10 to 16 | 2.30 pm | To 2nd Army School of Sniping, MONT DES CATS for 7 telescopic sighted rifles - 4 for 7th LEINSTER REGT and 3 for 9th DUBLIN FUSILIERS. Thence to BAILLEUL to O.D. Corps Troops for 14 air cylinders. Otherwise a quiet day. | |
| " | 24/10/16 | 12.15 pm | Wet day. About 12 lorry loads of stores at Railhead - 2nd Flemish coming up also one lorry emg. Delivered same to units. Orders from Corps to send 8 Lewis guns to units - 8 LEWIS GUNS from 7/R.I.R. Ricks Fusiliers to BASE - A.D.O.S. called for list of stores taken over - (acting A.D.O.S. in Temp. Captain C.J.T.A. ROBERTSON - late A.D.O.S. 55th Division). Draft to D.R.O. 20 pantaloons returned, approved. | |
| " | 25/10/16 | noon | Very hot - Mess hess cart for 155 Trench Fusiliers returned at Railhead - but since to remove it. | |
| | | 7.30 pm | To BAILLEUL in afternoon - Arranged for 12 pairs for Traffic cadets. To 2000 cafes backwater issued to Division. 87 will remain for distribution tomorrow after 15 have been issued for Traffic men. It seems that the plans to backwater issuing stores of which only small numbers are available had this in its favour - that it impresses to find out units known to particular corps will be of great value - it being that might be practicable involved in a general statistics. | |
| " | 26/10/16 | 6.40 pm | To O.O. 2nd A.T. at CASSEL this morning to collect 150 Belt × 150 Belt filler grande - also to BAILLEUL to purchase 100 yards of aft and 50 electric torches for a special purpose. A.D.O.S. assisted an inspection by D.R.O. Transport this morning. Recover 820 primers | |

D.A.D.O.S.
16TH (IRISH) DIV.

1875 Wt. W.593/825 1,000,000 4/15 J.B.C. & A. A.D.S.S./Forms/C. 2118.

# WAR DIARY
## INTELLIGENCE SUMMARY
(Erase heading not required.)

Army Form C. 2118

| Place | Date | Hour | Summary of Events and Information | Remarks and references to Appendices |
|---|---|---|---|---|
| WESTOUTRE | contd. | | Stores to go to O.O. Corps Troops - Also reserve 8/10 Soya Stoves - Wired BASE to consign the latter direct and wired O.B. Corps Troops that Primus Stoves were available for issue. 2/16 sent in a 2" T.M. Head to be sent to J.O.K. tomorrow - | |
| " | 27/10/16 | 10 a.m. | "WIND DANGEROUS" notified at 9.35 a.m. | |
| " | " | 4 p.m. | A.D.O.S. and A.A.D.O.S. 2nd Army inspected stores and billets about midday today. A.D.O.S. apparently satisfied with what had been done about building stores & condition of Kit. 4th Parade called for 12 grenade rifles for to-morrow - will be ready at 9 a.m. Promised 600 or 800 P.H. helmets to A.D.O.S. for O.O. Corps Troops for a special purpose. This will not affect reserve as 800 are surplus. Sent rather an urgent 2" T.B. from 2/16 to J.O.K. 4 more air cylinders for O.O. Corps Troops. | |
| " | 28.10.16 | 7 p.m. | Balance of horse cups received today. Issue into be completed to-morrow if possible R.A.O.C. called and will take A.C.G.In.9 verbal lowdown at once. Nothing special except for A.O.C. to LOCRE and WESTOUTRE - also Ordnance Depot - said that the Division now had to find Stamp in the Corps Applied to A.D.O.S. by wire for De CHASTY (A.O.C.) own bat expert would be finished with the Division on 30th inst. Orders to distribute 6 p.m. gum boots tonight treed. R.A. Bty. arrived for use of Expellers. WIND SAFE notified this evening 6 p.m. | |

Army Form C. 2118

# WAR DIARY
## INTELLIGENCE SUMMARY
*(Erase heading not required.)*

| Place | Date | Hour | Summary of Events and Information | Remarks and references to Appendices |
|---|---|---|---|---|
| WESTOUTRE | 29/10/16 | 9.15 a.m. | WIND DANGEROUS hoisted. Otherwise a quiet day. Very wet and cold this morning. 29-10-16. J.S. Onions Captain D.A.D.O.S. 16th Division. | |

**Army Form C. 2118**

# WAR DIARY
## or
## INTELLIGENCE SUMMARY
*(Erase heading not required.)*

Instructions regarding War Diaries and Intelligence Summaries are contained in F.S. Regs, Part II. and the Staff Manual respectively. Title Pages will be prepared in manuscript.

| Place | Date | Hour | Summary of Events and Information | Remarks and references to Appendices |
|---|---|---|---|---|
| WESTOUTRE | 30.10.16 | 10 pm | Wind safe; weather wet and stormy. Quiet day, no Lewis stores received from Base. Returns rendered – (weekly) No. 14 Percussion; (monthly) Indents reviewed and cancelled. Drew from O.O. IX Corps Troops further G.S. 4 pairs Boots Gum Thigh, making total of 4000 now in Division. H.Q. orders for distribution list. Paid detachment A.O.C. attached men. Ordered 2 rope ladders to be improvised and placed in various billets (upstairs) for use in case of fire. Repair of 4 Lewis Guns completed. Bicycles transferred from Armourers' Shop to Lake Detail from Motor Plus will free the cycle repairers more room to work. | |
| " | 31.10.16 | 7 pm | Wind safe; weather changeable. Another quiet day. 1 Trestle Store (3 tons) received from Base. Returned current to O/c Signals – Cable Electric and Telephone. Portable drive and phonevel. Received two 3" Stokes Trench Mortars complete for 47 T.M. Battery, also cut barrel one mounting complete for 3" Stokes Trench Mortar for 47 T.M. Battery. 7 Lewis guns repaired in Armourers' Shop. Run Boot exports sent to D.A.D.O.S. 41st Division having completed his duty with this Division. 50 P.H. Helmets issued A.D.M.S. for use of unconscious men in advanced dressing stations. A.D.M.S. reports that Box Respirators are useless in such cases. During the latter part of the month a Divisional Armourers' Shop has been established and turned out a variety of good work. Stores received from the Base this month amount to not less than 250 tons | |

31st October 1916.

A J Palliner Lieut RAOD

for D.A.D.O.S. 16th Division

WAR DIARY.

FOR

MONTH OF NOVEMBER, 1916.

VOLUME 12

D.A.D.O.S. 16th Division

**Army Form C. 2118**

# WAR DIARY
## INTELLIGENCE SUMMARY
*(Erase heading not required.)*

Instructions regarding War Diaries and Intelligence Summaries are contained in F. S. Regs., Part II. and the Staff Manual respectively. Title Pages will be prepared in manuscript.

| Place | Date | Hour | Summary of Events and Information | Remarks and references to Appendices |
|---|---|---|---|---|
| WEST OUTRE | 1-11-16 | 10 pm | Wind S.W.; weather fine generally. Public Show advised from Base did not arrive. Great frost this morning. O.O. IX Corps Troops on Candidates petition passed ordered to enable us to collect as camp tools on his back. This were handed over to H.Q. 47 Div. Bde. for trial. Collected from O.O. IX Corps Troops 3 Shrouds items & 5 air cylinders arrival of which was reported to D.A.D.M.L. Remainder returns of Park Repairs Coy. Ammunition repair 6 Lewis guns & C. today. 12,000 m. hessian (saw Timoti) over to new Div. Laundry at Lorne. |   |
| " | 2-11-16 | 9.15 pm | Wind S.W.; weather variable. Received Yorks Dragoon hockey boots to, also 4 tons of bottles water, wire, & in addition 1330 of rockets. Delivered to D.O.M. IX Corps for repairs amount of (3 French knife G). Visited Salvage Dump. 5000 pm Sacks wanted for the serving Div. Laundries. |   |
| " | 3-11-16 | 10 pm | Wind dangerous weather fair 11:10 a.m.; weather fine generally. Ordered Lt/From & O.C. IX Corps one barrel of 2" French knives repaired & spare parts. O.O. IX Corps Troops 1030 pm & 50 tin liners for gum boots. Ammunition repaired 3 Lewis Guns to day. |   |
| " | 4-11-16 | 9.30 pm | Wind dangerous; weather fine following wet early morning. 3 trips of Carts received from Base. Visited Regt Armoured, exchanging 2 armoured air cylinders at No. 3 Ordnance (Heavy) Mobile Workshop & receiving 36 mills cup attachments and 350 socks mufti & pairs (for Army with Friends) from 2nd Army workshop. Visited Salvage Dump. Issued 358 rubber thigh & 10 Div. cylinders as instructed by 2nd Army. Remade & reissue of machine fine French knives in Division. Ammunition repaired 6 Lewis guns to day. Further knitted clothing issued; also almost completed drop-out. Wind fairs for 50 pair Jamie Waders for our & under for fine issue to French. |   |
| " | 5-11-16 | 9 pm | Wind fair wind dangerous; weather variable. 8 tons of picketing poles etc. from Base. Collected from O.O. IX Corps Troops one 6" message for Div. Laundry & 2000 pair of Boots from Thps. 660 pair of the latter were issued to H.Q. each Inf. Bde as instructed by B.A.D.V.S. Received from Base 5000 pm 2080 inner pair from boots & 517 pm steel inners for boots F. numbe. Went from 2 3" Stokes T. M. to replace one put out of action by enemy fire. Issued 30 Grenade Carriers, Cable Patterns to H.Q. 47 & 75 Div. Bde. for no special purpose. Ammunition repaired 3 Lewis Guns to today. |   |
| " | 6-11-16 | 9.30 pm | Wind dangerous; weather variable. 2 Sons of NIR to received from Base. Visited by A/apcol who brought to Sniper Suits. Received returns of No. 14 Periscope. Took to D.O.M. IX Corps Magazine one mounting 3" Stokes T.M. Purchases refundable. 150 lamps electric torch as Bases has exhausted its for transit smith as army supply. Arranged for instant (visual purchase) of D.O. upto with handle, for drill purposes at Diet. School 1. Ammunition repaired 3 Lewis guns & one trench CB "Stokes T.M. R Gooty. |   |

# WAR DIARY

## INTELLIGENCE SUMMARY

Army Form C. 2118

| Place | Date | Hour | Summary of Events and Information | Remarks and references to Appendices |
|---|---|---|---|---|
| WESTOUTRE | 7-11-16 | 10 pm | Wind dangerous; weather very wet. Received from Base 3 "Stokes T.M. wind for one 6" Mark. Received 4 tins of stores from Base. Sent to join IX Corps and cleaned 3" T.M. barrel. Visited Stag. brown & exchanged some empty air cylinders at Mord & Ord (Mons) East, workshops realised. Corps & Telegs. for wilde, grenade from 2nd Army workshops. Completed yesterdays wt purchase in Bailleul. Rundowns returns of Cable & Cochic Telephone Batteries. Armourer repaired 2 Lewis guns, one barrel 3" Stokes T.M., 1 Telescopic Periscope to Tooley. Held kit inspection of detachment. | |
| " | 8-11-16 | 1.0 pm | Wind Safe; weather wet. Received stores of Boots from Base. Collected 6 air cylinders from O.C. IX Corps Troops. Issued 2 Snipers Suits to HHQ. and Duff. Bde. 76 pairs Boots from 51 HHQ. to 76 HHQ. air artillery under instruction of S. & Qs. | |
| " | 9-11-16 | 9.30 pm | Wind Safe; weather fine. Received 4 tins of stores from Base. Wind Base for 1 Vicker M.G. wind purchase in Bailleul - Long rifle covers, lamps, glasses and wicks. Rendered return of small arms reparations. | |
| " | 10-11-16 | 9.45 pm | Wind Safe; weather fine. Received from Base 8 cans of Stores, including our Vicker M.G. wind for yesterday. Issued Corp new beginning to arrive with horse-lines. To Hazebrouck exchanged 4 empty air cylinders at his S.O.D. (H.J. prot. workshops (Kandar) to Corps Twee 3" Stokes T.M. mounting for repairs & collected one 3" Stokes T.M. mounting repaired. | |
| " | 11-11-16 | 9 am | Relinquished Assumed Command of Office. | |
| | | | A.J. Dallinger, Lieut. A.O.D. for A.O.O. 165 Div. | |
| " | 12-11-16 | 9.15 pm | Took me duties on return from Base. A quiet day in the office. Most men Various Routine Orders. Published by Army Corps & Divisions during my absence. Together with various other papers. A.D.C. Called in the morning. | |
| " | 13-11-16 | 3.30 pm | No fresh at Railhead this morning. Visited 7/8 R. Innis. Fusiliers - KIPPETTE Advanced Dressing Station (1137a) ROSSIGNOL FARM and the LAITERIE. An the guide day and to cross Army. All Staff possible given leave of his absence. Arranged with the A.D.Q.M.G. for inspection of R.M.C. Stores tomorrow. | |

1875 Wt. W593/826 1,000,000 4/15 J.B.C. & A. A.D.S.S./Forms/C. 2118.

Army Form C. 2118

# WAR DIARY
## or
## INTELLIGENCE SUMMARY
(Erase heading not required.)

3

| Place | Date | Hour | Summary of Events and Information | Remarks and references to Appendices |
|---|---|---|---|---|
| NECTOUT R.E. | 13/10 | 5.30 p.m. | Visited D.A.D.O.S. stores & ask him in 4/5 & 4/96 Bdes. with the D.A.Q.M.G. this morning. On the whole the English amount of Ordnance stores in possession is not very great but several Cases & Blankets have ordered in. One or two of the others have not in such good order as to others. This is the fact is due partly to a bad Q.M. and also to bad & deal were accompanied. But there is no excuse for such rifles being about — rifles belonging to the Q.M. (return-staff — No is for any reason for hiding things away under stands & so on. Also found to 4 gun Bde. H.Q. and saw the Coys Captain — Apparently no questions outstanding. Tell him the banister equipment could not be issued, to the hd M. Gun Coy. Lieut. DASHMORE proceeded to BAVAIKOR to learn further his opinion and also to HARBROUCK to arrange an opinion. J.O.M. IX Corps confirmed two 4.5 How.s. belonging to C/17 Bde. and as belonging to D/17. Ix Corps asked for each in the jacket. Intended for new howitzers and improved XH Q. D/17 6-day for each in the jacket. Draft of D.R.O.s 26 telegraphic office and bicycles approved. One TRAVERSOR MAT received. D.M.G. asked for these orders. | |
| " | 14.10.16. | 9.5 am | WIND DANGEROUS notified at 9.5 am this evening by 486 Infantry Brigade | |
| " | " | 10 p.m. | Drafts for D.R.O. re return of Temp. Box Respirators and arrival of new drafts into that Schedule approved. Letter received stating that a number of Staff Officers are coming out from home and that a further communication will be sent later re — copy of compliance to A.D.V.S. Returned to chaps / GARCIA fuller Grande | |

1875  Wt. W 593/826  1,000,000  4/15  J.B.C. & A.  A.D.S.S./Forms/C. 2118.

# WAR DIARY
## INTELLIGENCE SUMMARY

**Army Form C. 2118**

| Place | Date | Hour | Summary of Events and Information | Remarks and references to Appendices |
|---|---|---|---|---|
| WESTOUTRE | 14/6 | contd. | Carried out 40 pairs of short gum boots from O.O. IX Corps Troops. 2nd R. Dublin Fusiliers entrain to-morrow (15/6 inst) to join his Division. Letter sent out by the D.A.Q.M.G. in regard handing over the surplus stores of 2nd R. Dublin Fusiliers on the abolition of that Bn. to 1st Bn. R. Munster Fusiliers. Lieut Dalkin re visits Calais to-day. | |
| " | 15/16 | 6.10pm | Cold morning. A.D.O.S. called — He wants an early statement of number of 60/75 gum boots evacuated from this BASE to replace "sent to PARIS for repair". Arranged to go to BAILLEUL to visit a chap of 20th Division and see that little of use for this Division — B Coms left Westoute 20 D Division. Promised to supply J.O.M IX Corps with 12 V rifles as soon as possible for convoys into breech-mechanisms for 2nd 7 inch. Visited 111 S.Z.A. at METEREN — only infantry above have Fortune. Draft for D.R.O. Re return of kit belonging no longer regiment officers. | |
| " | 16/6 | 5.25pm | Went to BAILLEUL this morning — Bought acetylene lamps for N.E. Hewle Batchijk with and 2 hrs for KEMMEL to join hunting R. affected of hostile aeroplane. Went A.D.O.S. Fularrup of stores left by Mess de bluff and agreed shortly to clear it of. Besides a considerable collection of Rd Clothing, had seven official tents and a number of things of actual use — Sent down 3 lorries to start to | |

# WAR DIARY
## INTELLIGENCE SUMMARY
*(Erase heading not required.)*

Army Form C. 2118

| Place | Date | Hour | Summary of Events and Information | Remarks and references to Appendices |
|---|---|---|---|---|
| NESTOUTRE | 16th /15 | cont | Chas. K. Dunlop. Arranged for D.R.O. in regard to the exchange of STROMBOS HORNS and an ofsicers horse Divisional Gas Officer. Visited Salvage Officer. Arrival of 2nd R. Dublin Fusiliers (17 officers and 702 O.R.) at NETRERN ASYLUM. Promised to give a lecture at the next Course on Balance in the Field. | |
| " | 17/6 | 6.45pm | To BAILLEUL with O.C. Divisional Coy S2 for local furnace - went to the Coy S2 as well. On returning found that 2nd R. Dublin Fusiliers had tried for 700 strombos to complete to a scale of one per man as they had one in possession. This number was (700) was collected and sent to the Coy by lorry in the course of the afternoon. 1400 demanded from the base to complete to 2 per man + to kept fuller demands. In the afternoon visited 2nd R. Dublin Fusiliers at NETRERN - Romeo Haas a few A.D. then in hands received. | |
| " | 18th /15 | 9.45pm | To NETRERN at 9.30 am with 20 pairs of L.A. Exceldoes to 2nd R. Dublin Fusiliers. France to BAILLEUL to see A.D.O.S. and to visit Dumps - collected a few items from Dump + returned to NESTOUTRE. Made a few notes for lecture at the Coy S2. The 3 4.5" How. returned from Base on 13th inst. not yet received from No. 3 Ordnance Depot - trailer lorries and for caules are hung up in the Railway stranslice. Except for trailer lorries and for caules are hung up in the Railway stranslice. knocked for information on tram wherewithal - also 8 Hotchiss - the weather has turned very wet. Out to NETRERN to O.R. | |

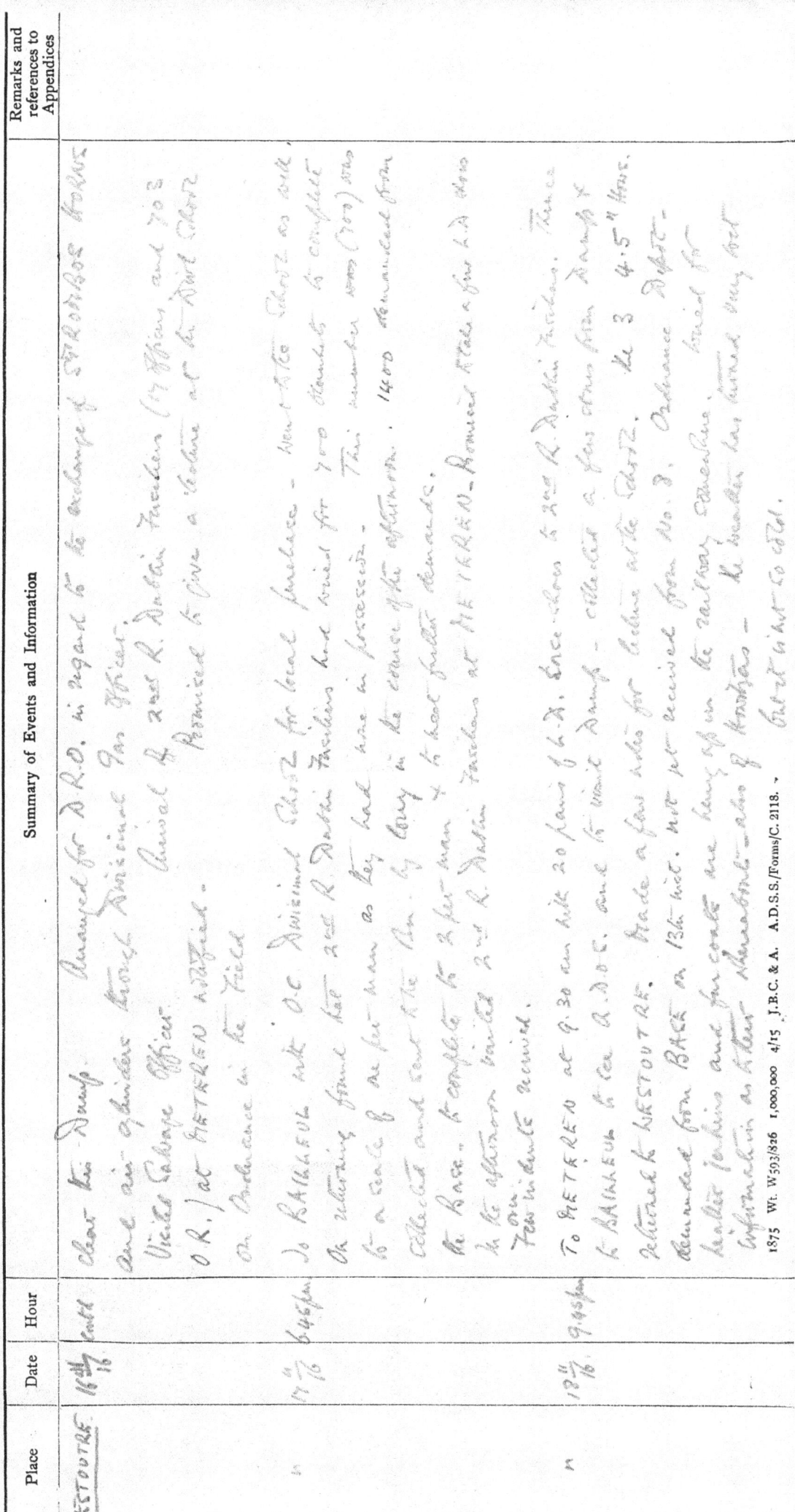

# WAR DIARY / INTELLIGENCE SUMMARY

Army Form C. 2118

| Place | Date | Hour | Summary of Events and Information | Remarks and references to Appendices |
|---|---|---|---|---|
| WESTOUTRE | 19/11/16 | 9.30am | To Railhead at 9 am. Nothing ArrD except grain and wood. The A.D.S. called again today. Went to No.9. Ordnance Depot, ABEEVILLE about 4.5" Howitzers. 58 issued for machine gun parts & LEWIS gun parts cancelled. Base adjmt again adjmt as well as units. | |
| " | 20/11/16 | 12.15pm | To HQ CoRE & saw Town Major re request to arrange for cache & had 2 horn cart for Sanitary work. Also 40 Canadian Division sends in to them. All in men— Also invited to QM's stores of 85 & 95 Dublin Fusiliers, 1st Munster Fusiliers & 7th R. Dub. Rifles — # Ordered in 290 surplus blankets. Otherwise the stores pretty empty except for shirts and cotton. Noted wind at Salvage as cool.  WIND SAFE N.Eat. | |
| " | " | 1.30pm | | |
| " | " | 7.30pm | Notified 95 R. Munster Fusiliers that all outstanding indents are cancelled on account of coming atrophin in 1st Bn.— arranged with A/Q & Q. A'Ttche new surplus stores on 23rd inst. HAVRE BASE cancelled indent for 3 Mallie carts for Signal Coy. to be transfer of pack animals horses only seal out supply.  Wounds being allowed animals are to be found in the Division from Remounts. Went to CARTS for 2 carts and 2 set S.D. harness — 1 cart and 1 set t harness will be drawn from 95 Bn. R. Munster Fusiliers. | |
| " | 21/11/16 | 9.10am | WIND DANGEROUS notified at 9.5 am. Officer Clothing Chap started in Cate Orchard. D.R.O. as open. | |
| " | " | 2pm | Went to RAIAREUL. R.A.D.O.S. (see Reid. M. Shephaind) to having relieved Captain Atherton who | |

# WAR DIARY or INTELLIGENCE SUMMARY

Army Form C. 2118

| Place | Date | Hour | Summary of Events and Information | Remarks and references to Appendices |
|---|---|---|---|---|
| WESTOUTRE | 21st 15 | contd | has returned to D.A.D.C. 5th Division) - Saw Fr Callier - and left 3 heavy G.S. and collected 3 line mess Apr. (Fr with hinges on to enable to facilitate cleaning -. Brought out a number of copies inaccurate from the Ambulance here at 11.4.6. Arrived on the telephone with the C.O.O. CALAIS to want the Base will be D.A.B.h. 9. on 23rd inst - (Thursday next) 2nd R. Anton fractions report that they have 10 LEWIS GUNS in possession and regum 402 Box Respirators complete. Fixed up December for below note Div Order. Wrote to a DDC. The Cafe in regard to the subject of heavy Rain, magazines, haversacks & magazine covers I.P.E. Ammunition in case of their divisions being in need of same or any other articles, to balance of the ammunition possibly be used to meet outstanding demands in the divisions. ABBEVILLE (No. P. Ord. Depot) have asked D.A.D.R.T. ABBEVILLE to wire asking 1) 2nd Containing 3 4.5. Howitzers. | |
| 22 16 | 2.40 pm | WIND. S.W.F. altered. Went to BAILLEUL with ... DAO h.9. to see D.O.h. 1× Cofse. Went to see 2nd M.M. also saw Senr Officer clothing Depot at 15 Rue D'YPRES. Great letter from A.D.D.S. ordering evacuation of 85 R. Munster Fusiliers to CALAIS. This crossed my letter of Yesterday, will wait further instructions. - Query from Cyls in Ath "abnormal" issue of 31,772½ pairs of socks the Division in July last - Replied the effect that 16000 here put into the Laundry | |

# WAR DIARY or INTELLIGENCE SUMMARY

Army Form C. 2118

| Place | Date | Hour | Summary of Events and Information | Remarks and references to Appendices |
|---|---|---|---|---|
| WESTOUTRE | 22/4/16 | contd | Held in readiness to complete to Doirin & 3 pairs per man in accordance with S.R.O. 1552 and the balance of 15,672 here issued to complete unit to 2 per man (Cattley). I Capt Q. 273 also 22-6-16. | |
| " | 23/4/16 | noon & 2.45pm & 6pm | Visited OKAPIS with A.D.V.S. & saw C.O.; sent out steers, ducks & workships - visited 8th R. Fusiliers facilities store taken over successfully today. | |
| " | 24/4/16 | 6pm | WIND DANGEROUS. Hostile flag at 9.55 p.m. | |
| " | 25/4/16 | 9.15pm | WET DAY. Many lines about 3 4.5" How. not yet received. Reported matter to officer who has taken the matter up. Trench Army HQ. | |
| " | 26/4/16 | 2pm | WIND SAFE. Hostile at 9.30 a.m. Visited rear bath at HOOGE - also 113 F.A. in regard to replacements of codes at HOOGE HOSPICE LAUNDRY. | |
| " | 27/4/16 | 12.30pm | To 115 Hants in regard to their inhabitation equipment envelopes also to 47th Rd HQ and SALVAGE DUMP. | |
| " | 28/4/16 | 6/pm | WIND DANGEROUS. Hostile at 4:58 pm. A number of occurrences in the offensive flag. A lung hit & praching from A.D.O.S. about 1½ hrs however. The 3 4.5" How. amounted in 13/16 N.R.O. 2y number of tents in processa. Invited flag & cases to lotop & Army. | |

# WAR DIARY
## INTELLIGENCE SUMMARY
*(Erase heading not required.)*

Army Form C. 2118

| Place | Date | Hour | Summary of Events and Information | Remarks and references to Appendices |
|---|---|---|---|---|
| WESTOUTRE | 29.11.16 | 9.30 am | Orders received from 2nd Army to complete the Division to 10 Lewis Guns per Bn. except Pioneers - Demanded 22 on 2nd R.A.F. are already in the accounts of Afwoles Rece ndln to ATPO at once. | |
| " | " | 6 pm | To HAZEBROUCK with 2 STROMBOS HORNS AIR CYLINDERS for exchange - RAOS called this afternoon - No General Questions - | |
| " | 30.11.16 | 9.30 pm | To BAILLEUL to D.O.h. 18 Caps in regard to T. Mortars also 112th ZA & SABUAG & DUMP where 16 Very Pistols (1½") were found & handed to by 40th M.G.Coy Taken possession of for immediate return to BASE. | |

30/11

F. Owen
Captain
A.A.N.T.C. 16th Division

WAR DIARY FOR MONTH OF DECEMBER, 1916.

VOLUME 13

D.A.D.O.S. 16th Division

# WAR DIARY
## INTELLIGENCE SUMMARY

**Army Form C. 2118**

Instructions regarding War Diaries and Intelligence Summaries are contained in F.S. Regs., Part II. and the Staff Manual respectively. Title Pages will be prepared in manuscript.

(Erase heading not required.)

| Place | Date | Hour | Summary of Events and Information | Remarks and references to Appendices |
|---|---|---|---|---|
| WESTOUTRE. | 1/12/16. | 9.30 p.m | No truck at Railhead. Altogether a quiet day. | |
| | 2/12/16. | 9.30 a.m | Bitterly cold. The 22 LEWIS GUNS mined for on 29th ult. received this morning - Reported to Army & Corps. - Also for 6 N.Z. Division. A.D.O.S. ex Corps reported that five live grenades had been found in a bundle of old equipment landed in at 1st Corps Railhead from the Chief at BAILLEUL - Investigated and reported to the A.D.O.S. 1 LEWIS GUN demanded from BASE for the 7th Muntshire Fusiliers to replace one found unserviceable in the Armourers Shop. No fuses to replace the gun mis on issue [illegible] limit. | |
| | 3/12/16. | 9.30 a.m | No truck at Railhead this morning. Supply train delayed. | |
| | | 9.15 p.m | To STEENWERCK to collect 5 bombs - handed them over the D.A.C. for disposal. LEWIS GUN demanded intervals for the Inniskilling Fusiliers arrived today - Applied to Army & Corps. | |
| | 4/12/16. | 4 p.m. | 1 LEWIS GUN demanded for 6th R. Irish Rifles to replace one condemned in Armourer Shop as unserviceable - Applied to A.H.Q. | |
| | 5/12/16. | 7 p.m. | A wet day. 1500 additional rifles handed over - 30 hospital containers - Lieut Dalbiner visited Salenque - received - 23 for 49th - 11 for 49th. | |
| | 6/12/16. | 9.30 p.m | Visited No. 1, 2, & 3 Sections. N.C.O. with Rifles 9 & Lieut. Dalbiner to inspect rations. Reported arrival to Army & Corps. 25 pairs - Special puttees received. LEWIS GUNS demanded for 6th R. Irish Rifles & 45 received. | |

**Army Form C. 2118**

# WAR DIARY
# INTELLIGENCE SUMMARY
*(Erase heading not required.)*

Instructions regarding War Diaries and Intelligence Summaries are contained in F.S. Regs., Part II. and the Staff Manual respectively. Title Pages will be prepared in manuscript.

| Place | Date | Hour | Summary of Events and Information | Remarks and references to Appendices |
|---|---|---|---|---|
| WESTOUTRE | 7/12/16 | 4 pm | To 2nd Army School of Sniping with 8 Offrs with telescopic sights for adjustment - Thence to BAILLEUL. Small bread purchased & lamp glasses - Thence back to WESTOUTRE - | |
| " | 8/12/16 | 7.15 pm | Wet day. A very quiet day - But little doing. A.D.O.S. called in the afternoon - Sent to No. 2 Canadian A.T. Coy. RE for T.h. bolts - also to Anti-Gas Shop for 15 air cylinders below pressure - sent same to HAZEBROUCK for exchange. | |
| " | 9/12/16 | 2.30 pm | WIND DANGEROUS - Very wet day. Visited Mobile Vet. Section - Further call for Chandeliers for 76 Leinster Regt. & U.S. Made for drafts. | |
| " | 10/12/16 | 10 pm | Quiet day again - No tin hats as Railhead until noon - Sent to BAILLEUL for T.h.s. also 15 air cylinders to Anti-Gas Officer - & 10 more further beds for 3r STOKES T.H. & 49th Res. A.O.C. Clothed for confusion of A.H.Q (9) report of 2 wristwatched gone lewis at Sivisemnal Regt. Accounted but the man Sig & that the Sergeant - in whose store had bought them - with him from LE TOUQUET. | |
| " | 11/12/16 | 10 pm | 3 days' stores collected from Railhead and issued. | |
| " | 12/12/16 | 3.30 pm | WIND SAFE. Went to BAILLEUL for morning. A.D.O.S. out - with General Division in regard to Recruit cast refused ADOS 1x Coy &c - | Correspondence |

# WAR DIARY or INTELLIGENCE SUMMARY

Army Form C. 2118

| Place | Date | Hour | Summary of Events and Information | Remarks and references to Appendices |
|---|---|---|---|---|
| WESTOUTRE | 13/12/16 | 9.15 p.m. | To Chief Cashier received yesterday delivered to the R.A. units which closed to-day. Another very quiet day with usual. No intervals, and no correspondence from the A.D.O.S. or Army. | |
| " | 14/12/16 | 12.45 p.m. | WAS DANGEROUS - to BAILLEUL for local purchase - booked out at a long ride even for 15 kmts - Had - Cal to WESTOUTRE - D.D.O.S. 2nd Army & C.R.O.M. came in for a few minutes - Otherwise a quiet day. | |
| " | 15/12/16 | 7 p.m. | To Divisional C.R.o.R. with A.D.M.S. This morning - a few have invited received them very quiet. | |
| " | 16/12/16 | 5.30 p.m. | Q.A.D.O.S. CONFERENCE notified for Monday next, 18th inst, at 11 am at A.D.O.S. Office - Visited the R. Demolishing Trainers this afternoon - took continues to be light. | |
| " | 17/12/16 | 4 p.m. | To J.O.M. for a Cheque signing. Thence to HAZEBROUCK to Defence Force Workshop to change 5 air cylinders collected from Division Gas Schools this morning. Thence to 2nd Army Chief of Supplies, Mont des Cats for 7 rifles with Cheques Sights - Released and Returned via KATZOUTRE. Afternoon - Lieut. Nathurne visited B.S.R. Demolishing Trailers, 1 Henri Farm arranged for by Rae. To BAILLEUL for Conference at A.D.O.S. Office - also present NADOS of 35 & 36 Div. + O.O. Ox Cyps Troops. No points of any great importance. | |
| " | 18/12/16 | 4 p.m. | | |

# WAR DIARY or INTELLIGENCE SUMMARY

Army Form C. 2118

| Place | Date | Hour | Summary of Events and Information | Remarks and references to Appendices |
|---|---|---|---|---|
| WESTOUTRE | 19/12/15 | 7pm | A quiet day. Snow fell this afternoon. A new return of the Staff called for shewing the men in Categories A & B. Arranged for the R.A.M.S. to medically examine the Staff. Report in regard to the number of Ammunition employed in the Divisional Staff called for by Corps HQ. through to Division. | |
| " | 20/12/15 | 6.30pm | 1 LEWIS GUN received for 3rd R. Inniskilling Fusiliers. Arrival reported to Army & Corps. Units received bomb stores, 47th Inn. Coy., & 496 Bde HQ with A.T. of 3rd Inn. Received from C.T.D. 1 x Corps Troops. 500 pcs bags from thirst received from C.T.D. 1 x Corps Troops. | |
| " | 21/12/15 | 5.15pm | 1 VICKERS GUN demounted to 47th M.G. Coy. & 1 3" STOKES TRENCH MORTAR for 47th TRENCH MORTAR BTY. demounted from BASE to-day. To R.A. & Fus. Thus training for local purposes. Also to SALVAGE DUMP. P. Collect unservicable grenade shells &c to be in the manufacture (local) of enter-party copies | |
| " | 22/12/15 | 6pm | WIND SAFE. Very hot. Asked 47th T.M.B. to verify last a complete 3" STOKES is required to replace one damaged by a premature. Sent out a letter to 3 Bden. D.T.M.O. & Q. (for information) in regard the necessity for accuracy in denunciation to the defect mortars. - Visited with R.A.M.9., C.Q.h.S., Signal Coy., in regard to the defect lessons of Vermorins [sprayers] into S.B. There may have been some deant exp. - advised them to Code them to E 11.25 T.A. for his info. Visit at WESTOUTRE Patho - Observer & very | |

Geo. T. Carr.

| Place | Date | Hour | Summary of Events and Information | Remarks and references to Appendices |
|---|---|---|---|---|
| WESTOUTRE | 23/12/16 | 4 pm | A violent gale blew from 4-1 pm today. No one but Bolt Pte 225 & Pte Ellis etc reported two lorries broken down. Sent Hotchkiss accompanied with Drivers to CARAGE DUMP. Nothing to collect. Also to Q.M. Coin 65 CONNAUGHT RANGERS — not back in the dumps and to Divisional STOKEHOUSE SHOP — these men are 15 been employed — all said to be fully trained — referring 3.6 & pairs of boots handed in — not a unit number but 4 regiments in each case on the extent of this repair articles on each pair of boots. Gum boots are also patched & ???? bts repair are possible. Am afraid they be attempted for the water. Stiles are never repaired. Books to and Divisional Kanotine and are a Q.M. Chown on Tuesday next — Set out | |
| " | 24/12/16 | 7 pm | On 2nd STOKES MORTAR received for repair T.M.R. Ho morning — Hotchkiss circular to units in regard to cancellation of hunts sent out today. United 9 no short about return of Box Respirators received prior to 31-9-16 — also SALVAGE DUMP and Supply Column. 500 pailasses issued to each Infantry Brigade for use as litter. A quiet day — also from a review by Tillochin in Rosam. | |
| " | 25/12/15. | 8 pm | Xmas Dolluring presented to 2nd Army SchoolR of Instruction for one office with Telescopic sight & to R.R.E.S., 1 copy for 1 pair special half sole utilise for expert & 100 pailasses from OD. 1 x Cafe Troop — Otherw Xmas Day. | |
| " | 27/12/16 | 8 pm | Very quiet day. Returns all signed before 1 pm. A.D.S.S. unable to infact Laundry on account of break down of car. Issue of 3rd Blanket to them in huts has been approved & 460 are being sent to the Division without demand. | |

# WAR DIARY or INTELLIGENCE SUMMARY

Army Form C. 2118.

| Place | Date | Hour | Summary of Events and Information | Remarks and references to Appendices |
|---|---|---|---|---|
| WESTOUTRE. | 27/12/16 | 6 p.m. | One LEWIS GUN demanded for 7/8 R. Irish Fusiliers to replace one condemned to Divisional Armourers' Shop. Visited Q.M. Stores of the following battalions:- 1st R. Munster Fusiliers, 6th R. Irish Reg't, and 47th Machine Gun Coy. No very great accumulation of stores beyond what had just been issued. It is difficult to see how a certain attitude can be helped as units are worn out of the trenches & stores received (e.g. clothing) when they are in bivouac until they come out. Programme for Bath stores received from 2nd Army circulated. Still await Returns for A.R.O. Applied for hearing station. This should promote. | |
| WESTOUTRE. | 28/12/16 | 6 p.m. | Visited all hut billeted to the stores of 75 Bn. herewith Resp. 75 & 85 Bn. Dwellings Fusiliers with the exception of 7 & 8 Bn. herewith these stores were and 85 & 95 Bn. Dublin Fusiliers. With the exception of 7 & 8 Bn. herewith & in to come, the 7/8 Bn. herewith hut was sorted with all pretty empty but no has always been to cases. All sorts of stores but specially C.B. clothing. Most take this question up with D.A.D. when their Bn. has been billeted. 2 Armourers sent out to inspect rifles of 155 & 157 Field Coys. R.E. also rifles of moulds present of 155 Field Coy. R.E. The question of the hurl rifles will be confronted tomorrow- 29th. Arrangements being made to inspect 8 Vickers Guns of 47th Machine Gun Coy. now in reserve and all average weapons to 9 at present in trenches when they come into reserve. - By instruction of Armourer Staff. | |

# WAR DIARY

## INTELLIGENCE SUMMARY.

Army Form C. 2118.

| Place | Date | Hour | Summary of Events and Information | Remarks and references to Appendices |
|---|---|---|---|---|
| LESTOUTRE | 28.12.16 (Contd) | 10 p.m. | Fighting strength of Division today - 19,557 ; Horses H.D. 623; L.D. 4555 = Total Animal strength 5179. + mules | |
| " | 29/12/16 | 9.15 a.m. | WIND SAFE N/East. Very wet morning. | |
| | | 6.15 p.m. | One LEWIS GUN demanded for 2nd R. DUBLIN FUSILIERS & replace one totally destroyed by shell fire - 39 magazines also demanded. One LEWIS GUN received today for 7/8 R. IRISH FUSILIERS - returned to Corps + Army. LEWIS GUN received today for ½ pr installment for new Coys — 460 Blankets also received as first installment for new Coys — Armourer completed inspection of 156th FIELD COY. R.F.E rifles. Inspection of Small C.O's, Lewis bull commence tomorrow - Saturday, 30th. | |
| " | 30/12/16 | 4.15 p.m. | To HAZEBROUCK via Gas School to exchange 6 air cylinders reported by Gas Officer to be below pressure. | |
| " | 31/12/16 | 7.15 p.m. | Verified Vickers Q. m. Stores (with Lieut. Dalhuine) of the following units:- 2nd R. Irish Regt; 7/8 R. Irish Fusiliers; 2nd R. Dublin Fusiliers and 7th R. Irish Rifles - All these Stores were fairly empty except for kit clothing - He last moved Residences has never been so empty before - Arranged with Q. to visit 7th Bn. Leinster Regts Stores towards the end of the |

# WAR DIARY
## INTELLIGENCE SUMMARY
*(Erase heading not required.)*

Army Form C. 2118.

| Place | Date | Hour | Summary of Events and Information | Remarks and references to Appendices |
|---|---|---|---|---|
| HESTROUTRE | 31/12/16 | Contd. | Week ending it became so exposed to report to H.Q. This completes the 12 Infantry Bns. Q.M.S. stores. Truck hire of last night upheld 24 hours Pans for the Division. This hill fire all Bns. except however 12 hours Pans. A.D.O.S. asked this afternoon — indent stores and clothing — Apparently satisfied. Also indent HESTROUTRE LAUNDRY and BATH. One Vickers Machine Gun demanded for 47th Bn. Coy. to replace one beyond repair in Armourers Shop. <br><br> The following Machine Guns and trench mortars have been demanded from to Base to replace others destroyed or rendered inaccurate during the 3 months ending to-night:— <br> Vickers Machine Guns:— 3 ; LEWIS GUNS:— 7 ; 3" STOKES TRENCH MORTARS :— 7 :— and 2" TRENCH MORTARS :— 2. <br> Nos. Rifles O.B.T. 18 fr. have been demanded and only 3 4·5 in Howitzer in last 3 months. 108 Cms Rifles have been sent up from BASE this month as expand till 250 last week who expand are 375 ; Rifles 38 ; Lewis pistols 42 ; Machine Guns, Lewis & Vickers 31.— <br><br> V.S. Orrad Captain <br> D.A.D.O.S. 16 Division. 31/12/16. | |

WAR DIARY for month of JANUARY, 1917.

VOLUME  14

D.A.D.O.S. 16th Division

# WAR DIARY / INTELLIGENCE SUMMARY

Army Form C. 2118.

| Place | Date | Hour | Summary of Events and Information | Remarks and references to Appendices |
|---|---|---|---|---|
| WESTOUTRE | 1/1/17 | 9 am | No kind of Railed today. Transport went out to Dranier to complete to Division to the Infantry Bn - 2 staff Pioneers also out this trip. Made up to establishment of 529 present rc 44 per Coy. Lewis Guns also received for 3rd R. Dublin Fusiliers to replace the defective Guns mended on 29-12-16. Also an 5th Training Hospital. This mustered 6 Officers. All new arrivals reported to Capt. & Adjt. Visited R. Hd. Qrs (Q.M. & Staff Practically empty). 44th, 47th, 48th, & 49th Infantry Bde (F.E. Appointed). All is quiet except 45 Bde. are in trouble about 400 pairs of boots from Repeated that Bn. took Staff Captain is going to look in all all the afternoon Ingt. of Orders & replenishment of these Bdes efficient — supplied GATES for these from 25 boots C.S.L. + felta etc 23, & others ac 30 ur SALVAGE. | |
| | 2/1/17 | 6.30 pm | List of machine ladies for assistance sent to A.D.S. 4 copies this morning. Visited 15 R.M.F training and Salvate dump. Arrived to Range to O.C. 15 Corps Troops 2 to-morrow with salvage dump. Stopped a quiet day. 48 Bde. went & sheltered cooker & 15 Prisoners for a special purpose to non-commissioned ranks. | |
| | 3/1/17 | 6.30 pm | 1 VICKERS MACHINE GUN received for 475 Machine Gun Coy demanded on 31-12-16 — Draft reported to Capt. & Adjt. Lieut. DASHMORE proceeded to R.E. DUMP CANADA CORNER to draw | |

# WAR DIARY or INTELLIGENCE SUMMARY

Army Form C. 2118.

| Place | Date | Hour | Summary of Events and Information | Remarks and references to Appendices |
|---|---|---|---|---|
| WESTOUTRE | 3/7/17 | Cont'd | 15 Mustanirs: Hence to BAILLEUL to purchase 4 electric Globes; and as to STRAGGLERS about 4 pairs of Wire Cutters. These Stores were handed over to 495 Fd. H.Q. He also visited SALVAGE DUMP and attached to M.G. periscope. I Visited O/c WAGON LINES A/177 Bde. also 495 MOBILE VETERINARY SECTION. Nothing special to note at either. | |
| " | 4/7/17 | Aftn. | A quiet day. Inspected Signal Corps Stores — Billets arranged and less in St Pann I have been — but it is a bad building. Otherwise a very quiet day. | |
| " | 5/7/17 | 7p.m. | Another quiet day. | |
| " | 6/7/17 | 7p.m. | Work day. To BAILLEUL this afternoon to purchase electric lantern for W/L Refs. for "a Scheme" purpose — also a lock for the repair of a Stationery Box. A.D.O.S. was out — Returned to WESTOUTRE R.E. | |
| " | 7/7/17 | 7p.m. | Most of the day spent in exercising laundry matters. The question of what Colt be carried in the laundry is one of some difficulty. Have submitted a minute to Q. on the subject. The lorries from 2nd R. Scots. Fusiliers apparent for duty to the Armourer Workshop. Two waistcoats fallen grenade carriers received + issued to 495 Refs. for a spare purposes. The question of Artillery armaments has come up again — WIND DANGEROUS R.Afoot. | |
| " | " | 10.45p. | Lieut. Mulhouse proceeded to HAZEBROUCK to exchange air exhausters for Gas Officers, + to BAILLEUR for spare punches + a drum of Field Cashier — Visited 8th R. Scots. Fusiliers and Salvage — the Special B/180 Bde R.F.A. & H.Q. for returning not-billetty Carts to be | |
| " | 8/7/17 | 10.15p. | Cancel 3rd Street T.M. for 47 T.M.B. | |

# WAR DIARY
## INTELLIGENCE SUMMARY
*(Erase heading not required.)*

Army Form C. 2118.

| Place | Date | Hour | Summary of Events and Information | Remarks and references to Appendices |
|---|---|---|---|---|
| WESTOUTRE | 9-1-17 | 7/am | 1 Vickers Machine Gun demanded for 49th M.G. Coy. to replace one beyond local repair in Div. Workshops - Applied to Corps - Army etc. Demands from 49th Bde. H.Q. for trench tackets, overshoes, cardies and gloves helping - Nothing arranged - To draw bag bomb tickets - Otherwise a quiet day. | |
| " | 10-1-17 | 8.35pm | 1 VICKERS MACHINE GUN demanded for 49th G.G. Yesterday received today. Applied to Army & Corps. Also having to local functions 6 coats to make 12 coats for additional working at 6 SALVAGE DUMP. 6 Arranged for hire for helping Rocket overcoats. To POPERINGHE LAUNDRY. This afternoon. 15 Tumbler kettles part of Vickers Test Q.M. Stores - explits that it has now been 156 R. Field Regt. in sent over. Vickers Valange | |
| " | 11-1-17 | 6am | Rec - This beginning smelling. SE character harmer complete - Some incomplete - arrayed for full collection. Also Shampo - 5 - 1/2 Very Pistols were complete - some the made to the Armourer. 6 Jusson one Boot Goes to draw one socket for petton of cows the 15th and 77 Bde. Notification received list to repairsher F.R.A. will commence a A.W.D. STAFF which will serve an Army Field Artillery Bde. will have the use of 185. Orders Notified today - 2° T.M. Carrel received from 5/16 & demanded on 9-1-16. 1° Dury to R. for Company duty under D.A.D. received today. | |

/S. Orover
Captain
A.A.D.S. 16 (Irish) Divison
11-1-17.

Army Form C. 2118

# WAR DIARY
## or
## INTELLIGENCE SUMMARY
*(Erase heading not required.)*

Instructions regarding War Diaries and Intelligence Summaries are contained in F.S. Regs., Part II. and the Staff Manual respectively. Title Pages will be prepared in manuscript.

| Place | Date | Hour | Summary of Events and Information | Remarks and references to Appendices |
|---|---|---|---|---|
| WESTOUTRE | 31.1.17 | 10.55 am | Captain T.S. Gno N/S having been appointed D.A.D.S. Rathyoul Division, Lieut A.G. DALLIMORE has been appointed D.A.D.S. 16th (Irish) Division — taking over on Jan. 1st 1917. Nothing calling for special comment has arisen between the 11th and 31st inst. 1/2/17 | Appointment List. D.a.D.S. 16th Divn |

1875 Wt. W593/826 1,000,000 4/15 J.B.C. & A. A.D.S.S./Forms/C. 2118.

WAR DIARY.

FOR MONTH OF FEBRUARY, 1917.

VOLUME 15

UNIT:- DADOS 16th Division

# WAR DIARY
## or
## INTELLIGENCE SUMMARY
*(Erase heading not required.)*

Army Form C. 2118

Instructions regarding War Diaries and Intelligence Summaries are contained in F.S. Regs., Part II. and the Staff Manual respectively. Title Pages will be prepared in manuscript.

| Place | Date 1917 | Hour | Summary of Events and Information | Remarks and references to Appendices |
|---|---|---|---|---|
| WESTOUTRE | FEB: 1 | | Received further 200 sets of ammunition carrying light, with buckles & Japanese silk. Some have but they do not seem to be very popular with commanding officers who are generally rather difficult to please. P.G. Taylor, Storeman A.O.C., entered hospital & suffering from exposure of the knee caused by a fall while off loading a lorry. P.G. Digard appointed Lance Corporal (without pay), appointment dated 15th Jan. 1917. | |
| | 2 | | P.G. Taylor invalided to Base and reinforcement applied for in the usual way. Wired for one 18pdr gun for 13/180 Bde R.F.A. to replace gun condemned by I.O.M. Received one 3" stokes T.M. Barrel and 2 mountings 3" Mortar T.M. for 47 Trench Mortar Battery. Owing to the snow, the hands are discovering our artillery positions. H.Q. Divl. Artillery accordingly asked for about 1600 yds of wattle & lashing wattle work owing in the endeavour to get authority for local purchase from A.D.O.S. IX Corps. IX Corps (D.) telephoned at 11.30 pm that | |
| | 3 | | Purchase would while starting for R.A. Transferred HQ, Bde (177H, 136) 77th Bde + C/180 Bde. R.F.A. to 39th Divn. as they were ordered from Calais Training Area. | |
| | 4 | | Transferred No. 1 Sec. 16 A.O.C. to 39th Divn also. Demanded one 18pdr gun with 13 M. and Carr. for A/180 Bde R.F.A. to replace others condemned by I.O.M. for damage caused by hostile shell fire. | |
| | 5 | | Wired for two 3" Stokes T.M. Barrels for 48 T.M.B. to replace others by I.O.M. for local repairs. Also for one 18pdr gun for C/177 Bde R.F.A. to replace one condemned by I.O.M. for excessive cartridge clearance. | |
| | 7 | | Received two 3" Stokes T.M. for 48 T.M.B. | |
| | 9 | | Attended at office of A.D.O.S. IX Corps conference with D.A.D.O.S. of 25th + 36th Division & O.O. IX Corps Troops. Much talk but nothing of value transpired. | |
| | 12 | | Received 2nd Reinforcement with appropriate magazine, carrying weapons, etc. This completes 1st Infantry Battalions to 14 Lewis guns each, & Pioneer Battalion with 8. | |
| | 14 | | Received 18pdr with R.M.V. Carr. for A/180 Bde R.F.A. and 18pdr with R.M. + Carr. for 13/180 Bde R.F.A. service the further 18pdr. and Carr. for A/180 Bde R.F.A. to replace others condemned by I.O.M. HQ, Bde. Battrs. 77th Bde + C/180 Bde. R.F.A. also No. 1 Sec. 16 A.O.C. returned to this area owing to know whether they are to be administered by this Division as it is understood they are to assist another Division with a re. | |
| | 15 | | Wired for one 3" Stokes T.M. Barrel for 48 T.M.B. to replace unserviceable. Decided to retain some & store such as Carr, O/R, Rifles, etc. | |
| | 16 | | Demanded one Carr. for 18pdr gun for C/177 Bde. R.F.A. | |
| | 17 | | to this Divn from BPP Divn. 17 Received nearly 1800 blankets for issue (3rd blanket per man) to men in inferior hutments. Received 3 braziers complete for warming hutments of L/ for 2nd R. Sub-Sec. Facilities. These have been extra Divnee Dept. Cart and the previous Divl. Hd. I.R.D.F. were sold to school to put them. Special steps taken have been however proved successful. | |
| | 18 | | Received one 18pdr. C.Carr. for C/177 Bde. R.F.A. and one 8" Stokes T.M. Barrel for 48 T.M.B. issued for H. complete turning of new pattern gun handguards for ports cont..., these, together with two new Peyper Bolt, will be duty attended on a personally from the manufacturing firm with refer the new withdrawn will be placed..... | |

# WAR DIARY or INTELLIGENCE SUMMARY

Army Form C. 2118

| Place | Date | Hour | Summary of Events and Information | Remarks and references to Appendices |
|---|---|---|---|---|
| WESTOUTRE | Feb 19 | | Received further 680 Rounds S.A.A. ammunition for S.M.L.E. Visited today by an Asst IX Corps who seemed satisfied with system in force. | |
| | 20 | | Wired for one T.M. Barrel for X/15 T.M.B. to replace one condemned for damage from premature explosion; also for one Lewis Gun for 101 R. Muntrs Fus. | |
| | 21 | | Reorganization of Divisional Artillery commenced. Received 18 pdr. gun and carr. for A/180 Bde R.F.A. also 7.0 more blankets for wired for one Lewis Gun for 7 R. Inniskilling Fus; and 2 for 3" Stokes T.M. with elevating stand for 48 T.M.B. | |
| | 22 | | Divisional Artillery reorganization completed. Artillery now becomes 177 Bde. R.F.A. (HQ, A, B, C Bdes. each six 18 pdrs.); 180 Bde. R.F.A. (HQ, A, B, C Bdes. each six 18 pdrs. and D Batt. six 4.5" How.); 16 D.A.C. (HQ, No. 1 Sec. "A" Echelon, No. 2 Sec. "A" Echelon, No. 3 Sec. "B" Echelon). Remainder goes to form 77 Army Field Artillery Brigade & 77 A.F.A. Bde. Amn Col. All concerned duly notified of above. Reorganization carried out as follows:— | |
| | | | Old Designation → New Designation | |
| | | | HQ. 77 Bde. R.F.A. — HQ. 77 Army Field Artillery Bde. | |
| | | | A/77 " — A/77 " | |
| | | | B/77 " — B/77 " | |
| | | | A/172 " (from 36 D.A.) — C/77 " | |
| | | | C/77 " & one Sec. C/172 from 36 D.A. — D/77 " | |
| | | | Altogether — one Sec. of D/177 Bde. & 1 Sec. to D/180 Bde. | |
| | | | No. 1 Sec. 16 D.A.C. — 77 A.F.A.B.A.C. | |
| | | | " 2 " " — No. 2 Sec. "A" Echelon 16 D.A.C. | |
| | | | " 3 " " — " 1 " " " | |
| | | | " 4 " " — " 3 " "B" Echelon " | |
| | 23 | | Pointed out to Staff Captain 16 Div. Arty. the necessity of returning all "U" gun components to Rear for repair or disposal. Reviewed to old schedule in proportion of 10-0 to 14. At dawn, this will help R.A. very considerably. | |
| | 24 | | Received :— one 3" T.M.B.; one 3" 3/4 gtes for 48 T.M.B.; 1 Lewis Gun each for 1 R. Inniskilling Fus; 7 R. Inniskilling Fus. Moved 77 A.F.A. Bde. & Amn. Col. (with outstanding incidents & truck ammunition) to H.Q. IX Corps Troops. Drew our Forward machine guns with French Mounting vice from O.C. 2nd Army Troops for issue to Div. Art. for anti-aircraft | |

1875 Wt. W593/826 1,000,000 4/15 J.B.C. & A. A.D.S.S./Forms/C. 2118.

# WAR DIARY
## INTELLIGENCE SUMMARY
*(Erase heading not required.)*

Army Form C. 2118.

III.

| Place | Date | Hour | Summary of Events and Information | Remarks and references to Appendices |
|---|---|---|---|---|
| WESTOUTRE | 1917 Feb 25 | | Wired for 3 "Stokes" T.M. as follows to replace others destroyed by premature explosions, viz :- one (with mounting) for 149 T.M. By. two (and one mounting) for 47 T.M.B. | |
| | 26 | | Received one 3" Stokes T.M. & mtg. for 47 T.M.B. Wired for one 2" T.M. for Y/16 T.M.B. | |
| | 27 | | Wired for one Lewis Gun for 1 R. Munster Fus. Visited by D.D.O.S. O.C. 2 Div. 2nd Army and A.D.O.S. IX Corps. O.C. "U" S.P. Clothing sent to contractors at hours to be fumigated to counteract majority in pockets Q.M.G. having no information hold in fittness all such clothing is to be examined in the area (divisional) before despatch, as it is considered to be beyond the power of the R.O.O. Arrangements are to be made for the work to be done by Salvage Coy. under supervision of D.A.D.O.S. To this end, A.D.O.S visited D.A.Q.M.G of arrangements can be made to bring Salvage Coy. to S area. | |
| | 28 | | Received 3" Stokes T.M. for 47 T.M.B. & 2" T.M. for Y/16 T.M.B. Several of the 18/pr guns overworked during this month have been several delays in coming up probably owing to the new Transportation Scheme. First delays necessitated our Div. Arty. borrowing Guns. Visits to Quartermasters Store this month show them to be amply and fairly satisfactory. Items which are habitually worst will be down to their reputation. Grenades have been rather heavy but explanations have been put forward in reply to queries. Steps have been taken from time to time, during the month to prevent waste but Lt 7/18 R. Dublin Fus. are at a standing Heart. | |

28 Feb. 1917.

A.E. Davidson Lieut. A.O.D.

D.A.D.O.S. 16th Division.

WAR DIARY
FOR MONTH OF MARCH, 1917.

VOLUME 16

UNIT:- A.A. & Q.M.G. 16th Division

# WAR DIARY
## INTELLIGENCE SUMMARY
*(Erase heading not required.)*

Army Form C. 2118.

Instructions regarding War Diaries and Intelligence Summaries are contained in F.S. Regs., Part II. and the Staff Manual respectively. Title pages will be prepared in manuscript.

| Place | Date | Hour | Summary of Events and Information | Remarks and references to Appendices |
|---|---|---|---|---|
| WESTOUTRE | 1-3-17 | | Wired for one 3" Stokes Trench Mortar for 47 T.M. Battery, to replace unserviceable. | |
| | 2-3-17 | | Received from Base one Lewis Gun demanded for 1 R. Munster Fusiliers. Q decided that something of all unserviceable S.D. Clothing (two waistcoats) could not be conveniently carried out by Salvage Section — Salvage Dump cannot conveniently be moved closer to A.D.O.S. Dump & it will be difficult to produce additional personnel. Divisional Routine Order therefore published instructing that all units will mark their "U" Clothing before despatch to Base (this to be carried out by an officer) and to issue certificate in duplicate that such search has been made and no papers or articles remain in the pockets; one copy to be enclosed in bale of clothing and duplicate to Craat & Siegner; all bales to be labelled with details of contents and name of unit. | |
| | 3-3-17 | | Commenced overhaul in Divl. Armourers' Shop of Vickers Machine Guns and Pistols of 48 M.G. Coy. | |
| | 4-3-17 | | Received Today Runnymede Hand II (to 7 to Divl. H.Q. to distribute 28 in detail indent) so long due. | |
| | | | Received from Base one 3" Stokes T.M. demanded for 49 T.M. Battery. Received was from 2nd Army Field Artillery Brigade. At determined by D.A.D.O.S. army on subject of administration of Army Field Artillery Brigade. It occurred to D.A.D.O.S. Corps that reduction in D.A.D.O.S. staff is desired? Replied that experience proves that present staff is minimum possible to ensure efficiency, that there is growing practice of taking detail wants to Corps to increase work of A.O.C. personnel and Army Troops Companies), and that already D.A.D.O.S. administers various Corps Troops (eg. Entrenching Battalion, Tunnelling and Army Troops Companies), and that duties on the army other units (eg. Heavy Artillery) became attached for Ordnance Purposes. | |
| | 5-3-17 | | Routine. | |
| | 6-3-17 | | Sent to A.D.O.S. IX Corps recommendations for promotion (M.F.) viz. Pte. O'H entitled to Corporal, Pte. T.C. Hanning to Sgft, Pte. O. Rayne to Cpl/Pt. & would if special accelerated promotion can be made as I am very short of N.C.Os. | |
| | 7-3-17 | | IX Corps and accompanied him on inspection of Divl. Baths, Laundries at Westoutre & Locre. A.D.O.S. went into system of accounting; stocks to inspected. Visited by O.Q.M.G. etc. went in place of Pg. Stitt, evacuated sick. Armt. Staff Sergt. Davies returned from hospital. P.Q. O.C. (48 M.G. Co.) reported | |
| | 8-3-17 | | Arranged programme for inspection of Rifles and Revolvers of 16th Bud. Train A.S.C. | |
| | 9-3-17 | | Wired for two 3" Stokes T.M. (48 T.M.B.) to replace others completely demolished by enemy fire; also one 18 pdr. gun without B.M. for C/177 Bde R.F.A. to replace one condemned by I.O.M. for wear and tear. Recommended to Brit. Commander Ord. Randolph for an award in Bingley Honours for gift for valuable services rendered. Although this W.O. rarely deserves some definite recognition, I am not sanguine that he will get any; all awards appear to go to the Padres and Fighting troops and HQ Troops other than A.O.C. | |
| | 10-3-17 | | Attended Q.D.O.S. Conference with D.A.D.O.S. 6, 2nd. O-O. IX Corps troops and Salvage Officer IX Corps Troops, 16, & 36th Divs. Usual chat on subject of Salvage schemes, show working of scheme with Salvage Officer. Others present finally agreed that Salvage system in force in this division is most satisfactory. A.D.O.S. decided to pay the D.O.O. a visit with A.A.Q. H.Q. IX Corps. 2353 Wt.W2541/1454 700,000 5/15 D.D.&L. A.D.S.S./Forms/C.2118. T.M. for 47 T.M.B. to replace one condemned. 7 T.M. demanded for 47 T.M.B. Wires for one 3 Stokes T.M. for 47 T.M.B. to replace one condemned. One Lewis Gun to 7 R. Dubl. Rifles to replace one condemned and one Dall Armourers' Shop. Armour repaired and Vickers M.Gs. & Lewis Guns etc. | |

# WAR DIARY
## INTELLIGENCE SUMMARY
*(Erase heading not required.)*

Army Form C. 2118.

II

| Place | Date | Hour | Summary of Events and Information | Remarks and references to Appendices |
|---|---|---|---|---|
| WESTOUTRE | 11.3.17 | | Received from store one 3" Stokes T.M. for 47 T.M.B. and two 3" Stokes T.M. for 48 T.M.B. Arrived for one Lewis Gun complete and 14 magazines for 6 Cavalry M.G. Range also two Lewis guns complete and 120 magazines for 7 R. Irish Rifles. Ammunition completed inwards. Vickers G. 9 + 4 8 M. G. Coy. Arrived for one 3" Stokes T.M. for 47 T.M. Battery. | |
| | 12.3.17 | | Received from store one Lewis gun for 7 R. Irish Rifles. Arrived for one Thombos Horn of air cylinders for 47 Brig. Role and for Steam Horse to air cylinders for Brit. Gas Officer. Received telegraphic instructions from D.A.D.O.S. Army that commencing midnight 14/15 March demands for stores in sections 14/15/16 (except 163 Steel Helmets & Body Armour) for Artillery Units and T.M. Batteries are to be made on Havre Base vice Calais Base. | |
| | 13.3.17 | | Commenced inspection of Rifles of 165 Brit. Trench A.S.C. Brig. from R.E. Park. Ascertained 30 Canadian Yukon Rocks and crews 10 to 110 each Sub. Role. Arrived for one Thombos Horn complete and air cylinders for Brit. Gas Officers. Shortly M.G. Coy. offering to overhaul Vickers M.Gs one per week. | |
| | 14.3.17 | | Received from Base two Lewis guns complete to 7 R. Irish Rifles and 1 Lewis gun complete for 6 Cavalry M.G. Range; also one B"Coy" T.M. for 49 T.M.B. Moved 1st Canadian Tunnelling Coy. to 41st Division from 16th and inclusive. All concerned notified, outstanding indent and bulk summary passed to D.A.D.O.S. 1 Can. Tunn. Co. Instructed to call daily for one week to draw stores and which will be consigned to us in that period. Other from routine work, the first half of the month has been fairly quiet. The Division is now in a fair state of equipment. The recent heavy demands for T.M.B. L.G. & Thombos Horn are chiefly on account of the recent heavy raiding by the enemy. No issues of 18 Pr. wind for an 9 Pr. as tasted today by wire. Routine. | |
| | 15.3.17 | | | |
| | 16.3.17 | | Received 18 Pr. 8— tr C/177 demand 31/3 + took 31/5/3. Also received from Base 25 sets of Body Armour of a lighter pattern. | |
| | 17.3.17 | | Notified all concerned that 6 Inf. Bat. Coy further light infantry required for this Division will be assumed tr Horse Shoes by one or two 16½ inst. | |
| | 18.3.17 | | Received orders from O.B.D. IX Corps that in future the H.Q. miniature cavalry expedition D.3.G. | |
| | 19.3.17 | | Travelling G.R.P. transferred from O.O. IX Corps from to D.A.D.O.S. 16th Division. Reported G.R.O. IX Corps my opinion that ammunition should be included in war Establishment of Div. HQ. take the Div. Armourers' Shop should become a permanent installation with a transit Officer in charge. A full attention of Workshop Lorry. Visited by D.A.D.O.S. IX Corps who came to see 16th Div. Q.R.C. in charge of Workshop Lorry. | |
| | 20.3.17 | | Visited by D.A.D.O.S. 38 Division as outstanding personnel number of 77 A.P.A. Bde. Routine. | |
| | 21.3.17 | | Arrived for one 18 Pr. gun (without Brig.) for B/180 G replace accidentally shown for wear and firing. | |
| | 22.3.17 | | Reconnoitred LOORE for Smith Shop, Store, Billets etc. Visited by A.D. O.S IX Corps revived during morning afternoon. | |

2353 Wt. W2544/1454 700,000 5/15 D. D. & L. A.D.S.S./Forms/C. 2118.

Army Form C. 2118.

# WAR DIARY
## or
## INTELLIGENCE SUMMARY.
*(Erase heading not required.)*

Instructions regarding War Diaries and Intelligence Summaries are contained in F.S. Regs., Part II. and the Staff Manual respectively. Title pages will be prepared in manuscript.

| Place | Date | Hour | Summary of Events and Information | Remarks and references to Appendices |
|---|---|---|---|---|
| WESTOUTRE | 23.3.17 | | Routine work | |
| | 24.3.17 | | Nothing extraordinary today when all clocks advanced one hour. | |
| | 25.3.17 | | Loaned for and Vickers M.G. for 47 M.G. Coy. to replace one damaged. Local repair. Received 3 of sum fim ripes 2 to use of B.B. (B.L.) Rammer Straps & ??? as immediate to Infy Batts and will B Lewis guns and 1 Inf (Lewis) A.B. on a Lewis from times wages. One 3" Stokes T.M. drum on received from 47 T.M. Batty. | |
| | 26.3.17 } 27.3.17 } | | Routine. | |
| | 28.3.17 | | Received three 4/8/35 ????? for 13/180, Vickers with ????? for the 3" Stokes T.M. for 49 T.M. B. A replace one damaged by shrapnel. Visited by new D.D.O.L. (D.C.) p. (L apt. Ira Mar) who inspected office recent & situation, interviews ??? Paraded (at 11:) D.O.G.Q.M.G. ? ???? ??? on office loan & arrange) to take over office from town Major. Loaned for 1 Lewis Gun for 7/8 R. Irish Fusiliers to replace one beyond local repair. Saw O/c 161 Batts also division Laundry re disposal of stores in view of coming movement. Closing of Workshops ? Stores ???. Commenced removal of Stores & Ammunition Shop to Locre. | |
| WESTOUTRE LOCRE | 31.3.17 | | Divisional Headquarters moved to LOCRE this date / Moved office to M.23.c.5.1. Stores to M.23.a.33.75.1 and Divisional Ammunition Shop to M.23.a.5.3 = all Longo Shut 28 Scale 1/20,000 Demanded 1 Showcase from and 2 Oil Cylinders for Divl. Sig. Office to replace unit destroyed by shell fire. Received from Bait Park by road 50 Lamps, hurricane oil, plus an additional 20. New the unit is independent as regards Stores except it is being made ??? | |
| | 31.3.17. | | | |

AHDammann Lieut. A.D.O.
D.O.A.O.S. 163 Division

WAR DIARY   FOR MONTH OF   APRIL, 1917.

VOLUME:- 14

UNIT:- DADOS. 16th Div.

Army Form C. 2118.

# WAR DIARY of D.A.D.O.S.

## INTELLIGENCE SUMMARY. 16th Division.

(Erase heading not required.)

Instructions regarding War Diaries and Intelligence Summaries are contained in F. S. Regs., Part II. and the Staff Manual respectively. Title pages will be prepared in manuscript.

| Place | Date 1917 | Hour | Summary of Events and Information | Remarks and references to Appendices |
|---|---|---|---|---|
| LOC.R.E. | 1/4 | | Wired Army for one Shoulder Hose Set complete to replace one destroyed by hostile Shellfire. (HQ 49 Inf. Bde.) | |
| | 2/4 | | Local purchase of material for making up disinfecting trays for Divl. Artillery. | |
| | 3/4 | | Transferred to D.A.D.O.S. 19th Divn: – 175 + 250 Turn. Co. R.E., 136 A.T. Co. R.E., 1st Entrenching Batt: Purchased 600 within square of whitewashing for special Artly. Stunt this afternoon, have known a heavy fall of snow today. | |
| | 4/4 | | Received from Base & 50 Rotn Haps Varity (today) by A.D.O.S. IX Corps (even pound Belts, knuckle, Boot hops and wrists)Armoury Shop and Store within HQ 7/8 - 9/19/19 Let it at Spanning, to put special trunk good in hope. Ammunition examined for the same  D.O.S., D.D.O.S. 2 = Army and C.O.O. IX Corps were expected today but unfortunately the train did not materialise. | |
| | 5/4 | | Have arose (taken into use up. 4/5 instead of 6/7). | |
| | | | Sent convoy of two lorries with Stores for 48 Inf. Bde. to NORDAUSQUES. Also visited HQ + units of 48 Inf. Bde. at & around NORDAUSQUES. Arranged system of supply while Bde. is in training area. Arranged with C.O.O., St OMER, to receive unserviceable stores for despatch to Base. | |
| | 6/4 | | Received from Base 10·00 Short pattern Greatcoats of Copes. Visited units. Routine. | |
| | 7/4 | | Visited HQ 47 & 49 Inf. Bdes. and settled arrangement of Armoury for work in Divl. Shops. | |
| | 8/4 | | Received from Base one Lewis gun for 7/8 R. Irish Inns. Wired for one 3" Stokes T.M. for 47 T.M. B. to replace one destroyed by hostile Shellfire. | |
| | 9/4 | | Visited 48 Inf. Bde. at RECQUES. R.F.A. WIZERNES. Visited A.O.D. depot CALAIS, with o/D.A.Q.M.G. Trained questions (eg. Supply of Clothes, replacement of F.A.Boots by Ankle Boots Puttees) Endeavoured to purchase large wingles for new Divl. Laundry — none available in Calais, so tried Boulogne unsuccessfully. | |
| | 10/4 | | Sent convoy (2 lorries) to 48 Inf. Bde. at 180 Bde. R.F.A. Comdr. Randall purchased 3 small wringers at BOULOGNE. Visited IX Corps HQ with A.D.Q. walk to inspect pattern of field constructed on principle of Division Boucher. | |
| | 11/4 | | Ammunition examined inspection of 11th Hauts. rifles, Lewis Guns &c. | |
| | 12/4 | | Inspection of arms (11 Hauts.) continued. Ammunition one Vickers M.G. for 47 Inf. Bde. to replace one beyond local repair. | |
| | 13/4 | | Ammunition Complete Bde. 11th Hauts. inspection – 917 Rifles, 8 Lewis Guns, 8 Revolvers. Report – satisfactory. One of this Lewis Guns condemned for wear and one new one wired for. Received Vickers with box for 47 Inf. Bde. (wired for yesterday). | |
| | 14/4 | | Sent convoy to NIELLES with clos. for 18 Bde. R.F.A. Hostile Bese for Smelling Is Pantaloons, Divl. Hosp. Bay Slose and Brevoc Base as now have been received for annual needs. Notified if provisioned of his A.K.Q.M.in to be... | |
| | 15/4 | | Received bearing for 11th Hauts. (2?) contd. (Temp. O.p.r. wished & A.O.O.) 16th Division. | |

Army Form C. 2118.

# WAR DIARY
## INTELLIGENCE SUMMARY.
(Erase heading not required.)

Bailleul
16th Division

| Place | Date 1917 | Hour | Summary of Events and Information | Remarks and references to Appendices |
|---|---|---|---|---|
| LOCRE | 16/4 | | Received one 3" Stokes T.M. for 177 T.M.B. | |
| | 17/4 | | Routine. Convoy to MEAQUEVILLERS for 149 Inf Bde (with 48 Bds now returned) and 180 Bde R.F.A at MIELLES. | |
| | 18/4 | | Routine. | |
| | 19/4 | | Sent for mud from 2nd army R.G. workshops 12 Boxes Ammn jars for carrying weapons/Lewis gun | |
| | 20/4 | | Routine. Great pressure of material for numerous columns & ammunition for training specialists. | |
| | 21/4 | | Units complaining of scarcity of butts only of Lewis. Specially wired Base in the hope of getting supplies. | |
| | | | Sent convoy to NORDAUSQUES with extras for 49th Inf Bde and 177 Bde R.F.A. (or BLINCOVE was 180 Bde returning). | |
| | | | Visitation of units. | |
| | 22/4 | | Armourer carried out inspection of rifles of 155 Bat C.R.G. and reports condition satisfactory, many indeed first-rate. | |
| | 23/4 | | Selected site for testing machine/Lewis guns after repair in Armourers' Shop. Said site not (being approved by the | |
| | | | Pampas Belgians, a less suitable site has to be reconsidered just off the road behind an ammunition dump. | |
| | | | Continued visitation of units. Lorries convoy petrol for training area. (Hd Qrs/Bde + 177 Bde R.F.A.) | |
| | | | Leave having been granted me from 24/4 to 2/5, handed over to Conductor J. Caudwell A.O.C. to carry on. | |
| | | | 23/4/17. A.P.Davisson Captain O.O.S. | |
| | 24/4 | | Routine. Convoy to NORDAUSQUES with stores for 149 & 150 Infanty | |
| | | | At 6:15 Showing that very heavy aerial fight at Ayf. and 177 Bde R.F.A. | |
| | | | what turned though not of Village School Mks. Aufs. aircraft shell (empennage vw?) | |
| | | | shell burst on coming in contact with kitchen door, apparently first had not been fused | |
| | | | burnt in pieces— | |
| | 25/4 | | Local purchase of details (44th Rds for Ammn tr training) 3094/Mr Booth Armb. & 3094/m | |
| | | | Lorry rec'd from Base to replace field service booti (Intelmen)– 16 Special | |
| | | | Brenether Durnet ditto received 9 Rifle Brigade – Head Granther | |
| | | | for trial | |
| | 26/4 | | Nothing special occurred | |

# WAR DIARY
## or
## INTELLIGENCE SUMMARY.

Army Form C. 2118.

| Place | Date | Hour | Summary of Events and Information | Remarks and references to Appendices |
|---|---|---|---|---|
| LOCRE | 27/4 | | Demanded 60 G.S. Wagons for X [?] Div. O. Train to replace 60 H.T. Special Wagons which were found too heavy for light draught horses. Auth. D.D.S. O.E.M. D/117/4 of 23/4/17. Armourer inspected the Arms of "15" Field Coy RE. | |
| " | 28/4 | | Nothing special occurred. (General Routine) | |
| " | 29/4 | | 60 G.S.T. Wagons received for 16th Div. Train (General Routine) | |
| " | 30/4 | | Sent 3000 Blankets (2nd Plunkett to Pool) (General Routine) | |

30/4/17

[signature] for Capt.
D.A.D.S. 16 Div.

Absent on leave

WAR DIARY:
-------oOo-------

VOLUME:- 18

FOR MONTH OF MAY, 1917.

UNIT:- DADOS 16th Division

**WAR DIARY**

**INTELLIGENCE SUMMARY**

Army Form C. 2118.

D.A.D.O.S. 16TH (IRISH) DIV.

*16th Division*

| Place | Date | Hour | Summary of Events and Information | Remarks and references to Appendices |
|---|---|---|---|---|
| Locre | 1/5 | | Armourer reported 3 Lewis Guns & 5 Bicycles. Court of Enquiry regarding accident in Armourers Shop (A.R.O. 2599). Received instructions re transport of Lewis Gun leaders. Undercarriages and gun cradles to be withdrawn for being leaders undercarriages. | |
| " | 2/5 | | Routine. Received from Base N.O.O. Perforators and Howsen asked Q.F. confirming re distribution of same. Armourers Companies returned: 136 at Cy RE, 148 & 236 Jamesburg Coys & 101 Pioneer Bn. Joining this Div. from 19th Division, in exchange for 5 Cylinders for stunken Army. | |
| " | 3/5 | | Routine. To Kayebrouck. Armourers General Repairs. | |
| " | 4/5 | | Field General Court Martial of a Sergt. Beard RE. in connection with accidental wounding of No. 36139 Dr Pariout and No. 36140 Dr Tower both of Q 180th Bde R.H.A. (accused acquitted). Four Armourers attended Court Martial. Other Armourers General Repairs. | E |
| " | 5/5 | | Car to 2nd Army RE Workshops, Jr. 16 Gun light Lewis Gun Boxes Two Lorries for Stores down Repaired by S.M. Hayes branch. Lic 14 H Special Wagons returned to A.M.S. Depot apparence making 53 in all returned. Armourers General Repairs. | |
| " | 6/5 | | Taking in Second Gs. Blinkt. Cle. Fatigue Party of 1 NCO & 8 men to assist. Received 19,400 Litigium pieces for Lewis Guns. Requested Car to C.O. 2nd Army Troops for Dr Caerens Amm. Q.F. 18 pdr. asked Q.F. re substitution. | |

Army Form C. 2118.

D.A.D.O.S.
16TH (IRISH) DIV.
No. ..................
Date ..................

# WAR DIARY
## INTELLIGENCE SUMMARY.
(Erase heading not required.)

Instructions regarding War Diaries and Intelligence Summaries are contained in F.S. Regs., Part II. and the Staff Manual respectively. Title pages will be prepared in manuscript.

| Place | Date | Hour | Summary of Events and Information | Remarks and references to Appendices |
|---|---|---|---|---|
| LOOS | 4/5 | - | Taking in Mens Clothing. Two smocks altered to white smocks clothing to Bns. Armourer. Two Lewis Guns repaired and general work. | |
| " | 8/5 | | 6000 Blankets returned to Base shop recently to Bns. Hargreaves establishing 2 Vickers Guns and unserviceable. Armourer. General repair. Air Cylinders. one Lewis repaired. | |
| " | 9/5 | | Drawing Ammo Shop, two Vickers guns & 2 Tripods repaired & 14 Magazines. DADOS returned of leave and handed over to him. | |

9/5/17

[signature] Capt.
Transport Officer

# WAR DIARY / INTELLIGENCE SUMMARY

Army Form C. 2118.

D.A.D.O.S. 16TH (IRISH) DIV.

| Place | Date 1917 | Hour | Summary of Events and Information | Remarks and references to Appendices |
|---|---|---|---|---|
| LOCRE | May | 10 | Took over from Capt. Russell. Found things in good order; preparations apparently being forward for some form of offensive. Received A.S.O. Tents Shelter. No. of Bivou[acs] that is reported to IX Corps 2nd Army that precautions would in my opinion be unsatisfactory with A.D.O.S. 2nd Army that precautions would in my opinion be unsatisfactory. Visited A.D.S. IX Corps. | |
| | | 11 | Received 50 Hammocks for men in dugouts + 250 (no. Sh.L.T. Bn.) Brown dispatched to 9720 Army from Hospital A.D.S. & Q Store. Booted & meet with Remount (manufacturing) at depot Echo to Raba. | |
| | | 13 | Exchanged by hostile shellfire. | |
| | | | Received 250 Tent Poles. Received for patrol 2970 Blankets. Attended A.D.O.S. Conference with D.A.D.O.S. of 19 & 36 Div. to discuss details in connection with proposed Army Gum Boot to be established near GODEWAERSVELDE. | |
| | | 14 | Moved to Base A.D.S. 19 Div. – 175 Tunnel Co. R.E., 26 th Tunnel Co. R.E., 136 A.D.Co. R.E., 151 Batteries Platt'y, also moved 16th Divl. Sdl. Co. O.R. IX Corps through our absorption of Sd. into IX Corps Art'y. | |
| | | 15 | Sent Convoy to 47 Inf. Bd. to 1st to replacing men. Arranged No. 6 Inf. Brd. Co. D.E.L. to O.C. 38 Div. Ammn. A.R. Transferred by G.O. from H.Q. Inf. Bde. to be devoted to Divl. Ammn. Shops. P.O.A. Ashley reported for duty from O.C. 3rd Army Troops, vice Pr. Warren | |
| | | 16 | Received for Advice 17 Wagons, 70 Cal. Tanks (cam) Yorkshire Ambulance Cars, Batteries class new transport convoys for 16 Divl. Art'y, 18 own ammunition sub-through in the spring and 1 am Yorksen Trinity for distribution to 3 Inf. Bds. Moved by Col. Co. D.E.L. 16 O.O. VIII Corps troops Vice 38 Div. owing to Communications from W.O. | |
| | | 17 | Employing orders for owners about the being more remaining those preventing of Cattle shortly from pill box. Spare A.D.S. Corps & O.S. Calais at movement arrived that indicate should be submitted for immediate needs. | |
| | | | Received Comm. 18t Div. for 15/1/80 attended Off. 17/5. Arranged with A.D.O.S. Corps to provide Tentage for approximately 113 Officers & 9940 O.R. (11th Sht. Arty, & Pr. Mtn. Bm.6) at short notice. | |
| | 18 | | Took over and strength for ordnance services 39th Div. C.B. arrived from IX Corps Area. Visited by A.D.O.S. cc & supply of Blankets, Spare, tripoline of Supp's, etc. Drew 250 Tents O/S + 132 Tents Shelter (vice 130 previous) for Art'y. – 3rd Convoy to 47 Inf. Bde. Rcvd. in Trenmey Area. Drew 250 Tents O/S + 132 Tents Shelter (vice 130 previous) for arrangements for attachment 5 Wheelers with Sht. Art'y. Service in all 6 Gun Ammunt. Lt. Col. Wiley, IX. Wheelers for Officer produces arrangement for attachment 5 Wheelers with Sht. Art'y. starte to remains gun in to mount gunning of saluting Penia through Ebbeken. He clearing us to have all the Wheelers rig in division fitted, references made to A.D.O.S. who inspected the arrangement & gave | |
| | 19 | | authority for modification to be carried out. Sent Ammn. Shop. Recd. 250 prs gloves Hosy'ey for official operation at 9 Inf. Pdn. addition of record water bottles then in use & impeding operations, reported application to IX Corps (O.) | |

# WAR DIARY
## INTELLIGENCE SUMMARY

**Army Form C. 2118.**

D.A.D.O.S. 16TH (IRISH) DIV.

| Place | Date 1917 | Hour | Summary of Events and Information | Remarks and references to Appendices |
|---|---|---|---|---|
| LOCRE | May 20 | | Forwarded applications for commissions in R.H. R.F.A. to Div. HQ. from Pte. G.A. Astley. Board of Survey held on 145 Rugs/Hair cord 2000 Strait. Sect from O.O. 22 A.T. Grande Carrieres, Amiens. C. 2888. A.H. Biggs. 600 J long wire cutting 2.50 - all for special operations. Rouclin. | |
| | 21 | | Appointments certificates A.O. Corps Stores. To Cr. Cr. Cpl (whilst ring) Pte A.H. Wheeler, J. Roger, T.C. Hawkins. Received 50 schwere Sateurs & Stoppers Cabin. | |
| | 22 | | Presented 20,000 antis shining SAB for S. Box Respirators. Drew 1500 Cases Packers to be converted to survey ration Carriers, 150 | |
| | 23 | | Indian Packs, 60 Tents G.S.C., 11800 sg. ft. Tarpaulins for covering ammunition. A.E. Applied to O Stop S. for A/c Cpl Dy | |
| | 24 | | Received another 130 Bandeliar Ed drew Tents C.H., 160 sg. ft. Tarpaulins (for covering ammunition). Capt Randolph allowed off leave. Sent away further consignments of winter clothing etc. SS Stanley's pending cost dispatch and branch department ringing. | |
| | 25 | | Purchased Poppinjus material for amb and A/c Corps. Drew from 2,179 Army R.E. Workshops at Amylie Iron Bedsteads T.M. (A/6). Wired for 2 - 18 pd. Guns Q.F. Per A/177 Bde R.F.A. to replace 2 exp at same range. Accounts 12 Labour Co. to 36 artic. + estimated amount of 148 Labour Co. (Grand Glenis camp) Admiralty Dept, Corps-Rd, for nightly return of machine funa in employ required - return of French workers to conclude. Wired for 500 Bomber Handcarts & 200 Limbers for that Howitz. The C.p.l.D. Stew | |
| | 26 | | Granted 10 days leave from May 28 to June 7. Applied for 10 days leave for Capt. B/of; Service Transferred 21 Labour Co. to O.O. [signature] Corps Troops under instructions from A.D.O.S. Ammunition started work on unloading 400 Rds attached at RailHead from 5 to 21/5. | |
| | 27 | | Indented for Arty units (see 14+18) to date Blue water from us. 27/18 way. Visited some local purchases. Remains. | |
| | 28 | | Returned to Base about 2000 pm Penn Bros wishing us an return to [?] Visited 2nd Army R.E. workshops and drew our Bands for 9 + 15 T.M. ammun. for 1/16 T.M. Batty Spoke to O. i/c Army Ord. Fire Aid - stated for use of Mining fire serum for magazine, also asked for Turbine for further do Trunk SEF Transferred 148 Labour Coy to O.O. [signature] Corps Troops under instructions from A.D.O.S. 2nd. Cpl. Dyson on leave from May 28 to June 7. | |
| | 29 | | Army Ordy; Stanley's painted 10 days leave from May 30 to June 9. Local purchases in Bacinghem. Visited 24 Army R.E. Workshops, Hazebrouck, re early supply of pH Staunchable Stoves 240 G.T.M. No hope of early prior supply. Received some 2" T.M., also 500 Bomber Handcarts. Loaned tarke received plus 21 which h. Visited Ordnance | |
| | 30 | | Gun Park + discussed details of various Arts Ord O/c, also talked over various details for immediate future and unproper. | |
| | 31 | | 16 DAC in Poperinge of Army Ord from Ord. Red Ford ball? indented for Paint. Plenty of ?can available, wide for our 18 pdr for 3/180 and placed and arranged for leaving and drew park for 2 R. Bertughis. Purchased 200 Tenella Brexit a (L, 16) for Special operations. Last washed at Ren Rey Bar preparing for operations. |  A.L.Orland [signature] C Colonel 31/5/17 |

H.Q.
16TH (IRISH) DIV.,
("A. & Q." BRANCH.)

No.....................
Date...................

WAR DIARY.

FOR MONTH OF JUNE, 1917.

VOLUME:- 10.

UNIT:- DaDoS. 16th Division

# WAR DIARY
## INTELLIGENCE SUMMARY.
*(Erase heading not required.)*

Army Form C. 2118.

D.A.D.O.S.
16TH (IRISH) DIV
No. I
Date.........

Instructions regarding War Diaries and Intelligence Summaries are contained in F.S. Regs., Part II. and the Staff Manual respectively. Title pages will be prepared in manuscript.

| Place | Date | Hour | Summary of Events and Information | Remarks and references to Appendices |
|---|---|---|---|---|
| LOCRE | 1-6-17. | | Demanded one Lewis Gun for 9 R. Dublin Fus. Received one Lewis Gun for 5 R. Dublin Fus.; two 18 pdr. Guns for A/177 Bde. & one 18 pdr. Gun for 15/180 Bde. R.F.A. Sn. issued diary out of special clean required for inspecting opening visited Bde. & Dept, CALAIS, & saw Q.O., O.I.C. field Issuing to most Group Officers. Received information that many up demands would not interfere with available & dispatched by next train. Brought back supply of disinfecting immediate, also material for use in Armourers' Shop. | |
| | 2-6-17. | | Received from A/16 Div. notification that Pte. ASTLEY has been selected for admission to an Officer Cadet unit in England R.F.A. | |
| | 3-6-17. | | Received one Lewis Gun for 9 R. Dublin Fus.; 50 Yukon packs for Division; one 9.45" Long trays T.M. and six 2" T.M. for operations | |
| | 4-6-17. | | Wired for one 2" T.M. for 2/16 T.M. Batty.; one Lewis Gun for 2 R. Dublin Fus.; one Vickers machine Gun each for 47 & 48 | |
| | | | with Col. Sent special Reserve to distaining Ordnance Gun Park for parts required to put in action Lewis Guns of 7/R.R. | |
| | | | Dub. Fus. and also for parts demanded in first trial wire. Supplies from Gun Park very small indeed. | |
| | 5-6-17. | | Visited Gun Park, with A.D.O.S. IX Corps in endeavour to get supplies of Lewis Gun parts — apparently no stock expected of. | |
| | | | Reported position to G.O.C. R.A. troops. Received one Lewis Gun for 2 R. Dublin Fus.; one Vickers supp. each for 47 & 48 Wg. Cos. | |
| | | | Demanded one 18 pdr. Gun for 15/177 Bn. & two more cardines for sealing. | |
| | 6-6-17. | | Recommended Pce. A. Cpl. WHEELER and Pce. DUNSTEAM BE ELLIOTT & advance in Capacity from St. Mt. M.C. Spare A.D.O.S. | |
| | | | about 6.30 pm. Arm. Staff Opl. ROSS proceeded to Armt. Staff Sept. A.D.D., previous report to Army north, we named. Drew various | |
| | | | Stores for Openings returned were trawles to Richland for Base. Stores containing Box Respirator reserve shelled today - serial casualties. | |
| | 7-6-17. | | Offensive opened at 3 am. most others really supplied by all units have been supplied. Drew various other stores for use in offensive | |
| | | | turned to Base Commend. Wired for one Vickers gun for 47 Wg. Co. and one 18 pdr. gun for 15/177 Bde. R.F.A. | |
| | 8-6-17. | | Pte. ASTLEY proceeded to ENGLAND for commission. Cupped 6 H. S.A.A. to relief. Wired for 3 Vickers supp. for 49 W.I. Co. | |
| | | | to replace "lost in action". Received one Vickers supp. for 47 W.I. Co. | |
| | 9-6-17. | | L. Cpl. SIGARS returned off leave. Sent away near founded & Authld for Base. Wired for two 3" Stokes T.M. for 4/9 T.M. By. | |
| | | | and Lewis Gun for 7/R. Dub. Fus.; one 18 pdr. gun each for 15/180 & C/180 (storing). | |
| | 10-6-17. | | Wired for one 18 pdr. gun for C/177 (storing); and one 18 pdr. gun with B.M. and Carr. for C/180 (formation). Received our Lewis | |
| | | | gun for 7/R. Dub. Fus. Arm. S/Sgt. FARRIE returned off leave. Received two 3" Stokes T.M. for 49 T.M. Batty. | |
| | 11-6-17. | | Demanded one Lewis Gun for 7 Dublin Fus. and one Lewis Gun for 6 R. Dub. Regt. Received 3 Vickers supp. for 49 W.I. Co. Carrying | |
| | | | 8/881. CASUALTIES returned to the unit. Wire firing 1/98 By/Rts S.Armenia manual. S/Sgt. INGRAM withdrawn from 49 Inf./R. | |
| | | | for duty in Div. Shop. This leaves no Armourer with each Inf. Bde. | |
| | 12-6-17. | | Returned Remble Spanworks to Requisled for Base. Demanded contains for Lewis Gun for 7 R. Dub. Fus. & sept. Strong regimental | |
| | | | certification from 9 Univ. (IX Corps half gum has been received). Wired up two to A/177; one to B/180; two to 575/177; | |
| | | | and one to A/180. Received onler for Division to move terrorrow morning to NIEURRIS area forward. | |

A.D.S.S./Forms/C. 2118.
2353 Wt. W25841/1454 700,000 5/15 D. D. & L.

# WAR DIARY
## INTELLIGENCE SUMMARY.
*(Erase heading not required.)*

Army Form C. 2118.

D.A.D.O.S.
16TH (IRISH) DIV.
No. 11

Instructions regarding War Diaries and Intelligence Summaries are contained in F.S. Regs., Part II. and the Staff Manual respectively. Title pages will be prepared in manuscript.

| Place | Date | Hour | Summary of Events and Information | Remarks and references to Appendices |
|---|---|---|---|---|
| LOCRE MERRIS | 13-6-17 | | Divisional R.A. moved from LOCRE to MERRIS. New Divisional location - Map 36A: Dump F.1.c.75.40; Office (Nappier) F.1.d.15.45; Staff F.I.d. 20.20. Demanded 18pdr gun for B/177 (Scarring). PTE. DUNSCOMBE (Groom) leave from June 15 to 25. | |
| | 14-6-17 | | Attended at IX Corps Conference of A.D.O.S. with D.A.D.O.S. 11, 16, 19 & 36 Divn + D.O. IX Corps Troops. Questions chiefly concerning working of Second Army Advanced Ord. Park. Strongly adverse to details of intended increase of steel and staff at Park. | |
| | 15-6-17 | | 023028 PTE. DAVIES, Storeman arrived from CALAIS for duty. Received one (new) fuse reel for 6 R. Irish Rifles, 7 Dismantling for same also one 2" T.M. for 2/16 R. Ir. Fus. Bty. Wired for one 18pdr for C/177 (Scarring). Army(?) wired CRA, CRE, + 11 HAUS.G. (P) re: supply of 18pdr. (Stew. until late Dump remains in front area. | |
| | 16-6-17 | | One 18pdr. gun sent for C/180 and one 18pdr. gun for C/177 notified available at Rail Head. Received one gun pair for R.A. Auffr. Demanded one 3" Stokes T.M. for 49 T.M. Battery. Divisional R.A. | |
| LOCRE MERRIS | 17-6-17 | | Divisional R.A. moved from LOCRE to MERRIS. One 18pdr gun for C/18 a notified available at Rail Head. One 3" Stokes T.M. H49 T.M. Bty. | |
| | 18-6-17 | | Divisional R.A. moved from LOCRE to MERRIS. Draper Hat proposed to look over 7 & 8 Stores useful for Corps Belt ammo. T.S. | |
| | 19-6-17 | | In view of impending list, broke up ammunition Stop returns. Gave orders to Unit's Stor. & Batteries took & handed over to 16 Divn. Sup. Co. to transport. All Battalions completed will complete turnout of Wagon Lindis(?), Pdr. for Convoy of Amm. Fuse. L.G. Howdart returned to 190 D.A. Army range at CASSEL. Demanded 18pdr Gun (H/177) replace one Condemned for Scoring. Also one 2" T.M. (Z/16) explosion unauthorized by armourers. | |
| GODEWAERSVELDE | 20-6-17 | | O.D.O.S. IX Corps to take leave. Divisional Ser. Artillery moved from MERRIS to GODEWAERSVELDE. New location - Map 17 Q.18.d.1. Wikham Richardson and returned to 0.0.; 2nd Army Troops at CASSEL. | |
| | 21-6-17 | | Withdraw balance of Richardson the Indian Pack, returned to 0.0. IX Corps Forage Attaint Carrel with information from A.D.O.S. Transferred HK HauB. Rifles (N), C.R.E., (SS, 155, 156 + 157 Field Cos. R.E. to 55 Div. (XIX Corps V? Army). | |
| ZEGGERS CAPPEL | 22-6-17 | | Division (Rein. Artillery, Divisional Field Co., R.M.E.) removed to ZEGGERS CAPPEL, new location - Col. 17, B.106 central. Transferred 87th Sanitary Section to O.O.G. 2 A.T. Visited A.D.O.S. VIII Corps (Major A.T. Fisher) and D.D.O.S. Fifth Army (Col. Hamilton) on another liar area. | |
| | 23-6-17 | | 63rd Division transferred 10 R. Dublin Fusiliers to 16th Division. First horses arrived in Div. area attached 48th Dif. Bde. | |
| | 24-6-17 | | Visited by O.D.O. VIII Corps ref. inspection of records, also by D.D.O. Fifth Army. Rations ARMEKE - underclothing Army, Sewn, Purse wired to Artillery units. Transport detailed into(?) for balance from Park to (?)CALAIS. | |

2353 Wt. W2544/1454 700,000 5/15 D. D. & L. A.D.S.S./Forms/C. 2118.

Army Form C. 2118.

# WAR DIARY
## or
## INTELLIGENCE SUMMARY.
*(Erase heading not required.)*

Instructions regarding War Diaries and Intelligence Summaries are contained in F.S. Regs., Part II. and the Staff Manual respectively. Title pages will be prepared in manuscript.

| Place | Date | Hour | Summary of Events and Information | Remarks and references to Appendices |
|---|---|---|---|---|
| ZEGGERS CAPPEL | 25-6-17 | | Stores received to M/180 Bde. R.F.A. at 2nd Army Artillery School, TILQUES. Demands met/ Spts. from C/180 condemned stores indicate workshops are not having profitable results, will [illegible] | |
| | 26-6-17 | | Received over 2 "T.M." for 2/16 T.M. Bty. Wire rope wheel for armature wheel Ordnance workshop will manufacture for this Division. 6 the sights [illegible] A.S.C., VIII Corps 15 armature wheels [illegible] returned to us. R.O.O. ARMEES has refused our A.S.C. and indigene as T. R.O.O. uncouverts stores, should be returned to, or R.O.O. ARMEES has refused units [illegible] nothing more [illegible] | |
| | 27-6-17 | | Wired for one 18 pdr recoil ( N/177 ) - appears condemned for premature; also for one 4.5" How. Recoil (D/177) damage shelter. Started Dir. Armourer's shop again. Revision. Pts damaged [illegible] | |
| | 28-6-17 | | Papers (final ones) reported available at Second Army Gunpark for B/177 C/177 Ma 16 F.A. | |
| | 29-9-17 | | Received extra lorry 15 will Bier, Armourer's shop mobile. Quite a collection of returns reached all infantry units and their units, workable or no not ones - all expected, all cases & only minor difficulties (Much shortage of soap), all incident upon mobile condition of Division & consequent dispersal of units. | |
| | 30-9-17 | | | |

30/6/17

A.D. Drewison Capt A.O.D.
D.A.D.O.S. 16½ Divn.

WAR DIARY.

FOR MONTH OF JULY, 1917.

VOLUME :- 20.

UNIT :- A.D.O.S. 16th Division

# WAR DIARY

**INTELLIGENCE SUMMARY.**

*(Erase heading not required.)*

Army Form C. 2118.

Instructions regarding War Diaries and Intelligence Summaries are contained in F.S. Regs., Part II. and the Staff Manual respectively. Title pages will be prepared in manuscript.

D.A.D.O.S.
16TH (IRISH) DIV.
JULY.

| Place | Date | Hour | Summary of Events and Information | Remarks and references to Appendices |
|---|---|---|---|---|
| ZEGGERS CAPPE | 1/7/17 | | I.a.m. No.5 Ordnance Mobile Workshop (Heavy) visited Division by arrangement and inspected vehicles for repairing repairs. General conditions considered to be repaired by Divl. Train. Received 4·5" Howitzer and Carrier for D/77 Bde R.F.A. | |
| | 2/7 | | Demanded one Vickers machine gun for 7/M.G. Co. to replace one condemned in Divl Armourers' Shop. P.G. ELLIOTT from Tukeaire 3/7 to 13 R July. | |
| | 3/7 | | Armourers overhauled Vickers machine guns from (48&49 Co.) & 2 Lewis guns (7 Leins Co.) etc. Orders for Divisional Routine Order 815 published to the effect that Lewis Equipment can only be issued to replace unserviceable - This club approach. Also from H.Q. Div attention to the fact that many unserviceable appear in Shorts - call form S.D. horses in continuation of D.R.O. 1850. | |
| | 4/7 | | Armourers overhauled & Vickers M/guns (48&49 Co.) 4 Lewis guns (7 Leins Co.) etc. | |
| | 5/7 | | Armourers overhauled 4 Vickers M/guns (48&49 Co.) 2 Lewis guns (7 Leins Co.) etc. Received from Base 140 sets of Pack Saddlery in special consignment. Received 1 Vickers M/gun for 49 M.G. Co. Wired for 1 Vickers M/gun (48 M.G. Co.) to replace condemned in Divl. Shop. | |
| | 6/7 | | Armourers overhauled 4 Vickers m/guns (48&49 Co.) & Lewis guns (7 Leins Co.) & Ambulance. Quartermaster that one water cart allotted to D.A.D.O.S. ref. Divl. H.Q. Cars inspected, D.A.D.O.S. must have final call on one (5th Army Q-A-4 1/933-17, d-27/1/17). Received 150 Lewis Pouches for distribution. Received 187 pr. gun for C/180 Bde and 1 Vickers M/g gun for 1 Buck. Co. | |
| | 7/7 | | Armourers overhauled 5 Lewis guns (7 Leins Bde, visited H.Q. 16 Divl. Artillery & 177 Bde. Battery & 77 Bde. Battery, 7 N.B. 16 D.A.C. Transport to 15 Div., No. 1 Co. Div. Train, all Div. H.G. + V, X, Y + Z T.M. Batteries, and machine gun Coys of XIX Corps Q. | |
| | 8/7 | | Received 100 Lewis Pouches. (marked total of 250. for authorised establishment for Division. 5th Army Q enquired the rough number should. As to establishment of Divl. Armvs. Shop on uniform basis throughout Army. Suggestions made in A.D.P.Q. reply in accordance with plan adopted by 16 Div. in NŒUX-LES-MINES, i.e. adoption of such a scheme was considered to be the ... Also recommended the placement of a workshop lorry to enable Shop to become mobile. | |
| | 9/7 | | Armourers overhauled Lewis guns - 3 of R. Munster, fus. - 3 of 7 Leinster, etc. | |
| | 10/7 | | Divl. Armvs. Shop on cycle Psty, having been apprenticing P.A.A.G. 16 Div. Shuffled his horses 15 Do. Buckingly attached Recommend that covers or conditions be continued to be employed in Divl. Arms. Shop. Also that D.R.Q. published. | |
| | 11/7 | | To effect that units drawing (?) said vehicles to for repair to Ord. Workshop must also attach mechanics expected by Divl. Train. Demanded 1 Lewis gun for 2 R. Dr. Rifl. Express condemned in Divl. Shop. | |
| | 12/7 | | A.D.O.S. VIII Corps called and went into ? various questions Arms, Tanks, Ammunition - Cook troubly &c. Visited 113 Fd. Amb., "Q 49 2 Fd. Amb, 708 Tramways, 7/8 R.D. Fus, Called G. A.P.M. XIX Corps orin his absence Saw A.O.M.S. and obtained authority to hand to O.R. Dublin Fus. to 15 Div. Local purchase of no. of spare material for toys. Visited town HQ. Wks. Workshop (Heavy) with h/c shop of manoeuvres (V repairs. [Manoeuv] 10 Dublins to 50Brig. Meant only KEMMEL. and 50Do. PLANT to DADOS 16 Div for duty while 16 D.D. Artillery in attacked to him. Armourers overhauled Lewis guns – | |

2353   Wt W 2544/1454   700,000   5/15   D. D. & L.   A.D.S.S./Forms/C. 2118.   (2) of 7 Leinsters and 10/1 R. Munsters & co.

# WAR DIARY or INTELLIGENCE SUMMARY

Army Form C. 2118.

D.A.D.O.S.
15TH (SCOTTISH) DIV.
II
JULY

| Place | Date | Hour | Summary of Events and Information | Remarks and references to Appendices |
|---|---|---|---|---|
| ZEGGERS CAPPEL | July 12 | | Received 1 Lewis gun for 2 R. St. Regt. that D.R.O. provided instructing units to render monthly returns showing numbers & pairs of boots required specially – ideas being to ensure sufficient quantity of finished boots being available for issue. (18(5th) Army Form to C/177 (amended) is 19(6) - arrangements accordingly. Visited A.D.O. of XIX Corps and arranged concentrated arrangements for drawing ordinary and special stores, informed that it is duty of D.A.D.O.S. to see that all units actually have all they are entitled to all times. This would be carried out visits outside the scope of a D.O.O. & all units known C.O. & OH.) Also informed that all "clothing" should be returned by units to D.A.D.O.S. Stencilled G.O.S. the "half" from the wearer on points over pair of pants of Return of Issue. Visited BADOT, Div. workshops of 11th Div. Articles for equipment overhauled. Issued 4 MG's from Co. to H'H Div. Visited 2 Batt 9 R. Dublin & 7 R.D. Reg, also 145 A.C. Armourers overhauled & finish gun &c. Called Q to call for returns from units showing (a) No. of this equipment (Armourers' War Reserve) & (b) State of same. Q.C.M.S. O.I.C(34. Received. Also as to numbers of Crates waiting from G.O.C. 1 Rifle reserves of R. Dublin Fus. Armourer attention to be paid. Advanced Staff Reports CHEL-CARTWHY VERE head level and after over 3 months & written representations in view of such increase made. Allowances Ammunition overhauled & Lewis guns and made available for increases. | |
| | 14. | | leave (19th July) for wiping the Batt: Grenades. Ordered to "destroy" ordered personnel who has been laundry from Batt: have been held. Also using the two Armourers reported above. | |
| | 15. | | Usual inspections & Brown Flag material. Visited A.D.O. of VIII Corps who has WESTA Army demanding further 160 sets for Boots Paschendaele to complete Div. to 800 sets in addition to Recto equipment. Other questions XIX Corps who separately Dec. L.G. Co. are complete to establishment in Armourer. Boxes R.L.S. Armr. Batt. Armourer Div. n.e.g. Offrs were to report position | |
| | 16. | | | Routine |
| | 17. | | Informed by 7th Army through XIX Corps that VIII Corps administered only for "local ordnance". | |
| | 18. | | Armourer overhauls all Infantry rifle & Armourers & under Corps/Div. Inspection reports to complete to authorised scale of 32 per Batt in lieu. | |
| | 19. | | Armour overhauled Lewis gun (2 R. Dublin Fus) & 10 day term granted Army Sgt. CALLAGHAN, Armourer Sgt. Received 160 sets Paschendaele, thus completing Division to 800 sets in addition to usual equipment. Armourer overhauled 4 Lewis guns (8 R. Dublin Fus) & Army Commander spoke G.O.C. re position of Companies supplies. | |
| | 20. | | Ammunition overhauled 4 Lewis guns & Visited Corps (OC I.A.S & endeavoured to persuade him to have settled list of articles adopted by Sub. Commander. Stencilled. No alternative but local purchase. Question of Return of Kettles etc. Corps/Div. Brown paper Commander. | |

A.B.S.S./Forms/C. 2118.

Army Form C. 2118.

Instructions regarding War Diaries and Intelligence Summaries are contained in F. S. Regs. Part II. and the Staff Manual respectively. Title pages will be prepared in manuscript.

WAR DIARY
or
INTELLIGENCE SUMMARY.
(Erase heading not required.)

D.A.D.O.S.
16TH (IRISH) DIV.
No. III
Date JULY

| Place | Date July | Hour | Summary of Events and Information | Remarks and references to Appendices |
|---|---|---|---|---|
| ZEGGERS CAPEL | 21 | | Details Arm: S/S/I. REDSTONE (S.R.) rejoining (June:) F. report to XIX Corps Salvage Dump for temporary duty, in accordance with Corps Salvage Scheme. Corp. BARR warned to proceed on same duties when officer is appointed. (Note: Divisional D.D.O.S 5th Army 2/3 Companies unfit for Salvage Dump + due to complete Division Armourers overhauls of Small Arms.) | (Appx 1(a) |
| | 22 | | Routine | |
| | 23 | | | |
| | 24 | | Warned to APP. & INVTE. Officer at Dist HQ. 28.G.Fd.G.1. — Surplus Ammunition stop notification shortly. Recd from Army through VIII Corps + 16 Div. Q. instructions to carry out Div. Ammn Supply in accordance with suggestions made by S.Army Q. Called in accordingly through Q. Ammn. S/Sgt B. PAGE (G.R.Dicks) and F/Q/M/S. (G.R. Darling) Rec'd instructions from Army through XIX Corps to visit all units frequently and ascertain real state of their equipment. | |
| POPERINGHE | 25 | | Applied for 10 days' leave for Sub-Cndr. CULLEN (financial reasons). Sub-Cndr. CULLEN granted 10 days' leave July 29/31/17. Handed over HQ returns of S.men. Keeps + without leave. | |
| | 26 | | Arm. HAYDON returned off leave 4.E. rate of Corps Pay granted from 30/6/17 to A. Cpl. WHEELER, Pte DUNCOMBE, Pte ELLIOTT. | |
| | 27 | | | |
| | 28 | | Called at D.O.S. XIV Corps for further warning of Horse Responsibilities being cared as Cavalry are assembling somewhere and horses, &c, unfitted for all but rest prepared for expedition in Sep.-Dec. Period. To discuss any ministry of preserving in reserve Armories supplied Defence from etc. Went to Corp. CALAIS asking further unit sends for 30 men. Obtaining Companies from Divisions on Army Reports - sending useless lots of disused sorts for 30 men. R.E. Redoubt Bty with Army Arch'y. Received strong muck of 25th indiv. ordering 35 wheels out, as much to have its Commdr. to hostile Trench armed at open - closed sight + Sing. Sights. | |
| | 29 | | Made no issue of yesterday's urging + the note issues is practically complete with armies, except Bn RE which are all very peace. | |
| | 30 | | YPRES/(Junior gained). Arm. S/Sgt. CALLAGHAN returned off leave. Received Indentamples for 1. Bty. Royal Gan list for 2. admirable fence - Also armed the S.B.R. fitted with ?. new (Cardwells) contusion Spring. Fine occupied during latter part of month in purchasing material for improvement of rotten armour and following. | Appoved by D.A. Commander. All units that were closing down sent follow — RITES. |
| | 31 | | | |

2353 Wt. W2544/1454 700,000 5/15 D. D. & L. Ad.S.S./Forms/C. 2118.

WAR DIARY.

FOR MONTH OF AUGUST, 1917.

VOLUME 2/

UNIT D.A.D.O.S. 16 Division

# WAR DIARY
## INTELLIGENCE SUMMARY

*(Erase heading not required.)*

Army Form C. 2118.

D.A.D.O.S.
16TH (IRISH) DIV
No. I
Date AUG '17.

No. .......... 16th DIVISION

| Place | Date 1917 | Hour | Summary of Events and Information | Remarks and references to Appendices |
|---|---|---|---|---|
| POPERINGHE | 1 | | Received further 30 S.B. Bandoliers distributed under Q instructions. Drew 33 Vickers M.G. Barrels from Ardent for W.G. Coys. | |
| | 2 | | Demanded 30 spare Trench Wire Plant for Divl. Training & Magnetic Compasses & Complete Inf. Batt. to issue scale of 4 to each. Demanded 325 G.F. Cord. 15 Div. for A/17, 18/MD. Gave to replace codements per Cavnl. | |
| | 3 | | Received 600 Groddh Carrying (two water Tins - attached to Packsaddles). Arrived for 2 Vickers M.G. equip. to replace gun sent of Shaftesbury W.G. Coy.). Visited HQ 48 Inf. Bde, HQ/16 Div. Train out 54 Cors. & 47 W.G. Vet. Sec.; Ratios; 1st Div. Tramway from 1st Div. to 16 Div. for Ordnance. -- HQ 16 Div. Arty, HQ, A, B, C, D/177 Bde. R.F.A., HQ 1, 2 & 3 Secs./16 D.A.C.; X, Y, Z & v/16 T.M. Bty; 16/16 Div. Train 47 W.G. Co.; also HQ. & Amnt. Div. Arty.; HQ, 49, 50, 51/13 Bde. Amnt. F.A.; HQ, S3, 54 & 57 and 114 How./14 Bde, Anct. F.A.; HQ, 11 & 2 Sec. & 13 Gal./Strut. D.A.C.; X, Y, 2 & v/15 Trench Mort. Btys and 10 Co. Amct. A.S.C. | |
| PLAMERTINGHE | 4 | | Moved with Divl. HQ. TO PLAMERTINGHE. Established Office. (Two Armour. Shops at (28) H. 7. d. 7. Transferred from 5 Div. G. 16 Div. for Ord. - C.R.E. 16 Div.; 155, 156, 157 Fd. Co. R.E., 11 Hants. (P). Sent A. D. of return showing share out of Portes (239). | |
| | 5 | | Visited Div. Sch. & Inf. Bn. Dulhinar & 7 R. Dubl. Rifles. Read 2 Vickers M.G. for 47 W.G. Co. Issued for one Lewis Gun for 2 R.B. Regt. - replace Jammed & Unfit. D.S.O.I. anxious about supply of Tickets - Ireland Anti-Aircraft Sights, Ind Lewis Haver lost unfit to experience position. Ord. Mer. knew nothing that they were being allocated by D. of Z. of 6% Div. is on war List, sent copying wire. S.S.D.I. | |
| | 6 | | Visited 6 R. Dubl. Regt, 6 Conaught, 7 Leinsters, 1 Munsters. Received one Lewis gun for 2 R. Dubl. Regt. Visited by A.D.O.S. XIX Corps. Visited 155 & 156 Fd. Co. R.E. | |
| | 7 | | Ammunion inspected army repects of defective amme - 1st, 155 & 157 Fd. Co. R.E., & 6 R. Dubl. Regt. Recivied Sps Watson 6/prolling trains. Visited HQ. 1st Div. Arty. & Strent. D.A. Wired for 1 Lewis Gun for 7 Leinsters - replace lost in action. F. U. Q. Corps. sd 6 taken into use 8/4 Aug. | |
| | 8 | | Ammunion wiled 6 Connaught Rangers. Finished inspecting of N7 Fd. Co. Visited Donway I/15 4th Div. + XVIII X IX Corps. Collected Bandoliers Plates & they D.R.S. Visited by D.D.O.S. Rifle Armoury, A.D.S. XIX Corps & A.D.S. | |
| | 9 | | Strent. Div. Visited HQ, 47 Inf. Bde. Received 1 Lewis gun for 7 Leinsters. Buts. Oft. C.W.T. returned 15 Lewis Guns for i.r. Ind. fm. (7 R. Dr. R.1/49) - destroyed by Shellfire; 2 (Lost in action) & 2 (by normal wear) - 8 Drivers; and 1 Vickers M.G. ( 48 W.G. Co.). | |

# WAR DIARY

## INTELLIGENCE SUMMARY.
(Erase heading not required.)

Army Form C. 2118.

D.A.D.O.S.
16TH (IRISH) DIV.
11 AUG.

| Place | Date | Hour | Summary of Events and Information | Remarks and references to Appendices |
|---|---|---|---|---|
| VLAMERTINGHE | Aug 10 1917 | | Ammunition inspected on arrival of Leinster Regt. repaired 2 Lewis Guns each of 6 Connaught Rangers & Leinster Regt. Received/Visited M.O. (4 & W.G.), 1 Lewis Gun (7 R.Dn. Riffs), 2 Lewis Guns (8 Dublins), Wired for 1 Lewis Gun for 6 Connaughts - replaced destroyed by shellfire. | |
| | 11 | | Ammunition Party (of R. Irish Fus. Rec'd 2 Lewis Guns (8 Dublins) and one (6 Connaughts). Wired for first Lewis Gun (7 R.Dn. Riffs) - replaced lost by shellfire. Rec'd from 18D.A. 3 Lewis Guns fifty for Lewis Guns belong'g to Brigade Bombers and Cylinders at Ord Workshop; visited 7 and 8 R. Irish Fus., 7/8 R. Ir. Fus. & 7 R. Dn. Regt. | |
| | 12 | | Visited No. 7 Ord. Depot to arrange for issue of Cartridges if required at short notice; wire to Ops Base for Lewis Ammunition repaired 3 Lewis Guns. Wired for 3 Lewis Guns for 9 Dublins - replace destroyed shellfire. Rec'd 6 Lewis Guns (7 R.Dn. Riffs) + 2 3 pm from Boots (S.A.A. & C.T.) | |
| | 13 | | Wired for 18 pdr. Gun Carr. for B/180 on B.C.I. Certificate that gun to completely destroyed by 6 direct hits from 5.9″ - at present unable to move to 9. Arm. Staff Capt. 16 D.A. asks to take 18 pdr. for early removal. Ammunition inspected armrs. of 8 & 9 Dublin, and Machine Guns of 48 M.G.C. Also repaired 2 Vickers M.G. Rec'd. 3 Lewis Guns for 9 Dublins. Wired for Lewis Guns (7 Inniskillings) to replace destroyed by shellfire. Amm. repaired 5 Lewis Guns. | |
| | 14 | | Ammunition to 2 R. Dublin Fus. today - Carried out programme. Wired for:- two 3″ Stokes TM (48 TMBS), replace destroy'd shellfire; 2 Lewis Guns (7/8 R. Ir. Fus), destroyed shellfire. Rec'd 2 Lewis Guns (7 Inniskillings) Carr. all fus. and repaired. | |
| | 15 | | Received two 3″ Stokes TM fas 48 TMB + 2 Lewis Guns for 7/8 R. Ir. Fus. Visited by A.D.O.S. XIX Corps. In view of tomorrows battle A Dm & Specials asked for 80 Shrapnel Boxes for Thomas applied by Army. Asked ADOS & DDOS for 10 ST. 7/8 LAISCars (for ascertaining availability). No car allotted to 48 Sudan Ambulance and so was able to draw Ambulance train. | |
| | 16 | | Battle of FRENZENBERG RIDGE commenced. Again asked for car to enable me to carry out various duties but was informed by A.A.Q.M.G. that no car was available for use - that it was useless to ask for one while battle continued. 5th Division Dumped action N of country supporters today. 10 & 16 Div. Administrative Instructions to Rifle Shoot Guards with all Guard duties action U of B.D.SS & Salvage Dumps. Wire conversation to attachment re. wired for 18 pdr. Gun (Stores) DAYSE and Cart (8 pdr.) (Shellfire) 24/11/Div. Asst. M.G. | |

# WAR DIARY
## INTELLIGENCE SUMMARY

Army Form C. 2118.

D.A.D.O.S.
16TH (IRISH) DIV.
No. III
A/C

| Place | Date 1917 | Hour | Summary of Events and Information | Remarks and references to Appendices |
|---|---|---|---|---|
| VLAMERT- INGHE Aug. | 17 | | Ascertained that 18 pdr. guns for A/180 & 180 Bgde. Corr. for 64/14 Aust. F.M. are available at Gun Park. Reception moved inside Div. HQ. | |
| | 18 | | To WATOU — Office. Short trip in 3 Nissen huts at Ell. 27. K. 4. d. 15.12. Moved from IVR 151 pts. Div. for O.D. Benn. all (6 Div., Anti-Tank No.1 Cap., Div. Train also Staff. Sgt. A.L.S., m.t. Tram. S/S Cutchin. CULLEN & ELLIOTT with Ad Div. returned after 10 DA. | |
| WATOU | 19 | | Armoured repaired & handed guns (2 Dublins). Wired for 15 Lewis guns for Armistice (replace lost in action) & drew SAA army Gun Pard. Withdrew special equipment (4 Pontoonsleigh, trench belt, &c.) | |
| | 20 | | Withdrew from 10 R. Dublin Frm. all equipment & ammunition on same lot. army a/c, sent their application & this Bn't. is to take over equipment of 7/8 Inniskillings. Issued 9 Lewis guns (throw 10 Dublins) to 7 R. Irish Rifle to replace a discharge obsolete. Division between to 3rd Army and 3 Cav.-A is now its supporting unit (5 changes in distrib to NAVARRE and ROUEN from 21/8. All concerned notified. Wired for 3 x 3"Stokes Trps for 49 Trw.B (rifles lost in action), 4 Vickers m.g (+) m.g.Co. (abortion), 6 Vickers m.g. - 48 m.g.Co. (shelling) | |
| | 21 | | Wired for 3 Vickers m.g. - 47 m.g. Co. (lost in action.) | |
| | 22 | | Moved from WATOU to ACHIET LE PETIT, then entrain vi Corps and Third Army. | |
| | 23 | | Wired for Lewis guns: - 11-8 Inniskillings; 2 - 2 R. Irish Rifl; 1 - 6 R. Irish Rifl; 4 - 7 R. Irish Rifl; 7-8 Inniskilling a/c applied for - a 7/8 R. Inniskilling Frm. 7 R. Irl. Rifle go to 49 Bde & 10 Dublins come into 48 Bde. | |
| ACHIET LE PETIT. | 24 | | Handed in equipment and transport of 8 Inniskilling to 10 Dublins — very many deficiencies. Wired for Lewis guns :- 10 - 9 R. Dublin Fus.; 2 - 8 R. Dublin Fus.; 12 - 7/8 R. Innish. Fus.; 3 - 3" Stokes T.M. (48 T.M. B.); 3 Vickers m.g. - 3 for 49 m.g. Co. and 1 for 47 m.g. Co. Drew from 3rd Army Gun Park Vickers m.g. - 4 for 49, 6 for 48, 3 for 47 m.g.Cos. Ammunition repaired 3 Vickers m.g. (4 7 m.g. Co.) DDOS 3rd Army called for report on why so many complete Lewis guns were demanded, enquiry made. Took spare parts into action. Wired Curtis O.D. to send Vickers & Lewis mellon | |
| | 25 | | issue to suspense! | |
| | | | Drew from Gun Park 3 Lewis guns for 7 Quinslus, 2 Lewis guns for 7 R Dublin, 3 Vickers m.c. 4 for 49 m.g. Co., 1 Vickers m.g. for 47 m.g. Co. 10 Dublins ammunition on arrival from O.D. & ix Corp arm to 16 Div. appr. 24/8. | |
| | 26 | | Recd. 3.5" Stokes T.M. (49 T.M.B.) and drew 11 Lewis guns, cap. equip for SON, CULLEM, Pte. ELLIOTT with Ad Sn. all returned. Detached and reformed to medical gall. 6 grd Gun. following units of VIII Corp. army; W.O., PLANT attached to VIII Corp workshop; 24 June Gun Ren. Co.; Renauvlt. B. 4th Div. wire CA. Rfr.; VIII Corp Supplies (Cars, Lorries, & worksp. (men.); Blyde on wksp. (Chs), R.C.S. III.; 357 & 538 Road Construction Co. Rfr.; VIII Corp Supplies (Cars, Lorries, & worksp. (men.); Blyde on wksp. (Chs), R.C.S. III.; 3) Lt. Railway Oppring Cos.; HQrts. II Army School, III Army Sch. 1 Corp Cav.; III Army Veterinary & 2) Canal Renayr Co.; HQrts. IX (IX Corps Cav.); Bug. S. Irish Horse (I Corps Cav.); III Army Ironmongery; 3) Prisoner of War Ref. 18 Labour Gr. Cav.; Engineer and Communications Troop. (IX Corps Cav.); 2-38 A.T.Co. R.E.; 5/Artly. Reinforce Battery. | |

**Army Form C. 2118.**

D.A.D.O.S.
16TH (IRISH) DIV.
No. IV
Date AUG: 1917

# WAR DIARY

## INTELLIGENCE SUMMARY.

*(Erase heading not required.)*

Instructions regarding War Diaries and Intelligence Summaries are contained in F.S. Regs., Part II. and the Staff Manual respectively. Title pages will be prepared in manuscript.

| Place | Date 1917 | Hour | Summary of Events and Information | Remarks and references to Appendices |
|---|---|---|---|---|
| ACHIET LE PETIT | Aug. | 27. | Ordnance Conference of A.D.O.S. with D.A.D.O.S. Points discussed were - to keep working stocks of Br. Helmets in accordance to Estr., reserve wastage system of Deivier undeclothing - Berl. Stores & Clean-to (to exchange for dirty); recover and re-establishment of A.O.C. personnel with Divisions; recommended to present A.C.IV.; Equipment otherwise likely to be difficult for winter campaigns; payment issues of ammunition to be made through D.A.D.O.S.; Canteen-vans D.A.D.O.S. Army proposes that D.A.D.O.S. should control payments. Boisleux au Mont - offices, stores, etc kept at S.g.c. 4.2. (Sht. 51 m) Dumps left in very dirty condition by XVII Div. | |
| BOISLEUX au MONT | | 28 | | |
| | | 29 | Surgeon Lieut. ROOTS sent to hospital with 16 Div. Art. Sgt. Ch. CULLEN and R.G. ELLIOT returned for Leave. Batteries from Front:- two 3" 10CoyRFA (48TMB); Pair'd DR Detachment, two DR RG'd TMy (48TMB); 1-6 R.Irish Rgt. 13-7/8 R.Irish Fusiliers. | |
| | | 30 | | |
| | | 31 | Sgt.Ch. N°2 reported 10 days leave from dept. Army Serj. ROOTS returned to duty. Reinforcements wanted Lewis gun Officer of 2.R.Irish Rg. & 1/B R. Irish Fusiliers. Staff Captain R.A. phoned that 16 DA. is short of 3-4 5" Hows. & 1-18pdr gun. Lewis guns repaired in Div. Shop. Spade axes, & iPicks cases to be ordered that usual procedure should be adopted & YPRES action - no indents received, full particulars cannot be furnished of bombs, numbers of picks - helmets, if D.O.M. certificate cannot be supposed accordingly. B.C. R.A. informs accordingly. | |
| | | | 31.8.17. | |

A.S. Ramsworth Capt. A.G.O
D.A.D.O.S. 16th Division

WAR DIARY.

FOR MONTH OF SEPTEMBER, 1917.

VOLUME 22

UNIT:- D.A.D.O.S. 16th Division

# WAR DIARY / INTELLIGENCE SUMMARY

Army Form C. 2118.

**16th (IRISH) DIVISION**
D.A.D.O.S.
No. 1
Date SEPT/1917

| Place | Date 1917 | Hour | Summary of Events and Information | Remarks and references to Appendices |
|---|---|---|---|---|
| BOISLEUX au MONT | 1-9 | | Weekly routine and supervision. Sub Col. NASH granted leave to ENGLAND 2/12 Sept. Dist. Artillery demands by telephone re 4.5" How. were (Spdr. and other equipment in important to demand in proper way. O.O.R.O notified no action to be taken to prevent or antedate deficiencies — questions punished only by him. | |
| | | | Wind dangerous notified. Routine. | |
| | 2 | | Received 17.8 Inch Howr. to D.A.O.S. Arty Troops, in reply to indent. Dist. - distributed Brigade option introduced on orders of A.D.O.S. Weekly indents — Courses on subjects. reg. — distributed | |
| | 3 | | to Division. Visits paid to Divl. Shop regularly for observation instruction, and to cross units R.H.Q. 6th, 4/7, 49 Inf. Bde., I How:ly, D.M. Gun Coy etc. | |
| | 4 | | Amm. Coy. ROOT to Amm. Sup. July, Pte. DUNSCOMBE to RuCpl.; Rue Cpl. DIGARD, WHEELER, FETCANS, HAWKINS Recommendation made for promotion: | |
| | 5 | | Amm. Coy. Bgt. VERE granted leave to ENGLAND Sept. 9/19 and Amm. S. Staff Sgt. COMERFORD leave (in FRANCE) Sept 8/14. | |
| | | | All indents and correspondence re Div. Arty, Sufficiency and to A.D.O.S. for instruction. | |
| | 6 | | Moved 32 by Railway Operating Co. to O.O. III Corps Troops and 3rd Army Troops No. 5. | |
| | 7 | | Wind notified. | |
| | 8 | | | |
| | 9 | | | |
| | 10 | | Cpl. ROONEY (5 Connaught Rangers) and Pte WALLIS (6.R. Irish Rifl) reported for duty as learners in Dist. Armr. Shop. On | |
| | | | instruction from A.D.O.S. Wind Board three 4.5" How. complete and carriages, D/177, replace destroyed hostilities in 62 Army. R.T.A. Bde. in same area. Army and another one 18 Pdrs. complete and carr., C/180, replaces transferred to 283 Army R.T.A. Bde. in same area. | |
| | 11 | | Sgt. KEARSLEY granted leave to U.R. 11/25. | |
| | | | First issue of denims (10,000) received. Moved No. 4 Supply Col. to 48th Division. | |
| | 12 | | Lieut. W.S. FIELD, A.O.D., Asst. Inspector of Armourers, 3rd Army, reported to carry out inspection of Vickers & Lewis guns and | |
| | | | units in Div. Q. and 1st army preparation. Moved 29 Canadian Forestry Co. to O.O. III Army Troops No. 1. | |
| | 13 | | Wind two Koons left Div. to refit & UBC. — replaces condemned in Amm. Shop. Sub Col. NASH returned off leave. | |
| | | | 16 Supply Col. moved from 36 Div. to 16th Div. Cancelled indents for 4 Entrenching Batt. being disbanded. | |
| | 14 | | Received Vickers W/Gun for 48 Inf. Bde. Co. | |
| | 15 | | A.I. of A. inspected armr. of Divl. HQ., Troops also Living from & Rifles of 11th Hants. (?). Amm. Staff Sgt. COMERFORD | |
| | | | returned off leave. Sub. Col. SANDERS granted leave Sept 16/26. | |
| | 16 | | Received (8Pdr. 9Comm. to C/180, without R.M. Wind Board to B.M. diversions surplus stores for 4 Entrenching Batt. | |
| | 17 | | Cpl. HAWRE notified that births & deaths (by Cpl. HAW) are arriving at home rate. Despatched all units to submit without | |
| | | | further ration. 4 Entrenching Bn. was disbanded, wiped off and all concerned informed. | |
| | 18 | | Our Corps Eng. Dwyer awarded (Ruc. Cpl. DUNNE, FERGUS, WHEELER, and HAWKINS, and Pte. PLANT, Deport & review | |
| | | | having been completed. A.I. of A. inspected Lewis gun, Rifles etc. of 4 Battalions of 149 Inf. Bde. | |

**Army Form C. 2118.**

D.A.D.O.S.
16TH (IRISH) DIV.
No. ..............
Date SEPT. 1917

# WAR DIARY
## INTELLIGENCE SUMMARY.
*(Erase heading not required.)*

Instructions regarding War Diaries and Intelligence Summaries are contained in F. S. Regs., Part II. and the Staff Manual respectively. Title pages will be prepared in manuscript.

| Place | Date 1917 | Hour | Summary of Events and Information | Remarks and references to Appendices |
|---|---|---|---|---|
| BOISLEUX-AU-MONT | 19-9 | | Cpl. HAWKINS granted leave Sept. 20/30. Routine. | |
| | 20 | | A.D.D.A. inspected Lewis guns 10/9/17 of 7 Leinster Regt. & Ammunition; also some Vickers M.G. am. of 47 + 48 M.G. Co. C/3 Army R.F.A. Btn. transferred for Ordnance from 50th Div. to 16th Div. Armr. S/Sgt. VETRE returned off leave. Lce.Cpl. FERGUS granted leave (via HAVRE) Sept. 23/Oct. 4 | |
| | 21 | | No. 53692 Pte. O. EVANS, Artificer of 47 M.G. Co. arrived for attachment to Div. Armourers' Shop. Recent Board interviewed for Perm. Note. (45567) | |
| | 22 | | A.D.D.A. inspected 6 Welsh lewis guns of 49 M.G. Co. moved 18 Lewis G. to 16th Division Mins for Vickers M.G. for 48 M.G. Co. — to replace out condemned in Div. Arm. Shop. | |
| | 23 | | Moved R.E.G. III to O.O. VI Corps Troops. Nickel & O.M. 13 + 14 to 2.5 + 3 Units Whatoyo (Pr.) or inspection of repair of motments in this Army; learned that no spare Carts are held | |
| | 24 | | Routine | |
| | 25 | | Sent local demand notes on for 8500 flannelets to complete to one per man. Bry J. KEMPSLEY returned off leave. Carried out an AMIENS road purchase (for special purposes of 47 Inf. Bde.) from G. PATTERSON, R.G.A. (Bethune to D.A.D.O.S.) Admitted to 111 Fd. Amb. Sick Armr. S/Sgt. CONNERFOR opened Reamly. Run. Sept. 27/Oct. 7 and Lce.Cpl. WHEELER (by Div) Sept. 26/Oct. 8 | |
| | 26 | | Asst. W.O. FIELD, A.O.D., Adv. Depot of Armrs, Third Army, left for XVII Corps (1st Divisional Horse), Received 4567 Rupe Horse from Base. Moved 238 A.T.Co. R.Z. to O.O. VI Corps Troops. Bt. Lt. SPANDER Field officer | |
| | 27 | | Visited by A.D.O. VI Corps to express concern for scoring. Visited by DA.D.O.S. VI Corps—D.O.O. 3 End Army. Routine. | |
| | 28 | | Visited by A.D.O. VI Corps & Salvy officer VI Corps Routine. | |
| | 29 | | Cancelled outstanding indents of 9 R. Dublins in view of impending evacuation with 8 R. Dublin to Brst from O'Keefe; three serviceable Lewis guns from Park for Bde. Artillery. During this week the workshops in Div. Armourers' Shop included :— | |
| | 30 | | overhaul of Vickers guns :— 47 M.G. 7; 48 M.G. 16; 49 M.G. 4; = 27, in addition to repair of Lewis guns — 47 Bde. 26; 48 Bde. — 30; 49 Bde. 64; Pioneers = 134. Bicycles — all Divisional troops and 47 Inf Bde. Group. | |
| | 30/9/17. | | | O.C. Drummons. Capt. OC/O<br>D.A.D.O.S. 16th Divn. |

2353 Wt. W2544/1454 700,000 5/15 D.D.&L. A.D.S.S./Forms/C. 2118.

WAR DIARY

FOR MONTH OF OCTOBER, 1917.

UNIT D.A.D.O.S. 16th Division

VOLUME NUMBER 23

# WAR DIARY

## INTELLIGENCE SUMMARY

**Army Form C. 2118.**

D.A.D.O.S. 16TH (IRISH) DIV.
Date October 1917.

| Place | Date | Hour | Summary of Events and Information | Remarks and references to Appendices |
|---|---|---|---|---|
| BOIS LEUX aux MONT. | Oct. 1917 | 1 | Notified by a.d.o.s. VI Corps that a Depot Battalion will shortly be attached to Division to be administered by 16 Division for all purposes. Lines drawn for Divisional Boots & kit. 2/Lt. HAWKINS returned off leave. | |
| | | 2 | P.G. FITZPATRICK (attached from Employment Coy) granted leave Oct. 3/15. Routine. | |
| | | 3 | Drew one Lewiston Bedford "Turnel Trailer from 2nd Army T.M. School. Conf. RANDELL granted leave Oct. 5/15. | |
| | | 4 | Ass. Inspector of Ordnance Services nominated Division to be completed inspection by Division of 6 R. Irish Regt. & 7 Connaught Rangers. Comny. PATTERSON, R.S.A.y. returned to duty from 111 Fd. Ambce. Pte. RILEY granted leave Oct. 5/15 - Amm. Sp. | |
| | | 5 | ROOTS (from Ba.) Oct. 1/22. - via HAVRE. Comny. Staff Sergt. W. CALLAHAN, A.O.C., L.R. nominated Administrator 111 Fd. Ambce. with G.S. wound caused by double fuse whilst starting Lewis gun on nose. M.O.H. declared no Court of Enquiry required. 16 Div. M.P. 732. notified. accident. Routine. | |
| | | 6 | Ammn. 8/04. D.A.C.F.T. A.O.C. (6 R. Irish Regt.) granted leave by Rr. Oct. 9/20, via HAVRE. Rec. Cpl. FENGS returned off leave. Received 300 special knot twine from Boots. | |
| | | 7 | Normal time received today; clocks put back one hour at 1 am. Received from Boots 2000 prs Boots - French Repair. | |
| | | 8 | Took on strength from Camp Commdt., VI Corps. No. 5 group, 2/ord. Rack for Ordnance duty. Drew from Gun Park four 6" Warrton Trench Mortars. P.G. A. PLANT granted leave Oct. 10/20. arrives for 1 visitors' lecture from (47 L.of C.) to replace one condemned in Armourer's Shop. A.O.C. | |
| | | 9 | Drew from Gun Park further four 6" Trench Mortars (Newton). Drew from G.O. VI Corps Troops 308 & 29 Tent Bottoms. Demonstration on 18pr. gun without R.M. (S)/160 Bde. R.F.A.) - replace condemning. Dewhurst & Br. French Mortars. Gun 3 Temple Silencer for 3" T.M. | |
| | | 10 | Posted Armr. Staff Sergt. ROSS (Cadiz) R. Irish Rifles) for duty at VI Corps School. Pte. EVANS, 47 w.a. Co., Rohyshi, returned to unit for leave - Submitted favourable report. as to suitability of 48 ind. Co. for carrier Shop. sustained by 16 Div (Q) Rest personnel of J (S.J Park Warden) R. Irish Rifles will arrive 14/10. | |
| | | 11 | Comny. G. PATTERSON (Balloon) granted leave Oct. 12/25. Received from Ammn. Reserves, 3 47 Roads Construction Co. " for Base " (A.D.V.S VI Corps min.). Base Repairs. Train on Enquiry to Ordnance Review. Comf. WHEELER returned off leave. Comf. FORD's leave having been extended. 10 Oct. by O.H. A.O.C. Received. F.O. Cpl. COMERFORD and | |
| | | 12 | Ammn. Staff Sergt. COMERFORD and R.O. Cpl. RECORD, Woolwich. Surrendered (300 assessed to complete 2 for use in Division. Visited AMIENS armoury weak. Purchase Co. Bre ("J) G.O.C. (6 Div) of 13 working running machines. Conf. 300 prs. = Total of 250 prs. | |
| | | 13 | Received from Base weekly issue of Boots T.S. - All gentlemen - with two out 8 prs. (without R.M.) & one Carriage for C/17. Bde. R.F.A. - replaced destroyed Shellfire. Pte. E.W. DAVIES A.O.C. granted leave Oct. 15/25. Delivery expected about 25/10. | |

# WAR DIARY
## INTELLIGENCE SUMMARY

**Army Form C. 2118.**

D.A.D.O.S.
16TH (IRISH) DIV.
No. II
Date October 1917

| Place | Date | Hour | Summary of Events and Information | Remarks and references to Appendices |
|---|---|---|---|---|
| BOISLEUX-AU-MONT | Oct. 1917 14. | | 7th (S. Irish Horse) R.I. Irish Regiment arrived in Division (49th Brigade) in place of 7 R. Irish Rifles, transferred to 63rd (Ulster) Division. Leave granted by Battalions to Armourer/Staff Sergeants INGRAM (7 R Irish Regt) and THURSPIELD (7/8 R. Irish Fus.) — Oct. 15/26, and (Military) M. FITZPATRICK (attached) armourer of above. Tour from Army Pool on anti-aircraft sights for Vickers machine Guns. | |
| | 15 | | Returned M/C FITZPATRICK to 27 Employment Coy. Routine. | |
| | 16 | | Moved 48 N.W.F. Indian Labour Coy. to O.O. III Corps Troops with instructions from A.D.O.S. VI Corps. Unable to attend A.D.o.S. Conference today as I would not obtain a car. Notified Bases arrival of 7 (S. Ir Horse) R. Irish Regt. from D.A.O. 6th, GHQ Troops, in advance of amount received in 6th. Routine. Capt. A.B. DALLIMORE to ENGLAND on Course 18/28 Oct. Handed over to Lt. Col. N.?. S/F pending return of Col. RANDELL. | A.B.Dallimore. Capt. A.O.O. 17/10/17. Nor Had |
| | 17 | | Returned off leave and took over from Nor Had | |
| | 18 | | Colla Kid 45 Lieut. Lieut. Boston from VI Corps. L. 17th R.I. Duk Fus (—) Returned No 27641 Pte ? Linsley and No. 5785 P.?R 8/R. Knight ? 75 O.O. VII Corps Troops Memories Burial and Removal No. 5343 Pte PUMFREY 47 Recordon and No 15158 Pte NUTLET N. Munster Fus burial Joint appointment in Dronville ? No. 03586 L/Cpl Noble ?A and Bizzelt Pte ROBISON R joined for duty from No III Cable Troops | |
| | 19 | | Relieved 105 Lets Tent Battery to 17th R.I. Duk Fus 1st R.I. Duk Fus 2nd Div. for 29th D.N. Lee q hustle and joined from No 17 L? ? for phant a list of ... ? to enable ... to be ... | |

**Army Form C. 2118.**

D.A.D.O.S.
16TH (IRISH) DIV.
No. 141
Date 26 Oct 1917

# WAR DIARY
## INTELLIGENCE SUMMARY.
*(Erase heading not required.)*

Instructions regarding War Diaries and Intelligence Summaries are contained in F.S. Regs., Part II. and the Staff Manual respectively. Title pages will be prepared in manuscript.

| Place | Date 1917 | Hour | Summary of Events and Information | Remarks and references to Appendices |
|---|---|---|---|---|
| BOISLEUX au Mont | Oct 20 | | Demanded One 18/pdr Carriage for C.23 A.F.A. Bde. Slim Work Normal. Armourers General repairs. One Vickers gun received for 48th M.G. Coy. | |
| | 21 | | One 18/pdr Gun received for C.23 A.F.A. Bde — One Battalion transferred to D.O. VII Corps Troops. Training Coy transferred to D.A.D.O.S. 15-17 Division. Slim Work Normal. Armourers General repairs. | |
| | 22 | | Routine — transferred C.23 A.F.A. Bde to D.O. 15th Corps Troops | |
| | 23 | | Routine — One 3" Stokes Mortar demanded for use with Morter Battery — 3,400 Coals fuze received from Divnl Armourer. General repairs. | |
| | 24 | | 16,000 Blankets received from River (2nd Blanket per man) The 18/pdr Gun without B.M. sent up for C.23 A.F.A. Bde. handed over to DADOS 51st Div for issue to C.44 A.F.A. Bde by Divn of ADOS 6th Corps. | |

# WAR DIARY
## or
## INTELLIGENCE SUMMARY.
*(Erase heading not required.)*

Army Form C. 2118.

D.A.D.O.S.
16TH (IRISH) DIV.
No. IV
Date Oct. 1917

| Place | Date | Hour | Summary of Events and Information | Remarks and references to Appendices |
|---|---|---|---|---|
| ROISIEUX au Mont | Oct. | 25 | Winter Clothing received. Took 2 in duplex stores of 9th. 21st Dublin Fus: for amalgamation. Gale blowing from 2 am joining to special state No. 11 and 24 Store tent blown down and destroyed with state D.D.O.S. 24f Army called and was very dis-satisfied with quantity of stores received. not understanding everything climatic conditions & quantity of stores received in that day (and only 15 men to handle it). Took in 150 arts anchordeing. O. 8943 Pte Clark 2/8 RIF Regt (Return boot expert). Joined from 6th Corps Troops. | |
| | 26 | 1100 | Prayers received from Regt. Returned surplus stores handed in by 9th Dublins to Base Depot. Sets of Saddlery to no 1st Corps. Mosfor D.A.Q.M.G. called to see condition of depot, informed him Place very unsatisfactory for winter months. Two Armourer overhauled 16 Jews Guns handed in by 2d Dublins Fus. Category "B" men joined from ETAPLES (No 41335 Pte Craig J 9th Gordons + No 296855 Pte HOLT H 10t Lanes Fus) 4/o S. Major A.J. Hagan granted 10 days special leave 27/10 to 6/11. — | |
| | 27 | | General clean up of Depot after storm of 25th inst. — Store work normal. Armourers overhauled repaired 5 Vickers Guns, 1 Lewis Gun, 10 Rifles & general repair. A.D.O.O.S. H.Q. called — | |
| | 28. | | Armourers general repairs | |
| | 29 | | Routine " " | |

Lieut Capt. Davenport returned off leave & resumed duties to him Jameson Capt. on did such to him J Nash Lyn

WAR DIARY

FOR MONTH OF NOVEMBER, 1917.

VOLUME :- 24

UNIT :- AAQMG. 16 Div.

# WAR DIARY / INTELLIGENCE SUMMARY

**Army Form C. 2118**

D.A.D.O.S. 16TH (IRISH) DIV.
No. I
Date: NOV: 1917

| Place | Date 1917 | Hour | Summary of Events and Information | Remarks and references to Appendices |
|---|---|---|---|---|
| BOISLEUX- AU- MONT. | Nov. 1 | | Indent for one 3" Stokes Trench Mortar complete – 49 T.M.B. – to replace exchanged by staff Sgt. Jebb our Vickers machine gun – 49 M.G.C. – to replace condemned Ammunition Shops; also two 18 pdr Guns – C/180 Bde R.F.A – Completed for service. Lather ammunition cancelled by orders of A.D.O.S. VI Corps – replenishment being arranged from R.C. | |
| | 2 | | No. 46226 Pte. CLAYTON, J., 4/6 Innis. Adjutant reported for duty in Armourers Shop. 5th Div. and 151st Div. 77 Army R.F.A. Bde, Hqs, H.Q., A, B, C & D Batteries and B.A.C. | |
| | 3 | | 2nd Lieut. Read of Elephant Huts is sent to HQ of Inf. Bde. 2/31 convert in Armament Shops with an amount field repairing to attached field Stokes Armourer. Received III Corps Cyclists S.A.A.O. III Corps Troops. XIX Corps Troops moved to 16th Div. 5 Army R.H.A. Bde, HQ, O. + Z. Batts, RHA, 402 Batt. R.FA 118.AC Received Vickers machine gun for 49 MG Co. Wired for substitute faith (Q. order) 203, 460 Pte. MORGAN, T., 9 Seaforth Highs, G.B.Strgt. Armourer via OO of M.G.P.L.A.N.T, A) reported for duty from O.D. 29 Div. | |
| | 4 | | Wired from 16th Div. to O.O. III Corps Troops No. 13+4 O-D LLutchinot workshops (L) on instructions of M.G.C VI Corps. | |
| | 5 | | Received 6–18 pdr Guns – two R/177, two B/177, one A/150, and C/180. wired from 4 to ask 15, 16th Div. 93 Army Bde R.F.A. original HQ, A, B + C Batts 118 A.C. | |
| | 6 | | Received 2 5 Tube Rocket; one 3" Stokes T.M for 49 T.M.B., one 18 pdr Gun for 3 Army R.H.A. Bde, O. Smith son late of Armourers. | |
| | 7 | | Received 18 pdr Guns – one 15/93, two C/93/3, one B/177, one 18/80, one exchange C/177; two 18 pdrs for 93 Bdes handed over by O.O. Ammunition direct 6257 B. and Workshops (Ch) Lee Cpl. DICARO, EE., FERGUS, J., WHEELER, J.A., J HAWK 102 T.C. appointed Craftsmen workshops from 11017. Sent annual. 8/. Recrts (113 Hands (R) to armoured arms. | |
| | 8 | | Routine. Plenty of work. | |
| | 9 | | Dine 12.68 to 5 P. holding G. Spencer O.C. VI Corps Troops S. Routine. | |
| | 10 | | Routine – quiet day. Army still plenty of independents. | |
| | 11 | | Attended C. of E. Confirmation meeting of importance. Routine. | |
| | 12 | | Collected 100 pgs Rebuilding Off. from B.O. II Corps Troops and sent to Div. | |
| | 13 | | Annl. Sgt. Root native issues from (113 Hands (R), having overhauled 8 Lewis guns, 6×8 Rifles and 10 Revolvers. Wired Nantes – 3 | |
| | 14 | | Routine 3 – 4.5" Howrs 28 Cartridges (D/177) but an Breach mechanisms. Wired for 3000 Field drawing for same guns. | |
| | 15 | | Received 3 – 4.5" Hwtrs, "D Cart/(D/177) but we had ordered Pearce to despatch A. wire to the Auth. Pte. BELSHAW praised leave CO/25 later Telephoned Field D.O.S.L. Paid detachment. | |
| Nov 16/30. | 16 | | Wired Pearce to suspend issue for 5A R.H.A. Bde, 77 A.R. Bde, 93 A. R.F.A. Bde. I agree to use of any dumps etc. as EARWICKER on Monday, & wired all concerned accordingly. | |
| | 17 | | Visited A.D.O.S. + G.O.A. now W. recd. S. to O.C. IV Corps Troops SA RHA Bde, 77, A. R.F.A. Bde, 93 A. R.F.A. Bde, two 3" Stokes T.M. complete (49 T.M.B), returns of deficiencies by 17 0/11/17. Wired Guns Rds about 3 Pairs for D/177 – and amount Pte A. PLANT A.O.C. proceeded (HAVRE) 16 Base. Ordnance, HAVRE, on a category "A" wear. Ogum wired Pearce re C/F for R. 3 army Regl. Battery out of support of DMO. Shill were to be handed for Salvage via WMC, LE NR, L.C. at upon it of D.M.O. | |
| | 18 | | | |

2353 Wt. W3514/1454 709,000 5/15 D.D. & L. A.D.S.S./Forms/C. 2118.

Army Form C. 2118.

# WAR DIARY
## or
## INTELLIGENCE SUMMARY.
(Erase heading not required.)

D.A.D.O.S.
16TH (IRISH) DIV.
No. I
Date Nov. 1. 1917.

Instructions regarding War Diaries and Intelligence Summaries are contained in F.S. Regs., Part II and the Staff Manual respectively. Title pages will be prepared in manuscript.

| Place | Date 1917 | Hour | Summary of Events and Information | Remarks and references to Appendices |
|---|---|---|---|---|
| BOISLEUX—AU—MONT — ERVILLERS | Nov. 1 19 | | Moved offices, Stores and shops to ERVILLERS (Sh.57c.B.19.b.6.6.) — with quarters. Purchased in ALBERT 100 carpet glue Tools, spare heavy spares wanted from Army for artil. work, and mechanics — awaiting arrival. D.A.D.O.S. Dav. went into action for handlift operation. and on [illegible]. C(177). [illegible] no lorries detailed. Butterfly CAMERAS seated today. | |
| | 20 | | Spare parts for Vickers machine guns (4 Nos.) and replace broken shafts. Became exchanged [illegible] & delivered to HQRs. 183rd Batteries. Returned to stores book (v.2) supplies delivered B/177 during Sept to HQrs. C. 8/9/177. Final v.5.T How. Can. dumped as unserviced to HQrs. C. 5/17. Visited M.G. dos. — nothing claiming. | |
| | 21 | | Visited 107 Divl's HQ. (148 M.S.Co.) also 1 Coy. [illegible] (D.E. Irish Rifles) also 1 Coy. (M.R. Irish Rif.) — replacements of Shell. breastplates from Park. also new blankets' depot. (Guns not ret. with Co.) and delivered direct to owner's HQ. Ind. for no 3" 2"CStaff.T.M., one complete and limber. (48 T.M.B.) replace damaged Shellfire. | |
| | 22 23 | | Collected Rolex, Riverhear from Corps Cemetery Station. Received from Rolex two 3/4"Stokes T.M. (No 9 T.M. Bs.). Routine. Pte G. RILEY, A.O.C. spec. KEEN, A.S.C., M.T., reported for duty. Moved X., Y., 2/5/9 T.M. Ba. to 59 Divs. under orders of A.D.O.S. Visited by D.D.O.S. and announced his decision. Did not secure stereoscopes except with authority of Brit. Boonerkist Dept. Spare A.A. veg. M.G. about field. | |
| | 24 | | Amm. Staff Capt, COMERFORD sent to 1st Aust. Dublin fus. to overhaul amm. Brow in Sub.Reb for 6" Newton T.M. from 3 Divl. Inst. workshop (M.) Handed over 3 instructional lorries from to VI Corps Reinforcement Camp. Visited A.D.O.S. — no confirmation to be taken under, | |
| | 25 | | Received two 3" Stokes T.M. (1 complete and 1 barrel only) — 48 T.M.B. and Bullets to left.B. Bro.III Corps T.M. L. and Bullets S.B.G. Bro. IV Coy: Rifles. — received from 6 Connaught Rays for 4 how fired. 4 Bags Spare Pats. v.s.5, 1587 magazine C.S. — all sent away by lorry, received. Saddlers from horseman-up in charge & wired for balance. Brow from gunburst. and delivered to 6 Clog. 2 Lewis guns (A Batt., Spare parts plus, also Saff with Cov. 1) Trepo mounting. Amm. Staff Capt. COMERFORD returned to park. Amm. Reg. | |
| | 26 27 | | Routine. From today all gun Ports to be made by units on S.O. rec. and demands for machines and spare Parts to be sent to A.O.D. Drainage from Park. No.3 BAPAUME instead of to O.D.S.P. No.3 ALBERT. | |
| | 28 29 | | Drew from Arm. Corps. Gunboaters two 18pdr pieces replacing A.C. 4188 of A/177 and 4837/C/190. Repaired work-shop (3); handsaw and spares from O.D. II Corps. Params to Old 110 Battr's. Visited by A.D.O.S. when by 17 confirmed that D.O.D.S greased in W (4) at MOB.P.M.G specified from Staff at 1st LEGER'S Archway. "U" Spare paks wheeler, any other purpose weaponized (i.e. work supplied by) the advance through the infantry of machine arms. A.G.G whenofer ship private carving, Artifr. CLAYTON (48 M.G. Co.) to Regt. announced through am't Saf[?] his certificate of Routine. Pol.Cpl. NASH T., Hospital today. Rcvs to advance with Bt to Keillu Wheeler forms and lorries fitted and whole. | |
| | 30 | | Invisible in Inqy. Visible in mount... and sundries standing moult. Announce cleaned overnight. Higher wheelerforms and knife-fans during the mount, wind [illegible] and [illegible] today 3/N.S.O.C./B.O.— upheaveracing. | |

A.A. Drennan Capt.
D.A.D.O.S. 16th Division.

30/11/17

WAR DIARY,

FOR MONTH OF DECEMBER, 1917.

VOLUME :- 25

UNIT :- D.A.D.O.S. 16th Division

Vol 24

Army Form C. 2118.

# WAR DIARY
# or
# INTELLIGENCE SUMMARY.
(Erase heading not required.)

D.A.D.O.S.
16TH (IRISH) DIV.
No. 1
Date DECEMBER 1917.

Instructions regarding War Diaries and Intelligence Summaries are contained in F.S. Regs., Part II. and the Staff Manual respectively. Title pages will be prepared in manuscript.

| Place | Date | Hour | Summary of Events and Information | Remarks and references to Appendices |
|---|---|---|---|---|
| ERVILLERS | Dec. | 1 | Wired for one Farrier (R Irish Reg't) to replace Sergeant by shell fire. In view of early snow, Cos. Artificers and 47 Inf. Bde. leaves up for inspection next. | |
| | | 2 | Pte. BELSHAW returned off leave. Moved to Ordnance 40 Div. — 338 + 347 Road Construction Cos. R.E., 6 O.D. Works Workshops (Divl.) & 284 A.T.Co., Mob. Workshop (Bn.), 5 Troop Broad Gauge, all 16½ Div. Artillery, 1ST, 176 & 177 Field Cos. R.E. and 11 Hants. Regt. (Pioneer). Also 14 Division (Bn.) U.S. Army. Drew leave for from Advanced Tank Park for R. Irish Regt. | |
| YPRES. | | 3 | Moved to LITTLE WOOD, YPRES — no official information available. Received instructions from 16 D.S.C. for move but have withdrawn by 16 Div. Q, this making two journeys necessary. Infantry A.D.O.S. that from 5th ind. 18 pdr 04.5" how Lowers will be demanded from Gun Park, and moving sub. Corps area. | |
| | | 4 | Every order recommunicated in morning. Received Lorries from I.M. T.O. 1st Corps | |
| FLAMICOURT. | | 5 | Moved to FLAMICOURT, near PERONNE (7 kilometers). Very bad accommodation — none for stores. | |
| | | 6 | Wired Bases to send up trucks. | |
| | | 7 | 16 Div. Q communicated stores. Moved to VILLERS FAUCON — two journeys, as a result. Took over dump from 48 Div. Stores at | |
| VILLERS FAUCON. | | | 2nd. 6 T.C. E. 15. d. 6. 3. – absolutely accumulation of stores, salvage dump Armourers Shop Supply of unserviceable shoes. Moved from 55 Div. 16 Div. — "G" Special Coy — Troop C.R.E., 166 Labour Coy, 50 Sanitary Section, 2nd Coy. I Engineer (Reg't) U.S. Army, Moved from 40 Div. to 16 Div. – 1ST, 176 & 177 Field Cos. R.E., 11 Hants. (P.) Wired for Viewer N.F. (47 & 7/8 Cos.). 8 R. Inniskilling Fus. approaching. | |
| | | 8 | Visited A.D.O.S. VII Corps at CATELET and ascertained procedure for demanding funds etc. in this Corps vs. Gunner McROBERT. Paid Detachment. Returned & drew stores from 7 Sufs. Corps. MAYRE (indents supplied by A.C.W. VERE, supplies from M.D. 050 Armourer happy, and MAYRE is enough. Sent No. 2050 Armourer happy and F.A. VERE (surplus) | |
| | | 9 | Strength of 8 R. Dublin Fus. (5T Coy. MAYRE) holds. Truck Driver impecuniously. Loaves, huff, is reported from after. Loaves, Corporal of Stores received entirely from Base. Truck Driver reception awaits at ERVILLERS also arrived. Received ordnance machine gun (47) W3 Co. Paul 7 B.L. F.O.R. Corp. Chose restrictions with maximum | |
| | | 10 | Recommended to 3 + 60 Pte. J. MORGAN of Scottish Rifles (C. Armoury) R.O.C. as Armourer. Issued SOS Sanitary Section "G" Spec. Coy R.E. | |
| | | 11 | First Sept Divs. Wired for 1 Violin and one fund (49 W.B.Co.) replace destroyed by shell fire. 3rd ST Div. moved to 16 Div. 1st Div. Arty., 3, 7 HQ., A, B, C & D Battns. & 175 & 6th and HQ., A, B, C & D Battn. 276 Bde. R.F.A.; HQ., 1, 2 + 8 Secs. 5T D.A.C.; HQ., Z. Subviv. Train A.S.C., X, Y, Z & V 55 Trench Mortar Batteries. | |
| | | 12 | Took 7 Cd. F.U. P.C. Bde with rest from windmill. (Hd.) Dec. and destroys 6 set by fire. Visited by A.D.O. S VII Corps who went at length into explosive faults, indents etc. Inspected Div. Armourers Shop. Appeared not dissatisfied. | |
| | | 13 | 48 Inf. Bde. HQ. declined to send lorries to Divl. Armrs. Shop as they have no new to spare. Received promise of VII Corps troops on Sunday and arrived for funds. Rifles ruined by hot (RHQ) U.S. Inf. Rifle. Received one Vickers machine gun (Reg W.O.A.) | |
| | | 14 | Gilstrap's & Ind. Roll for 2 Canvas for Dual Armrs. Shop. Routine. | |

2353 Wt. W2544/1454 700,000 5/15 D. D. & L.    ADSS./Forms/C. 2118.

# WAR DIARY
## INTELLIGENCE SUMMARY

**D.A.D.O.S. 16th (IRISH) DIV. DECEMBER 1917**

| Place | Date 1917 | Hour | Summary of Events and Information | Remarks and references to Appendices |
|---|---|---|---|---|
| VILLERS FAUCON | Dec. 15 | | Routine. | |
| | 16 | | Lieut Col. T. NASH returned to duty from hospital. Wired for 1 Lewis gun for 1/(S.S.P.) R. Innisk. Regt — replace destroyed by shellfire. Routine. | |
| | 17 | | Returned to O.Gunner 55 Division their personnel (1 Sergt., 2 O.R. Staff) which had administered artillery under orders of A.D.O.S. VIII Corps. 7564 Pte. M. LANNON, 2 R. Innisk. Regt. attached to Divl. Armourer's Shop. | |
| | 18 | | Armr. Staff Sgt. INNIS reported for duty in Divl. Armourer's Shop. VII Corps transferred from 3rd Army to 4th Army at noon today. | |
| | 19 | | Drew from O.S. Park/Bn. No. 3 our Lewis gun for 7 (83rd) R. Innisk. Regt. also one 18 pdr. piece for A/275 Bde. R.F.A. | |
| | 20/21 | | Routine. | |
| | 22 | | Wired to O. Ordnance 55th Division all S.S. Div. Arty. (including X, Y, Z v/55 T.M. Bt. + 149 Co. S.S. Train) our instruction A.O.T.S? | |
| | 23 | | Visited by A.D.O.S., who went into this matter at length with current practice of accounting & report to any examining this department by present methods and up to date that this application — use will be putting in on useless 16 "B's" instead of showing how A.O.T.S. Supplies the Corps and being based on issues. O.O.T.S. never refuse to procure of Service Regt. issue of statements required of "Unhelpful" in which respect it had never to. A.O.T.S. would not forward any report being on a form not Q. to Corps Commander, his terms of being quite unreasonable. Replies we tone a complaint partner and will write him a report having been a form by Q to Corps Command ascertained from the O.O.C. that the question of issues of Sock. Lost. is quite satisfactory and that all elements of units had been with... | |
| | | | And A.O.T.S. full statement of position — 4/5 co. prior accession Seine and G Divs & S. Corps actually showing situations continued by Armourer. Wired for 1 Vickers m.g. (47 A.S. Co.) to replace one cancelled; no record of cancellation received here 6" mortar T.M. for 1/55 T.M.B. (D.T.M.O. S.S. Div. notified that indent was cancelled & instructions that there or later referred A.D.O.S. was with A.D.O.S. an issue.) Refund was/off/A.D.O.S. who issued instructions that there has been referred further. Received office records of two Bands and their Mountings 3/4 Field T.M. (N.B.T.M.B.) | |
| | 24 | | | |
| | 25 | | XMAS DAY. The restrictions ordered from upon to-day; later cancelled owing to unexpected wire for one Vickers machine gun (47 M.S. Co.) — replace destroyed by shellfire. Received 5 trucks of wire at Villers Faucon 4.30 pm. Staff dinner at 6.30 pm; participants being W.O.D. M. Corps — officers of detachment. Armourer. attached fatigue work, long distant Sgt. of A.S. Corp & W reserve (Sana fma) & Divl. Laundry Depot and demanded further 10,000 pc from Base — under instruction from A.D.O.S. | |
| | 26 | | 405 Division wound all (16 Div. Arty. and HQ Corps) Red Train to T. Bn. Received one Vickers m.g. (47 M.S. Co.) | |
| | 27 | | Bahman, Gunner G. PATERSON, admitted to hospital. Received one Vickers m.g. (47 M.S. Co.) wired for one 18 pdr. piece (A/177) — to replace one unserv(iceable) for Savoy. (10/5973) | |
| | 28 | | Armourer completed overhaul of 15 Lewis 800 rifles. Salv from III Corps/also from III Corps — 140 unsafe Serviceable rejoined to D.A.D.O.S. 4 Army. One serv. unloaded & British offic. n.b. All R.I.U. B. R.F. in.t.? in.t.v.sig. and all bach rifles returned to Base. Pte. Q. DOHERTY Detachment cook, admitted to hospital. Pte Persons took over as detachment cook. Received 30 bath or (un) wen 2 lorry (9) from m.p. flanes. Gunner ASMITH on instruction of/W.A. R.F.d., two handrails/wagon tripled for Divl. Sock. replacing. Absuntasta.... | |

Army Form C. 2118.

# WAR DIARY
## INTELLIGENCE SUMMARY.
*(Erase heading not required.)*

Instructions regarding War Diaries and Intelligence Summaries are contained in F. S. Regs., Part II. and the Staff Manual respectively. Title pages will be prepared in manuscript.

| Place | Date | Hour | Summary of Events and Information | Remarks and references to Appendices |
|---|---|---|---|---|
| VILLERS FAUCON. | Dec. | 29 | Arranged with Colonel in Divl. Bookkeeping Staff commencing 1st Jan 1918. Received 10,000 prs boots winter. | |
| | | 30 | Visited Fifth Army Burying School to see certain method of erecting Ridge pole Telescopic Bell tents in this Army. System practically the same as that followed in Second Army, with slight alteration in parts. | |
| | | 31 | Lieut Col. RAMSDEN, T., mentioned in despatches. Lieut Col. CULLEN, R.K., proceeded special leave Dec 31/1/18. Drawn from 2nd Indian Cavy. Corps. (part of 2000 allotted to VII Corps) waterproof sheets 153 of Battle took over officers Indian Cavy. Regt., C.L.A., promoted to Honr. Staff. for it. from 6/9/17. Handed over total 19,000 prs boots to Divl. Returning Depot. Arrangements carried out in respect of Reinvigorator machines for use during the month. | |

1/1/18.

A.V. Dawson, Capt. A.D.O

D.A.D.O.S. 16th Division

WAR DIARY,

FOR MONTH OF JANUARY, 1918.

VOLUME :- 26

UNIT : D.A.D.o.S. 16th Division

# WAR DIARY / INTELLIGENCE SUMMARY

Army Form C. 2118.

*(Erase heading not required.)*

Instructions regarding War Diaries and Intelligence Summaries are contained in F.S. Regs., Part II. and the Staff Manual respectively. Title pages will be prepared in manuscript.

D.A.D.O.S
16TH (IRISH) DIV
JANUARY 1918

| Place | Date 1918 | Hour | Summary of Events and Information | Remarks and references to Appendices |
|---|---|---|---|---|
| VILLERS FAUCON | Jan. 1 | | Attended Conference of D.A.D.O.S. with A.D.O.S. VII Corps. Weekly returns wanted from D.A.D.O.S. (i.e. summary in report of preparedness). Arrangements for war not being collected from units on Friday and would ask all machine gun etc. pointers for distribution the Corps – reminder of first 5 to be reported at next fortnightly conference. Everything going on well and nothing important to bring forward. Orders received from 3rd Western Cavalry over from 217 Divl. Employment Coy., 11/Irish Regt. Brooklyn with 1/M.G.B. and 5/Staffords. | |
| | 2 | | Attended review of 2000 watermen-in-prisoners. | |
| | 3 | | Arranged for C.O. VII Corps. Troops, 16th D.A., inventory, 100 numbered units as Regt.tation. Base guns from O.C. VII Corps. Troops. Besides balance of 9 battalions and 7 Divisional Field Artillery, (R.M.G.AY, 217 Divl. Emp. Coy. attached as work in place of P.C. Details & Sec. Corps E.E.T.CARDO Brigade here from 14th Jany. Today visited all Battalions and regiments to check installment of complete equipment of all in patchwork, by Companies, Squadrons, minenwerfers, Band, Brees, etc. All regimental informed me they were up to date or had indented even where. However many indors to add others, bags to find the following day: Balfour & games, BAYERS 60 not printed Company Commanders visited 3rd Artillery and received complaints of shortage of stores through inability of N.D.D. to supply Deft fell extent to get D.D.S. as his instruction staying that any interpreted work in otherwise there on the front of yards dis, as he had anticipated importuinment to forward but could be practically earned through inspection & gone the data. Visited by A.D.O.S. who continues to touch and touched under of Wagons of patches & artillery complaints. | |
| | 4 | | Their impediments into to visit Corps etc. Stores always ready, to arrange with A.D.M.S. for establishment of Runners here, and to arrange etc. in field. Confidence instead of evacuating them with 500 numbers C.C.S. (numbers applied half in them has been done, but it cannot allow trench Count & Equipment where there are records of C.C.A.'s and C.G.R.O.P.), to arrange provision of supply of others refusing for issuance of uniform & Finland, G.S. to Corps Opening Depot, & Depot State have been shelved by my name and made, & to Corps the said Return Records for artillery assisted as followed & Bde (Flanders Companies) – as Battalions of they desire to known to 31st Infantry Records & nearly adequate demands on Depots were received at (official). Sent Ord 40 Div. to suspend of all accidents to 16 Div. Arty. on day of the ammunition, to sent to A.D.O.I. statement showing latest arrival & 16/8n. Arty. from 40 to 16 Div. and date of receipt of notification that dispatch A.D.O.S. Test with his way of service a mountings of 21/12/17, rule 40 & 21, containing 24/12/17, 20 Div. acts received 26/12/19. All clear. | |
| | 5 | | Received from Pour 100 TAHH, 154 Trailer, 1st with marches & Ring fend Coalry Depot to replace attack horses sent to 42 Div. O.A.D.P. enlightened about duties & any, had wet tadre-mest; 2/Lat Bde. Arty, arr. | |
| | 6 | | 11.03mm – ab 9.58 am far Section. Stress from the troops. O.A.D.P. ordering S.G. 184. Hewewing, 18/64, C/177 Bde R.M Con. 5/15 Bde Arty, an intelligent can be made and arrives at having about any 5/17; Mhr, ref. reviews & last find him tup. Pistols or we ng. 16/6384 (ref-see 6868 & 39 & 17 roph. continuously have from tup. Rule & 55e; (rj. 16/6365, 2) 177 Bde R.M + Ord to 4.5 ("Huss 5" (units)), Ord-see 1108 cancelling demand by tup. Mhr mountings 40/22. On the working demands for Rule only arrived at 10.15pm 57/m from 40 Div., after warning 16/ajum junction | |

Army Form C. 2118.

D.A.D.O.S.
16TH (IRISH) DIV.

No. II
Date JANUARY 1918

# WAR DIARY
## INTELLIGENCE SUMMARY.
(Erase heading not required.)

Instructions regarding War Diaries and Intelligence Summaries are contained in F. S. Regs., Part II. and the Staff Manual respectively. Title pages will be prepared in manuscript.

| Place | Date | Hour | Summary of Events and Information | Remarks and references to Appendices |
|---|---|---|---|---|
| VILLERS FAUCON | Jan. 1918 | 7 | 40594 Gnr. AUSTIN, 7/8 R. Inniskilling Fus. temporarily attached to Divl. Ammunition Shop as Carman. Wired for one 18 pdr. Spare Carriage for C/180 Bde. R.F.A. to replace 2252 condemned for repair at Base. Received 18 pdr. Gun D/16/5973 for A/177 Bde. R.F.A. from Ordnance Gun Park No. 3. Reported to 61st Division Q branch establishment of Field Kitchens viz. L 6399, L 4028, L 3482, due to carelessness and neglect of this Company. Order to be sent to Divl. Ammunition Shop for overhaul and once every two months to be accompanied by their Officer in Charge to D.A.D.O.S. for inspection for acknowledgement. Received four 18 pdr. 4.5 Hwz. Spares from Gun Park No. 3 — no further additions completed. | F.893 |
| | 8 | | Altered note, Pte. RILEY, R. issued 156 Labourers. P.T.E.Q.VII Corps Trps G/1/1 All units advised (re: 18 pdr.) Rtry. Ammo. Res., D.A.C., Divl. Trning, D.3.C. Personnel (D/I/8 unit advised issued every six months reported to Corps according recommendations cancelled lotion (re: serious eye trouble) and transferring mobile: B. mobile res. of A.N.D.F. Ranches | |
| | 9 | | Denied that had 6" Howitzer T.M. Bomb. (Revised May/G/T511d. HHQ 10/2/18) 9 x 11" T.M.B. | |
| | 10 | | Rates working in times train yard. | |
| | 11 | | And R.T. BERESFORD, R.F.A./A.O.S. joined from HAVRE (C.O.O HARVE Depart. G.A.D. Order No. 31870, 10/1/18) for two days attached to study Ordnance methods in the field. Cpl. DIGM R.O.D. proceeded on leave from 14-28 Jan. | |
| | 12 | | | Routine |
| | 13 | | | |
| | 14 | | One from Gun Park one 18 pdr. Carr for C/180 Bde. R.F.A. (returned at same time (A/Cr ROSBOTTOM) to O.O VII Corps Tpr 9.8 arms 3 Shoulder Harness with chain Q for 4.5 Hwz. #49 US Cav. (wired Armoured Sleeve for 60pdr. while opening for Reber late 6 pm) and being overhauled. Visited by accompanied by 4 gas rounds etc. | |
| | 15 | | Returned Gun Park one 18 pdr. gun to Corps: (C/177 Bde R.F.A.). Obtained A.G.S. Configures, accompanied by R.E.F. BERESFORD also proceeded in morning. | |
| | 16 | | S/sgt. CULLEN returned off leave. Routine. (Reinstated) | |
| | 17 | | Paid attachments. Pte. WRIGHT, G.R. Innis. Regt., 11th Innis. Divl. Bomb Shop from Camp Commandant. Pte. DUNCOMBE, 1st Innis. | |
| | 18 | | Down from 11 Div. t. 49 U.S. Artillery returned to the Unit, Ammunition wires for Bump (7/18 R. Inniskilling Fus.) replace one Captured. | |
| | 19 | | 269 Divl. Units from Company ammunition from Base. HAVRE announced. Rerun completed overhaul 49 (medium) Gun machine guns. | |
| | 20 | | Capt. REED (United States Reserve), attached HQ 16th Division for instruction in his duties, spent day in Office and Shops and was shown general organization of duties of a D.A.D.O.S. - everything shown and explained. Appeared. Special Conference with A.D.O.S. of forwarding of Division. Reorganisation of N.D.O.S. arrangements for the 26th postponed until further orders. Placed of N.D.O.S. | |

Army Form C. 2118.

# WAR DIARY
## INTELLIGENCE SUMMARY.
*(Erase heading not required.)*

D.A.D.O.S.
16TH (IRISH) DIV.
No. III
Date. 1 MARCH 1918.

| Place | Date | Hour | Summary of Events and Information | Remarks and references to Appendices |
|---|---|---|---|---|
| VILLERS FAUCON | Jan. 1/18 | 21 | Pte. DOYLE (sick. Bootshop) proceeded on leave from 21/1/18 to 5/2. | |
| | | 22 | 2nd Lieut CLAYTON joined 2nd Armourers Shop with 48 M.G. Coy. Collected from Canal S Ammn Ration, Rifles, Pistol, breech Mtd Mitrailleuses, Bayonets &c. Rendered to C.O.I.Q.M.G. wounded roll of I.M.O. (Auton. Division), Clerk (Rag). # June 1918), Armre (P.G. Amy.), Artificer win (...........) + 3 Armourers (2 R.O./5. COMERFORD, BA[illeg]GAN + ROOT) temporarily attached A.S.O.? VII Corps when collectr. Rendered to A.S.O.? (copy to) returned loaning use of Fidder M.G. per body Rifles of onloading during 15/7 - 1/j. - 220 Veriss [illeg] Ammn 70 - Vinis Armn, 12,539 Rifts - average of 9 Armourers employed. | |
| | | 23 | Reported unemploymt dhowing use of Boots issued to cashlaims [illeg] by Battaleon during Oct, Nov, Dec. 1917, also quantities of Boots repaired by Bootsrepairers. Sent copies to A.O.O. V.G. Corps & vide note. | |
| | | 24 | 2nd Lieut. BERESFORD R/H HAVRE (I Corps Armn) S.N. 2748 or 23/11/18). Routine. | |
| | | 25/26/27 | Received notification from A.S.O.? VII Corps that Capt. DALLIMORE will report to O.O.I.G. Ordnance Depot on arrival of Jan. 29 for ammunition Courses lasting through 30/Feb.14. | |
| | | 28 | Proceeded to 14 Ordnance Depot, handover to Comdt. T. RANDELL A.S.S. Allsanimon Capt. a.O.O. | |
| | | 28/1/18. | | D.A.D.O.S. 16 Div. Armourer |
| | | 29th & 30th | Ammurerrs inspected "D H.F.P" Brefg. Lee Byn & reported on remarks on work now on Stire [illeg] | |
| | | | Routine. | |
| | | 31st | Charged 23 Air Cylinders for 16 M.H. Div Gas Officer. It C.A. Walt Inspectr I/Armourers arrived for duty. Work in Shops & write. | |

[Signature] [illeg]
Captn
D.A.D.O.S. 16 Div.
absent on duty

WAR DIARY.

FOR MONTH OF FEBRUARY, 1918.

VOLUME:- 24

UNIT:- D.A.D.o.S. 16th Division

# WAR DIARY

## INTELLIGENCE SUMMARY

**Army Form C. 2118.**

D.A.D.O.S.
16TH (IRISH) DIV.
No. ........
Date: FEB. 1918

| Place | Date | Hour | Summary of Events and Information | Remarks and references to Appendices |
|---|---|---|---|---|
| VILLERS FAUCON | 1918 FEB 1 | | Lt. Waite Assistant Inspector of Armament of Infantry Div. visited all units of 48th Infantry Bde. and approved of machine guns carried out. Inspection of the 49th Infantry Brigade now being carried out. A.D.O.S. VII Corps paid a visit & inspected outstanding armament of machine guns & Rifles. Stores stock normal. Armament despatched to Base. Salvage from salvage overhauled cleaned. | 1/2/18 |
| " | 2 | | Routine - Armourers repaired at Vickers guns & general small repairs - Lt. Waite and Supply of ammunition. Army Heavy Mobile Workshops - Mobile & and branches joined Div. all armourers notified. | Left Div. for 5th |
| " | 3 | | Visited A.D.O.S. VII. Off. in connection with re-organization of Infantry Battalions & disposal of surplus Stores - all technical Equipt. to be taken in & returned to Base. Any stores required to meet incidents to be utilized (except Lewis Guns, Rifles, Tele. etc., Pistols, Elephants Buggies. Swords etc.) Routine Armament General repairs. | |
| " | 4 | | A.A.Q.M.G. paid me a visit in connection with re-organization of Infty. Bns. Asked for plan to be published indicating units handing out their transport to 1st & 2nd Divisions to send returns showing quantity they handed over. Ammunition returned to Vickers Guns & general inspection. Stores left normal Cyl. Collected 300 S.B.Regts. returned for reviews by Veteran Cyl. Armament of 8th Inspected. Wire A/507 of 4/2/18. | |

2353 Wt. W2544/1454 700,000 5/15 D.D.&L. A.D.S.S./Forms/C. 2118.

# WAR DIARY / INTELLIGENCE SUMMARY

Army Form C. 2118.

D.A.D.O.S. 16TH (IRISH) DIV.
No. II
Date FEB. 1918

| Place | Date | Hour | Summary of Events and Information | Remarks and references to Appendices |
|---|---|---|---|---|
| VILLERS FAUCON | Feb | 5 | Routine in Stores. Armourer overhauled & repaired 32 Pistols. Very little overhauled repairs and general annual repair. | |
| | " | 6 | Routine in Stores. Armourer overhauling Rifles received from Salvage. Offr. in lieu of Pistol, Auth. No. to be issued. 1000 M.G. Ammo S.A.A. vide G.R.O. 3292. Machine Gun undercloth'g ordered by VII Corps. & handed into D.D. Laundry Dept. | |
| | " | 7 | Issued Stations Coy. with 22 Revolvers, O.B. request that army unit or extra blanket for men A.P.O. Cyls. & Coys. approved from Armourer General Refuse. Stoves work Normal. | |
| | " | 8 | Two O.P. #5 Signal Pistols (1 Long Range & 1 Short Range) with cartridges. Received over to 6 x VII Corps Supply. Refused Completion to Col. Wen. A.149. 16 D.T. M.G. & Ammunition. Received from reserved Lewis gunf. S. incident to Dr. nightfire. One Gunmm. Maglum Gun Station Coy. Musketry Range #5 #5, Supply Buttates etc. Issued 23 light M. Stores Normal in Stores Supply. | |
| | " | 9 | One 6" Newton Chambers ammunition from 16 D.R.O. & handed over to D.A.D.O.S. 39th D.V. Reporting Completion to Capt. Weir A.069. R.E. Died. Inv. Taking in Surplus Stores from 1st 2nd Irish Regt 7 1/6 R. Died Inv. vide H.S. No A.115. Armourer overhauling Machine Guns guns in L.G. working whan. | |

Army Form C. 2118.

# WAR DIARY
## INTELLIGENCE SUMMARY.
*(Erase heading not required.)*

Instructions regarding War Diaries and Intelligence Summaries are contained in F. S. Regs., Part II. and the Staff Manual respectively. Title pages will be prepared in manuscript.

D.A.D.O.S.
18TH (IRISH) D[IV]
No. ...
Date FEB 6 1918

| Place | Date | Hour | Summary of Events and Information | Remarks and references to Appendices |
|---|---|---|---|---|
| VILLER FAUCON | 10 | — | Lubring in Rifles Lewis guns from 8/9 Rl Inf Fus — Armourers overhauling Lewis guns within ordinary routine | |
| | 11 | — | Took part of 10th Rl Dublin Fus stores over. They are to retain all clothing utensils by order of B.Q. Routine returnment. | |
| | 12 | | Sent one Lewis Gun stores to Boris (Lt Rl Irish & 7/8 Rl Irish Fus.) Armourers pushing on with machine gun maintenance. Transmond in (when completed to be sent to 5/2 army gun park) Preparing 7/8 Rl Irish Fus stores for Boris | |
| | 13 | | Numbered one 16 Elewelas rifles complete & at old eighth to Comdt 5 Army Sniping School. 32 Lewis guns overhauled & ready for despatch to gun park. | |
| | 14 | | Sent two heavy lorries of stores handed in by fit armty paper to Boris Lent 32 complete Lewis guns to 5th Army gun park. 4th Leinsters standing in their stores. | |

2353  Wt. W2544/1454  700,000  5/15  D. D. & L.    A.D.S.S.J/Forms/C. 2118.

# WAR DIARY / INTELLIGENCE SUMMARY

**Army Form C. 2118**

D.A.D.O.S. 16TH (IRISH) DIV.
No. IV
Date: FEB. 1918

| Place | Date | Hour | Summary of Events and Information | Remarks and references to Appendices |
|---|---|---|---|---|
| VILLERS FAUCON | 15 | — | Granted 14 days leave – Handed over to S/Cab. Nash. O/C Officer Ordnance Depot. No. 14 notified in Capt. Sullivan's 16 Div. had left on 14 F. instant. 16 Jan' 1918. | |
| | 16 | | Took over from S/Lieut J. Nash on return from Mob. & Ordnance Depot. Move – from OO VII Corps Troops to OO 16 Div. – No. 9 A.A. Rowleys Stn. Returned to O.O. from Part No. S-32 Lewis guns (ex 9/7 to R. Dublin Fusiliers); also drew 31 Lewis guns for A.A. defence as vice 9 Battalion @ 2 a.a. 8 Battering. R.F.A. @ 1, 3 Field Coy RE @ 1, MM Rowleys Sec @ 2, Div from Ord Fmn Ref No 3, part 4, 57 How. (B/177) off 16/6385. To Base – two fourths of stores surplus on reorganization. Returned to St. Army Sniping School Telescopic Rifles – Gen'l Sniping Rifles etc – and Mor Opt. by 3? Echelon G.H.Q. Ret 203+60 Pte. Morgan, 31 of Leinster Rifles, a compulsory transport. O.C. (with Corps 170). 036+48D on from 31.10.17, at present rate of pay for receipt of the service. | |
| | 17 18 | | Move – from O.O. 16 Div. to O.O. VII Corps Troops – 5/Lt. (Heavy) T.M. Battery. Y, Y + Z TM Batteries are returning in X + Y. all outstanding indent of V + 2 Batteries cancelled. all concerned notified. Division from a.a.o.y VII Corps? Returned to 03 Gunbull No. 5 – 16 Lewis Guns (ex 7 Leinsters); drew 1 Lewis gun for MG defence (2, 3 B.A.T. Coys RE.). Thus reduction on/or crease in armaments. Pte. D. V. M.S. Combe returned off leave. Routine. Indent for :- 1 Waistcoat each for HQ 16 D.A.C. & C/177 replace condemned 9.0 m.; 18/ar. Coy (aux) – B/180 – replace 9.9.17. 6 condenser from - shelter (16/R397). Demanded from OO, Gunboat No 5. Sheepskin firing for A.A. defence. amount to 75 Lamp Signs for drivers, Pte 19 30 Convoy to H (Brit and Sly) CA 3 32 army but not wearer away (S.R. warn occurs). | |
| | 19 | | | |
| | 20 21 22 | | | |
| | 23 | | | |
| | 24 25 | | Visited by O.O.O. Inspected stores of clothing, lately held by field ambulances acting as Rest Stations (11/R95) four all convd. Routine. Sent 120 set Packsaddlery a.s. & 00 KWW Corps Troops by lorry. Returned to O.O. Bunbull No. 5. 600 Beginnings Lewis guns applied? Hopkins Companies conflicted for help Gpecrs. Drew from OD, Fmn Ref No 3. cart 18 pr. Carr. (B/180) of mbl, 11/8347. Demanded 26 Lewis Guns for Anti Aircraft outposts and for Lieut Shep but for exception+Green + Type Battery RFA. | |

Army Form C. 2118.

# WAR DIARY
## INTELLIGENCE SUMMARY.
(Erase heading not required.)

Instructions regarding War Diaries and Intelligence Summaries are contained in F. S. Regs., Part II. and the Staff Manual respectively. Title pages will be prepared in manuscript.

D.A.D.O.S.
16TH (IRISH) DIV.
No. V
Date FEB 1918

| Place | Date | Hour | Summary of Events and Information | Remarks and references to Appendices |
|---|---|---|---|---|
| VILLERS FAUCON | 26.2 | | Attended Conference A.D. of S. with D.A.D. of S., A.D:O.S., 49 D.V., 16th, 21st & 39th Divisions. Chief questions raised:- Salvage arrangements of unit and 5th Army; Pack Nos. 17 (38); booking rooms of Pack Gp by Corp of ammunition of unit; fitting of wagons; Auxo Horse Butts - 16th Division to take over of 21st Div.; A.D.O.S. invited to position of spare battalion, F3 Corps HQ (moving over); ampla horses required by station lattine Co. to be raised from... Visited Q16 c/c in set of Q4, 7, 1, 4, 8 & 9 R3. in Companies of 15oth... statement of BROGTORLING Stores during 20st. & 21st. tasks for 6 pack of planation of equipment Demurrage letters to Battalions down delivered transit horses. | |
| | 27. | | Drew from Jumbo Park No 3 = 26 pairs from Stretchers from her onti ambulance + 3 from 2.5 per bdf amb Co. Lowery 1.25 per batter 72HA. 1 hose-tho [?] pass Brit Inc. and Brit Engg Co. 188?] Ma. MCENRY I.A. Dublin Jos. to Brit Ordnance Stores on Loadly supply of Lo. AUSTIN, 1/6 R. Ennisbilling Fir., returns to us. Heit Hospital. 1000 pairs from mrd 24 Jun 27/28 Rd for ordinary drainage, in plaas [?] and. Jumbo Park No 3. A.O.C. 4th Bdg. requests to supply garrison in courses of Cho Jerly 2. Boots (welcome which potatoes) nullus report is made in initial. Wrote horse stays. Q/Bonito | |
| | 28. | | Questionnaire by A.D.O.S. or position of Burying plant ammunition carried in Div. Hrg. Replies all complete except 13/30. due 20 on 1/3/18/18 ID 94/5/9, Indoor 24/2/18. [?] Ordered for 24/2/18. | |
| | 1/3/18 | | | |

A.I. [signature] Capt.
D.A.D.O.S. 16th Division

# WAR DIARY

## INTELLIGENCE SUMMARY.

*(Erase heading not required.)*

Army Form C. 2118.

| Place | Date | Hour | Summary of Events and Information | Remarks and references to Appendices |
|---|---|---|---|---|
| VILLERS FAUCON. | Mar. 1918 | | 1. In view of impending operations following 28 yds. to 2 yards, immediate plans to carry out first instructions. Packed by H.Q. reports announced this unit to move to TINCOURT. R.E. party ordered. (visibility completion) 2. A.D.S. & M. Hospital to dismissive purposes. ("U") to W. Southern Mr. 8 to was to evacuate pt. Commander somewhere (18 pers.) Refer from OC. VIII Corps Transport. trial & Stella Ramp. Indication for Vickers machine gun knocks. O.M. Stellunch C., V. OC. VIII Carps or ops. Tooting 283 Army Troops Co. R.E. from S2 Corporate. "Information from Brid. Corp." Wires to be hot in tree of Carp. to chary port. | |
| | | | 2. Visited Divl. M.O. — A.A. HQ. 14 F.S. Considered & juste arrangement for transport, the news board advised the O.P.S. Called for inspection we lay on bringing up of 115 (Haute) O.K. to 3 Coy, Hav + Rev.S. Bey. from 4 undertake from Coi. and arrangements to take it up. Loaded Troops in Lorry only (Reorhs) of Messieurs advance notify Som Junction 6Y(6:10?). Have consulted with A.D.T.S & Mr. R. G. Jusarden? Weisfusion Pioneer manneless to only. Sent R.A. (Hewe)S.R. from R.E. Copt. (N) (fb.) (R.F.KEARSLEY, A.S.C.) about initial change. B. 9 am 9 to my sure. 0.4 am 0.4.3. Instructor. Wholvilly 68 4.9am heavy O.P.S. Placed him under the asst. Fasted Camp Commandant. (L2 flores) P.M. Comp. Corps. | |
| | | | 4. Real (Rundell?), Registration, Notintransuse reports. Promise to TINCOURT the. Mr. Lent 2 Am. Runlord Ambas to Stretch Finance for Installation. Attended with Returns. N.S. CK. BULLEN, Lecture to PERSONNEL, Subject "Recovery" by Capt. F. G. A. UTTING, ADP. O/U/ (SEN ALLEY ordered by Camp Commandant. Some situated Capt. Borsh ADS. to arrange his postion of SMTCASC Captl. ETE. WOOD at Capt. A. W. F. J. & Fish as ordered on Cont. Real now cashed of SMTC.A.S. from OM Cavalry Corps Transport. OS. & two enforcements and Shaff conferred. Handed over to (Capt. S.M.A.) Corporate arrival of O.C. KAYSELL this morning. | |
| | | | Report 118 to Unit for Purple examine for 2 9307 S R.E. A.Balmein Cpl. 6/S Div. D.A.D.S.O.C/6 Div. | |
| | | | 5. Notified by O.O. Can Corps that this unit down from first is an defence rearranged by Mar of Main the remainder (Turk. mo.) medical all properate stores in Select dump attend to Railway by line O. Main. similar formation carried over on two M.T. III. deposits. | |
| | | | 6. C.D.R. Randall returned from leave. A.D.O.S. visited W.shop on Commence sanitary requests, reported consultation sanitary port. Honored over to CDR RANDELL 3 Lorie Carptuing arrived. Arche Spets A.D. Corps | |
| | | | 6. Returned of leave and took over from O.C. | |
| | | | May. | |

Army Form C. 2118.

# WAR DIARY
## INTELLIGENCE SUMMARY

*(Erase heading not required.)*

D.A.D.O.S.
16TH (IRISH) DIV.
No. 11
Date March 1918

| Place | Date | Hour | Summary of Events and Information | Remarks and references to Appendices |
|---|---|---|---|---|
| VILLERS FAUCON | 7 | — | Collected 5 Lewis Guns from A.O.W. VII Corps. Armourers working in with Armourers and Armourer Sergeants of unit concerned. Repaired for 275 Battery &c. also nos of pulleys for One Lewis and various repairs. Store Work Normal. | |
| | 8 | | Armourers still busy with Armourers of Armourers of Brigades. One Lewis Gun for Munster Battalion demanded for. 16th M.G.Bn. Store Work Normal. | |
| | 9 | | Armourers still working on Armourers & A.D.O.S. VII Corps paid Lewis and machine guns. Armourers of 6 Div. Sent 2 Bren guns to 16 Div. Store Work Normal. | |
| | 10 | | Re-organization of 16 Div. Supply Column & 16 Div Amm. Park (known now as 16 Div. Am. Coy. (Reg. 48, 49 & 361 Coys) All concerned notified. Re-organization of Machine Gun Coys. now known as 16th (D) M.Gun Battalion all concerned notified accordingly. Armoury still working on Armourers. Few small repairs. Store Work Normal. | |
| | 11 | 1300 | 2/VII Trench Completed work on G.S. pipes & ropes & Y/VII Tay Battery. One Vickers Gun received for 16th M.G.Bn. 11th Hants Having in surplus stores on re-organization. Armourers Store work Normal. | |

# WAR DIARY
## INTELLIGENCE SUMMARY

**Army Form C. 2118.**

| Place | Date | Hour | Summary of Events and Information | Remarks and references to Appendices |
|---|---|---|---|---|
| Villers Faucon | 12 | | Wed 16 New Pattern Lewis Gun Butts from Ord W N° 5 Heavy Armourers Employed another 1350 springs and fingers C.I. ad by what was handed over to CRA 91st Div. Col. Welf. AA/QMG visited DAOS during my absence to workshop and left me two hours with me at 2pm full Sgt. Armourer Rug W. & in the M.T. Store workshop hour later. Armourers worked at night on M.T. Stores W.O.R Normal no new guns Afternoon if on to 8 P.M. Store hut W Normal Empire gun received N.O. Ammunition & No 3 grenades sent to store two 2/Drakes hoses to shelves watched | |
| | 13 | | Armourers still busy with M. 2 Gunners Gunnick'd 16 Lewis gun Butts fitted them to Lt. Connaught's Sqn. Afternoon ? After alteration to MA Z Gunners Regt. Infantry- Sqn Butts sent to Draw of Col we Alterations = CRA 16 Div decided to take them already Corrected & 2 rifles. (Although not very safe) as some were very urgently Required. = Shrs with Normal = | |

# WAR DIARY
## INTELLIGENCE SUMMARY

Army Form C. 2118.

*(Erase heading not required.)*

| Place | Date | Hour | Summary of Events and Information | Remarks and references to Appendices |
|---|---|---|---|---|
| VILLERS FAUCON | 14 | | Sect. 16 New Lath. Bank to O.R. from N.P.S Ord. Wks. Hospt. &c. Armourers. Converted 600 Syn.Rs. and Smal. Arms from sling up to standard. 3rd Pul. Parcel off at 10 P.H. About up 22 standard — Unit attended and 01 Guben 90 and an arrived fresh unit — Two type standard. Demonia 9 nights. 1 Lyn. Bury. Lewis rifles strip 111 wants are holding as of wings today for General Smith to General Counnghill. Remaining Personnel repaired. | |
| | 15 | | Work normal. | |
| | 16 | | Obj. E 3 Snipers to 10 New 1 to N° 3 Ord Wyp Shop Armourer's 5th Army Chair School, Lt V. Penn with 2 L.G. Inspection Guns Park and 390 Myragron. Relieved two Lewis Gun No.5 Gun Park. — Work about normal. | |
| | 17 | | Iss. 16 New Battery Btn 14 Lewis Buns N°5 Gun Park Issued Guns to Br.d Lewis Gun Demand. Drew from O Rep Crp b ygne. Let to H. Hump ft. 3" Stokes Gun new type 4/27 Aus Inf Bn Pen Battery. 400 Syn.Rs L Converted and issued to 16th Divisonry — Work Normal. | |

# WAR DIARY
## or
## INTELLIGENCE SUMMARY.
*(Erase heading not required.)*

Army Form C. 2118.

| Place | Date 1916 | Hour | Summary of Events and Information | Remarks and references to Appendices |
|---|---|---|---|---|
| VILLERS FAUCON | March 18 | | New in New Pattern 2 am Butts 1 am Gun N2S H.W WSK.f. Accident to Cpl Wylie took No 1 Sgt Lt. favor Limp Re Cartlet of Bridge Relative F.G+FLET Buick 18/Div Lo (Camp) Cnr d 16 D" 7 16/D" on his Cpl accident. | |
| | 19 | | Armourers Convey Equip 400 M.E. Syrebis and served normal So 16th Div Artillery Store work normal Nothing etc etc occurred. Armourers Converted 400 H. synches were served by batty etc. Star W/H normal Received 300 C.S. Lewis Guns + 9th Division | |
| | 20 | | Demanded 16 Vickers Gun Spares (Pip 319 oyd) M Gun O+ 7 Mel in Ammunition 50 (R) Louis Lost 6 Glen Rifles 2 Armourers Recount Single a mode... All other work normal. | |
| | 21 | | at 4.30 am Germans started very heavy bombardment of front aread Received no orders from Div 16 now move to line of communication during ..t... Commenced moving to Trevent of V..... + cleared all Sml arms Store Staff etc. Nearly 700 shells dropped in and around dept, but no casualties. On arrival at Trevent reported to O. who ordered me to Move to Peronne - Capt. Willmann Apt Sambre Authy Att the Completely destroyed 16th had Lewis Dehaut at a Vickers Gun for 16 D" my Cpl Need Verbally that 16th D.A. had lost the whole of their Guns, but received no demand. | |

2353 Wt. W2544/1454 700,000 5/15 D.D.&L. A.D.S.S./Forms/C. 2118.

# WAR DIARY / INTELLIGENCE SUMMARY

Army Form C. 2118.

| Place | Date | Hour | Summary of Events and Information | Remarks and references to Appendices |
|---|---|---|---|---|
| PERONNE | 22 | | Received 12 Vickers Guns to to (sic) in 9 M.G.Bn. & issued immediately Awaiting orders from 9 M.G.Bn. Remained with 16 Bde pending orders at 9 and 23rd Lbs & with 1st Div which orders did not come — Managed and to debut any 3 times during night - to get 2 Lewis Guns & 1 Vickers gun on rail for Bray. | |
| CAPPY | 23 | | Arrived at Cappy. | |
| " | 24 | | Demanded 135 Lewis & 50 Vickers guns to replace others lost in action. Sent Div lorries to Gn Park but they managed to get 2 Vickers & 25 Lewis — About 6 p.m. sudden order received from Cappy and rationing Officer which could not be moved from Cappy ordered to Vickers at the time. Rail Gn Carried improbably 2 hours to unite Own Grup & closed with traffic. He arrived really this way many Lewis Guns followed with Stores. No point of Bleary intelligence seriously destroyed. – Moved to Guerrieu. | |
| | 25 | | Arrived at GUERRIEU at 3.30 A.M. Rejoined Division Receiving equipment from Gen Randell Officer to await further instructions Made further application to Gen Park for Vickers guns they might have. Sent 21 Lewis Guns to 1 goss & 97R & 47R & 49R Bdes. (13 Lo 4yth & 14 to 49R) Issued to Vickers guns to 1/A Div when Capt. Hallinan arrived back (N.A. D.V.G. 16 Div Orderly rm to Capt. Darling) — Moved to LAMOTTE EN SANTERRE (8462.b. Q.30.c.) | |

## WAR DIARY or INTELLIGENCE SUMMARY

Army Form C. 2118.

| Place | Date | Hour | Summary of Events and Information | Remarks and references to Appendices |
|---|---|---|---|---|
| LAMOTTE au SANTERRE | March 26 | | Moved at 11 am to HAMEL (62.D. P.10.a.6.3) with 118 Bde A.Q. under orders of A.A.Q.M.G. Brig. Genl Pavelli. S.O. to view new dispositions of plans — Division A.D.M.S. Lieut Col Ray Loring Jones - 6th Field Ambulance HQ + 2 sections at 47th F. Amb. (Division of A.A.Q.M.G.) | |
| HAMEL | 27 | | Moved at 6 a.m. to direction W. of VILLERS BRETONNEUX with (Division HQ) Transport (62.D. P.7.a.4.y) Detachments of Infantry Bdes delivered I.B.D.A.C. & Divl. M.G. Bn. Moved at 5.30 pm. to FOUILLOY (62.D. O.10.b.1.4) rejoining 16 Fd. Ambce M.Q. | |
| FOUILLOY | 28 | | Out visited HQ of Inf Bdes at HAMEL with Adj, Genitourin, Infect, Ammunition sections all available when 3 stated. | |
| | 29 | | The 47 Fd Amb forecast as went from Shore Row CARAIS not available... [illegible handwriting] | |
| | 30 | | ...[illegible] CARAIS. | A.O.C. 1372 d. 26/3/18. |
| | 31 | | Visited Surg't KIX Corps at ST FURIEN. Suggested... [illegible] ...HAVRE (CALAI) - A.O.C. 1061 d. 26/3/18. | |

31/3/18.

A C Dawson Lyt.
D.A.D.O.S. 16th Division

# WAR DIARY
## or
## INTELLIGENCE SUMMARY.

Army Form C. 2118.

| Place | Date 1918 | Hour | Summary of Events and Information | Remarks and references to Appendices |
|---|---|---|---|---|
| FOUILLOY | April 1. | | Draft finding Army Ord. Gunboat No.1. Received reels empty Q.Stores handcart. Lance Corpl. of Valuable. Issued 236 (D.T.) G.R.A.C. to Gds. Scarch Corp Troops Ord. No.9 articles of Separate/Lip section 1609. J. Mann. Brig. from No. 3 m. D. A.C. | |
| | 2. | | 2 motor ambulances to Rudaux. Cancelled owing to D.A.C. also 5 Vickers machine Guns. Salvia stores coll. at BLANGYTRONVILLE "Camp" forms. Cancelled at 10.30 a.m. 1st 16 D.A.C. in line at 10.3/18. | |
| | 3. | | Moved at 10.30 a.m. to LE PETIT BLANGY, joining 2nd Echelon 16 D. H.Q. Joined XVIII Corps, 3rd Army | |
| SALEUX | 4. | | Moved at 9.30 a.m. to CERISY with 16 D.H.Q. Moved to Ord. 14 Div. all 16 Bn. Artillery moved w/Depot. | |
| CERISY | 5. | | Boys to send much. ... units to XVIII Div. ... "B" Echs. Field Location Vickers arty. ... information from No. 8 m. | |
| | | | notified units to avoid appearing ... MA.Q. 16 Bi., in view of early move to Front Army. ... Rec. Puttees, Socks + two lectures from No. 3 m. | |
| | | | Suspended issues from Bde. res. and ... XVIII Corps at PORT REMY (nothing of importance transpired). Recommended | |
| | 6. | | Dept. - wo S.O. Gilkinf available. Vickers Guns XVIII Corps at PORT REMY ... A.O.C. Ord. 397 L 21/3/18 Vol I Lopt. E.E. DIGNED, A.M. Corpl. E.E. DIGNED, A.O.C. J.S. to acts. Bn. in Reg. Card. ... A.O.C. Ord. ... J.T. WHEELER, J. FERGUS and T.C. HAWKINS all advanced to 3rd of Corps ... par A.O. Corps 9/1/18. Recommended Pt. R.J. KEARSLEY, A.O.C. on ... A.I.S. for Army... advance at line. Recommendation to A.O.F. W.P. ... 2 Corp. (A/Colo) J.T. ... RANDELL, A.O.C. for Military Cross and AcpCpl (A/Cpl) I.E.E. DIGNES, A.O.C. for military medal, for obvious action, full ... | |
| | | | Conduct on 31/3/18 and 2 ... Bn. Ammunition + as brazenarl. | |
| | 7. | | Returned Pt. KENNY (R. Antilla) from Ammunition Shop to his Unit + returned to Base tradies to Camp, Command, 16 Bn... Re... | |
| | | | Drew more Boots each from No. 8 Ord. Depot. Received ... from Bade much of Hornetons, 1000 Boys May 5th ... and of Army Gas Corp. | |
| | | | 1 Mess Cart. Visited all units with O.A.D.V.S. re allowment of supplies + comp. dispersion from 19 Bomb. Reg. 16 R. Real R. ... | |
| | | | ... 16 Ord. 14 Div. H.Q. Co. 16 Bn. Train A.S.C. No. 3 Sec. 16 D.A.C. Supplied by a.i.O.M.G. Pte. in read of the ... of Div. ... | |
| | 8. | | of putting reinforcement, No. 165 (Brid.) Division will probably cease to exist as a fighting division until moved to rebuild when ... reinforcement. | |
| | | | Went at 9th Tooth Army and Q. ... intimated movement of machine Guns to complete Division, viz, Bn. from 140 complete ... | |
| | | | Notified by 16 Bn. that Repair Battalion will be reequipped with and always for transport to Vickers M/G. for ref. | |
| | | | other Division. | |
| FAUQUEUXBERGUES | 9. | D.4/p. | Moved to FAUQUEUXBERGUES. Received 3-15 pm from "Various" Army. R.P. per Lorry to 1st/15 Air Army Ind S. (Demands to 16 m. etc.) | |
| | | | Demands from Ord. from Part No.1 and ... telegrams ordered from Ord. XIII Corps, Joined XIII Corps and First Arny. Inform... | |
| WISMES | 10. | 10.15 a. | Moved to WISMES. Wired Bayer to C/Inf/p mets. Notified HAVRE + ROVEN to forward indeed to CALAIS. | |
| | | | Received Bn. Arn. Reqt. F.T. COERUZE FORS from S. Ord. Workshop (Navy.) | |
| VAUDRINGHEM | 11. | | Moved to VAUDRINGHEM. Visited Q.Bn., XIII Corps. - to bring out, Field Corps Artillery to and ascertained location of Div. Artillery. Visited Arty and ascertained their deficiencies. Demands from Bays to meet these deficiencies. | |
| | | | Sub/Lieut. J. MA..., joined off train. Pur. SIMPLE Lattclots from 217 Div. Engr. Co. ... admitted to Base. Hospital over. Brough All 16 Bi. Cooking + H.Q. 16 Bn. Train A.S.C. on one truck. | |

# WAR DIARY / INTELLIGENCE SUMMARY

Army Form C. 2118.

Month: APRIL 1918

| Place | Date | Hour | Summary of Events and Information | Remarks and references to Appendices |
|---|---|---|---|---|
| YVBRINGHEM | April 12 | | Amended 1-4.5" How. (D)(180 Bde) reported 977 Cartridges for issue; 2.18p.m. 61st Army Cavalry with A/5 (S/177 Bde) absorbed, while (3mm) Jrs. Cancelling which information sent in April. 133 Reinforcements completed transfer of officers & men mounted (56/157 Fd. Co. R.E.) & 16 Bn. Unicycle (Prov. Bn. 60th XVIII Corps Tr.). Received notification that Divisions will hold 6 months reserve & 6 battalions of horseshoes from Ord. Field No. 1. Now to be complete frame saw 30 to 40 & pound punch frame saw D saw from Ord. Field No. 1. Amended all 16 Div. Estab. x T/T.M Bn. 2/14 Hd. Qr., 16 Dn. S.R. 16 Bn. Train A.T.O., 16 Dn. Signal Cy., A. Cov. & 10 DAC. Amended trench stores scales from 1335 to 40. Amended (Rgt. Gen. Coy.), and first Army scales of articles authorised from 155. 16th Div. Unicycles & 152 +157 Fd. Co. R.E. henceforth to be on VIII Corps tr. troops.) Received warning order for departure of 15th & 16th Div. unidentify receiving units to 4 Battalions. |  |
|  | 13 | | 1st Bn. LEINSTER REGT. — consisting of 7/Leinster Reg. & 6 Connaught Rangers; 1/2 R. DUBLIN FUSILIERS. — " " 1st " " 2nd " R. Dublin Frs.; 1/2 R. MUNSTER FUSILIERS. — " " 1st " " 2nd " R. Munster Frs.; 2nd Bn. R. IRISH REGT. — " " 2nd R. Irish Regt, 7 (S.9.A) R. Irish Rep. & 7/8 R. Leinster Reg. to form Bn. 48th (Composite) Infantry Brigade. |  |
|  | 14 | | Orders from Railhead about 20 tons of stores (8 horses). Received Regt 7 completed Lewin from. Composite Brigade for 6 Connaught Rangers, 2 R. Leinster Regt, 2 R. Dublin Frs, 7/8 R. Inniskilling Frs, 7(S.9.A) R. Irish Regt. arrived in 4 Coys. — Consisting of 21, 3, 2, 28 & 34 Inft. Bns., 4 H Coy, Engineer and Signal Coy, 1 Wireless, (Heavy.) 1st Portuguese Inf. Bde. visited by D.A.D.O.S. 1st Portuguese Division, who explained a feature of mine recruiting and improvised M.G. Sends Portuguese speaking Sergeant to Amoi. Received orders from Q.16 & Div. Inst. 140. will ensure movement to AIRE. |  |
|  | 15 | | Received notification from Gen XVIII Corps that sufficient 3" Stokes Trench Mortar shall be allowed to complete Brigade. Left Inst. Col. CULLEN and party of 1 M.G. R.I.G.O.T. to probably draw & rump Clear Rattles Unit by 5/4 D.S.O. 2nd Army (Major ORMOND, A.Q.) during my absence visiting units. A.L.m. 1st Army Corps |  |
| AIRE | 16 | | refined off leave. |  |

Army Form C. 2118.

# WAR DIARY
## or
## INTELLIGENCE SUMMARY.
(Erase heading not required.)

| Place | Date | Hour | Summary of Events and Information | Remarks and references to Appendices |
|---|---|---|---|---|
| AIRE | April 1917 17. | | Sent W.O. R Brown (Surg. Cpl. SANDERS, A/C. Sgt. W. BROWN) to 3rd Echelon to administer 16th Div. Artillery. Sgt. T. HUTCHINSON, A.O.D., joined from D.A.D.O.S. Reinforcement, for duties with 1st Reinforcement Buf. Bde. Sub. Sec. C. Clerks and party (two Privates) joined from VAUDRINCOURT. Visited A.D.O.S. XIII Corps (who was out), D.D.O.S., A.D.O.S., 1st Reinforcement Army who had issue of future of 16th Division. Issued 10 f.s. wagons & limbers to the Railways. | |
| | 18. | | Closed dump at VAUDRINCOURT. Notified Base to send cheese for W.O. etc. on receipt Schedule to be reduced at once. | |
| | 19. | | Cleared Railhead. Notified by "Q" Brand that 18th Div. Ammunition Column are analogous to Mr R. Munster, which leaves Division tomorrow. Next Ammunition. R.G.A. CALLAGHAN, 12th Jun 18 R. Munster & leaves tonight, rest proceed with 1st Munster and ... Salvo... from MARIE, DELETTE, & is complete. Order for Panel 13 to be sent up. Is delivered to 1st Panel Park. Mr is in charge of part of XIII Corps. Ammunition of 1st Brigade R.A. ... Completed train of 7 brigade F.A. Trays.  | |
| | 20. | | 1st Bn. R. Munsters on leaving 16th Div. Bn. personnel and Guns(?) ... to O.C. 57th Division all concerned notified. Cancelled all outstanding indents of 1st 7 2nd R. Munsters, 6 Connaught Rangers 7/8 R. Dublin, 7th R. Immoskilling Fus. 17/(D. of W.) R. Irish Regt., 11th Hants Regt. (R.), 7 8 1600 Rounds from. Instructed D.R.O. that no issue of Ordnance stores are to be made except from D.A.D.O.S. of Div. from Park. Ammunition R.G.F. Commerfords returns to R. Dublin Fus. Reported to A.D.O.S. XIII Corps completion of replacement and evacuation of 1st & 2nd R. Munsters Guns return to 1st 7 8 Divs. on & Bn. of 1st Bn. R. Munster Fus. | |
| | 21. | | Sent A/19352 Ammo. S. Sgt. J.G. PAGE (as from 16th Bn. Welsh Regt.) to C.O.O. CALAIS. (Auth. D.A.G. 3/862 A.D.C./1061 d. 20/3/18.)  16th Div. having notified duties of persons carrying on accounting & reporting of Ammunition and stocks showing disposal of surplus Ammunition, made further recommendations:— | |
| | | | To 6 Connaught Rangers — A/22063 Am. S.Sgt. G.N. FAULK (Sub at 3/4 R. Berkshires), vice A/2357 M.S. Sgt. A. BEARD; To 7 R. Innskilling Fus. — A/5765 " — C. J. INNES ( " — 10 — ) — A/2497 — F.L. DAVIES; To 11 Hants Regt. (P.) — A/17/15 " FRYERFIELD (" — 7 R.2nd Bn.) — A/7742 " E.L.A. ROOTT. Writ... Horns. of Units. See Table with Q.M.O.Z. 2 R. Irish Regt., Z Royal Irish Regt., 7 R. Dublin Fus. approved by no all in part 6 of 4 same...  | |
| | 22. | | Notified by O.C. XIII Corps that first Ammunition will depend at end of 20th to 29th Division. Notified by A.D.O.S. that 2 R. Irish Regt. & Brig. Artillery will be administered by A.D.O.S. Reinforcement. Camp 16 Bn. Ammunitions will ... Mr METHUEN rejoin after duty with R.Es. Received from A.D.O.S. XIII Corps instruction (Q Copy) regarding disposal of surplus stores in of retire of Division. | |

# WAR DIARY or INTELLIGENCE SUMMARY

Army Form C. 2118.

D.A.D.O.S.
13th (Indian)
IV
Date April 5/18

| Place | Date 1918 | Hour | Summary of Events and Information | Remarks and references to Appendices |
|---|---|---|---|---|
| A.I.F. | April 23 | | 2 R. Irish Rifles (at present at R. Irish Rifles, 7 (S.D.M.) R. Irish Rifles, 7/8 R. Inniskilling Fus.) amounts to 63 (R.M.) Divisions) justified at 2 Divl Staff. (In extending it was G. Cavanagh Roughly). — " 29 Divisions Casualties outstanding indents reported to O.C. XIII Corps replenishment and issue of this two Battalions. Notifying O.O. XIII Corps that First Army reinforcements has detailed 15 Drums which will be reinforcing with DAPOS 1 B.E. Div sent to O.C. 7 (S.D.M.) R. Irish Rif — 1st complete finish from 2 Drums only = 16 R.M. remaining ex S.D.M. prisoners of |  |
| | 25 | | 7 (S.D.M.) R. Irish Rif. left for Camiers Depot. |  |
| | 26 | | 1 R. Dublin Fus. (Agreement of 1 R. Dublin Fus. amount 22 Battalion amounts to 39) notified that centre of reinforcements and issue of this Battalion |  |
| | 27 | | Returned 22 / 49 Pts. G. BROWN to O.C. 2/7 (Dvn) Hampshire Rgt. (In extending to DAPOS XIII Corps notices of this been and abandoned duties (permanent) rendered (including wounded) wandering INDIA on B.A.O.O.S (Rule Rudey). Recommended Rs Cpl. E.E. DISHARD per promotion to Crchy Sergeant. Volunteered for service in INDIA on B.A.O.O.S |  |
| | 28 | | Cpl. HARNETT returned to 16 Intl Reg. Y.B. at request of O.C. 3 Cpt. GARCIA N2 (General In absence of reinforcements. |  |
| | 29 | | Brought rear through 156-157 Field Coy. R.E. in absence of reinforcements. |  |
| | 30 | | Re.Cpl. E.E. DISHARD promoted acting sergeant from 16/3/18 [A.O.C. 2034 496 d. 29/4/18]. Routine |  |

A.H. Cameron Cpt!
D.A.D.O.S. 16 Division

# WAR DIARY or INTELLIGENCE SUMMARY

Army Form C. 2118.

D.A.D.O.S.
16TH (IRISH) DIV.
I.
Date MAY 1918.

| Place | Date 1918 | Hour | Summary of Events and Information | Remarks and references to Appendices |
|---|---|---|---|---|
| AIRE-sur-LYS | MAY 1 | | Received from "Q.B." Div. copy of "BAB" Trench Code for first time. Ordnance VII Corps Troops received 150-157 Fld.Co. R.E.S.G.Ordnance 16 Div. Visited 150-157 Fld. Co. also 7/8 R Ir. Inniskilling Fus. | |
| | 2 | | 11 Hants. Regt. (Reinforcements) today received 11 Hants. Regt. Battalion Drawing Stores, Equipment, Clothing &c to restock down to unit draw 1.7, or only 8½ Bde. F.U.P. Code and destroyed 7 Bn. Battalion Drawing Staff of Rostrings. Liverpool Regt. (Liverpool Scottish) joined 16 Division. 2/6 Bn. R.T. Kearsley A.O.C. | |
| | 3 | | 16 Div. joined XI Corps at 1200 today. | |
| | 4 | | Personally on through by Div. O/C Divisional Bn. Training Staff in absence of unanmoh. Great jend bot of units to D.A.D.O.S. First Army. A.D.O.S. XI Corps rCorps CALAIS. Supplementary Replenishment N.S. Ar.A. and No.1. | |
| | 5 | | 02.66.100. R.T. KEARSLEY A.O.C. assisted by Capt F.M.O. Indenture Carry by Chief Ordnance 164 Div. Rowlin Visited by A.O.S. XI Corps and brought S.D. Quirke in Consoleter with R.T.R.S. Division of the 6 Division to | |
| | 6 | | Visited by A.O.S. Rejoined by A.O. Servind this activity tomorrow and shall with suffices and engineers of the eq. expected Col. Cpr. SMITH A.A.C.P. Lt-Cpl. PATTERSON detached transit 5/5/18, by ADOOS Div. | |
| | 7 | | Visited D.Gun Party at CREQUY was FRUGES. Beyond by Lieut. HANNAH OPS R. XVIII Corps. nearrr 16 OS R.I Corps. heard HO 1st Div. Arty, in ranks of R.E.A. Bde. and opprsenthwy is our visit. Reve. Carlo from S.H. Carters. Visited HQ 16 & 37 Div. Arty. in ranks of R.E.A. Bde. | |
| | 8 | | 16 D.A.C. under reval of our transport. New BDOOS M Div. has left area. S.L. Col. SMITH Reach Capt. PATTERSON returning to BDOOS O.A. under instructions of ADOS XI Corps. Visited by ADOOS Div. drawing rdeptrind otror of R.A.P. Pl. 16 B.A.C. previously returned to Calais in a Camp, kit out | |
| | | | Visited BDOOS 61 Div. on Riv. Sector Visited BDOOS 6 Divn. 500 Pa. 16 B.M.C. with live camps visited Rejo MIR from return to Railhead, vehicles movement. | |
| | 9 | | Visited BDOOS 4 pence 14/18 Surf. Res. Bn. Tearing Pty 8/9 Commayf Ktr Regg 2/10 K King's Liv Regg, 2/R Dub. Fus. 2 R. Manning fus. Army, 11 Hants Regt also 200 113 Fdf. and and 143 7/10 Co. R.T.C. Visited by A.O.S. in my absence | |
| | 10 | | Sent in 11 Fdt. Ambt. and 112 and 2061 P.tr. R.T. KEARSLEY A.O.C., has been evacuated sick to 51 C.C.S. on 10/5/18. Applies to O.O for 2 returns, under instruction of A.O.O.S. Div with whole whom | |
| | 11 | | visited by 111 Fdt. Ambt. and 112 and 2061 Ptr. R.T. KEARSLEY A.O.C., has been evacuated sick to 51 C.C.S. on 10/5/18. Applies to O.O for Returns. 11 Hants Runston with 107 ptr. 0007 11 Inft. R. Ir. Rift. 0.043 Bc L.A.H.O. Kare approved following transfers viz: | |
| | 12 | | 42 of R. Ir. Clar. to R.I.R.S.A. (Lahk attd P/q R Battalion) To 6 Connaught Rangers viz 1/23 Pu.Connaught Rangers — CJA Qurt A O.C 11/23106 Gunnin Staff Pte G.A. FAULKS AOC (Late attd P/q R. Battalion) To 6 Connaught Rangers viz 1/23 Pu. — C.J.A. Qurt. A.O.C — 11 Hants Regt — O.L.A. Qurt A.O.C. A/27145 5/15 Evgr. A o.c.(G. A.C. Reinforcements 5/106/87 of 7/5/18). Promotion of 6 Connaught Rangers to delayed Bn. O.M.O. R.T. KEARSLEY A O.C Reinforcements 11 Hants. Regt. of 1 NAH/c 11 Hants. 165 Roatt Levered 1/5 Fdt Ambt 51 O.R.s 11 Hants Anninn Div. CALAIS. Notifies 11 Hants Rept. of transfer of R.S.R. 11 Hants Ac. S.S. RoitT. Leverend 1/5 Fdt Ambt 51 O.R.s 11 Hants Annuni Div. on visited Capt M.R. BULLIMORE AOC Sent A/2745 — A/F S.J.CLR Report Hos. C.Can CALAIS Notifies Rect. D.O.J. QMG in MSIR (XI Corps O.Stnt 11/5/16; Ford Army O/3B/11) 11.4/5/18;) |

2353  Wt. W2544/1454  700,000  5/15  D.D. & L.  A.D.S.S.Forms/C. 2118.

# WAR DIARY
## INTELLIGENCE SUMMARY

Army Form C. 2118.

D.A.D.O.S. 16TH (IRISH) DIV.
No. 11
Date: MAY 1918.

| Place | Date | Hour | Summary of Events and Information | Remarks and references to Appendices |
|---|---|---|---|---|
| AIRE-sur-LYS | MAY 1918 | 13 | Visited nr. C.T.O. 16 Div. Major Gen. A.S. RITCHIE, Comdg.) Applied for special leave for Gutch, J. NASH, A.O.C. on account of serious illness of Mother. 16 Div. Approved that it would be given. There are at least hand to deal with affairs. Recommended O.R.S. 531 Pte. R. RILEY, A.O.C. for change of unit calling from Armoire (48 Road) to B. Depot Exeter(Wash 47 Bath). Sent A.B. 64 and App. B.122 of Pte R.T. KEARDEF, A.O.C., to B(A.O.D. Record), 3 Reg. Delivery Group.) | |
| | | 14 | Visited D.O.D of final army for interview approximate to INDIA of Capt A.G. DALLIMORE A.O.C. is non-committal received byt from D.O.D. of S.Sgt E.E. DIGARD A.O.C. awaited military further by Commander of Second Army for Pollara warrant 21st driver(subseq. promotion) 4 O. promotion of army S.Sgt F. THURSFIELD, A.O.C. to 7/8 R. Irisscilling Fus, vice Army. B.Sgt. F.L. DAVIES, A.O.C. (Cadet), A.O.C. Reinforcements S/1061 Pte. d. 11/5/18. | |
| | | 15 | Visited by D.A.D.O.S. 14 Div. re taking over from us of certain use of Portuguese troops & 156+757 Pot. Cos. R.E. Visited HQ of Q O.R.S. X1 Corps(Maj. HEBDITION) who introduced incoming Maj. (Lt. Cal. HEBERT) Notified O.R.S. CHRISTIE and O.R.S. 14 Div. all these for Portuguese troops: Supplemental service from O/Capt S. CAL T.C. MEDCALFE, A.O.D. arrived from Q.D. Final army to ration Capt. R.F. DALLIMORE, A.O.D. on his being posted to INDIA. Applied for special leave from 17/31 May 1918 for Capt. DALLIMORE. Cancelled move of 11/274 Labr, to O.D. 27 American Div., and moved to O.D. 39 Division. | |
| | | 16 | Moved to O.D. 14 Div. 156+757 Pot. Cos. R.E. and all Portuguese troops, viz H.Q. 1st Br. Bde, 21st, 22nd, 28th & 3rd Inf. Bns. 4th Coy, Pegsieres 1 Signal Bn, 3rd Batt. M.A. 153 Bde, 15 Bad M.A. 1 Bde, 1 Pie. A.T. Troops, Horse and Car, 2 W.G.C & Ind.C.B. Retinues Pl. Pegsieres 1 Clearing Stn., Boes, Park M., T.C. MEDCALFE, A.O.D. will act as ADOS 16th Div. from 17/5/18 inclusive. Moved to same R.H. with HQ. 16 Div. Followed meds. sections MATFIN in evening Pte 45 W. Read, A. Reg., 4 W.B. R. Inniskilling Fus, will remain meanwhile. Official 16. Div. ammended in 583 Gen. Hospl. BOULOGNE as were M/054 133 Pte. A.E. JONES, A.O.F.C. awaits a Bd. at 10.30pm attempt from a lorry. Under in charge of Q.16.B Reports 17/5/18 195 16 Div. accidental with details of Army Sgm W/1546 Dvr, W.J.G. WHEELEY under Escort of Q of to 1st relief Hospl. BOULOGNE at 6am 17/5/18. Reported O. Rn444 Request remove to O.D 14 Div. approv 200 S.B. R.v too often containing. Captain of bus, diagram by Royal Shottums beg W1 x1 Corps Tpt Deposit. Handed over to O.D 14 Div typt Bde, Keepers and Store from St. OUENTION Camps for Advance Purchase. NewcastleB Commerce 1978 (Lamach v. Roy) MEDCALFE as AWS 16. Div 5 JSB. Offered guide to adherence Army that Immediate appointment to command 2. verbal inspection from O.P. of D.B. Notified by Pt. Roy first Army. that immediate appointment is made under Capt. F.G. DALLIMORE | |
| | 17 | | | |
| | 18 | | | |
| SAMER | 19 | | of 828 Ctl Tank bring consigned to one first bunch of American horses arrived tonight. Divisional Farewell Letter special train from N.G.I. Out. Lx/Corps S.L.15th A 17/5/18. Paid Farewell and Tribute Compliments to Cal. J. RANDELL detailed by Q5 proceed at 9am today to A. RENVIEW Staff Cap. 16 Dist Train to take over transport for Divn. Recent Ply officer is Lt. J.C. MEDCALFE and meanwhile ENGLAND on leave. Handed over command Old Berniere Capt. D.A.O.S. 16 Div. 19/5/18. | |

O.S.BEENVILLE
Capt AR. DALLIMORE.

Army Form C. 2118.

D.A.D.O.S.
16TH (IRISH) DIV.
No. .........
Date May 1918

# WAR DIARY
or
## INTELLIGENCE SUMMARY.
(Erase heading not required.)

Instructions regarding War Diaries and Intelligence Summaries are contained in F.S. Regs., Part II. and the Staff Manual respectively. Title pages will be prepared in manuscript.

| Place | Date 1918 | Hour | Summary of Events and Information | Remarks and references to Appendices |
|---|---|---|---|---|
| SAMER | MAY 20 | | Took on from Capt. M.G. Salmon A.O.S. the whole of Sh/16th Div. arranged with O/C Salvage regarding his stores & disposal of salvage. Dr. Nenneret R.J. Regs. acquired for clerical work in my Salvage Office. Bought 6 Bonnets for American Drivers, as uniforms they had been wearing were worn by the Portuguese who had left in a rush. Returned to the American S.W. Q.M. who abandoned back to the Ordnance Officer. The Drivers are in & from the 77th American Div. they are a very keen set of young lads & hard they were dumped. are arriving every day. We sent 8 Lgt Lorries. Half these were very useful. | |
| | 21 | | No.3 lorry 9th Pk Bn. 50th Regt. A.S.C. arrived with 8 men from the stores of Pkt. 2nd & 3rd Bn. 58th Reg't. (who attached) had to be sorted out & sent by Ordnance Officers. Arrived privately. Shirher, 1 Sergt who is being instructed by the Chief Worker Capt. Morris also 1 Sgt. & 57 m Sgt. & 9 M m arrived Checker and transported the stores of No.12 M.G. Coy 57th Regt to then arr Clit. Received Spare for Stokes Suppies Copper Units. Bomb etc. urgently required. 800 C.S.Y. Tent. Are issued today, not to hour. Returned "13 & 12 Truck sold to H.Q. 16 Div | |
| | 22 | | Arranged for American S. Sgt - & now & 3 lags with the Division, as the repair of M.A.T. cars not for American S. Sgt. Shuihs G.P. to have formed. Drivers & Drivers must by 1st some send of with armourment with the American Ordnance officer, they have kept the Main. Is to go to another branch of the Division, as he cannot unite the to be issued with British equipment & is arranging for them to keep as near Southern Stores from British Sources. Two before going to go the Americans to retain an Officer & be included. | |
| | 23 | | Reborrow. Work. Recommend cont from Colonel for Commendation Camp. | |
| | 24 | | Recd Reqt hd'lrs to be charged Sloven the American Government Immediately be left our Area when Div moved. | |
| | 25 | | Routine Work. Demounted 12 Lewis Morter, 37 m.m. for D.U.A. Hd' American Div. | |

2353 Wt. W2544/1454 700,000 5/15 D.D. & L. A.D.S.S./Forms/C. 2118.

# WAR DIARY or INTELLIGENCE SUMMARY

Army Form C. 2118.

D.A.D.O.S., 16TH (IRISH) DIV.
No. .......
Date .... May 1918

| Place | Date 1918 | Hour | Summary of Events and Information | Remarks and references to Appendices |
|---|---|---|---|---|
| SAMER | MAY 26 | | Received 6 Officers Mens Outfits & 5" Ambulants have been sent over to Infield 11th Div. 1st Div Sundys. Div. 15 Ambulance Pans over to Infield 4 th American Div. & Inf. General Stores received. Lt. S. C. Medcalf admitted to N° 3 Canadian Hospital both NYD from 4 th Midlands | |
| -do- | 27 | | Received 12 Lovelry Platoons and 3 Unshian & Supn guns to complete above. Sent 2 ammunition Training Ety. Guns to touching truo to American Div. Some guns & 6x40 all of Met. Equipt. for American troops | |
| | 28 | | Routine Work of the a.D.W. Puchand arrived H.Q.R. D.V. and took over duties S.A.D.W. | |
| | 29 | | Commenced duties as S.A.D.O.S. Arranged with O.C. Rest Camps that he a hymn. Close small quantity of S.A.A. & grenade for Training & Supply for American. Demanded Seven Lewis guns (one each for training Staffs of Divs) from N° 1 Gen Park. | |
| | 30. | | Inspected S.A.A. Dump at Rest Camp Nuted fair full. Inspected Sloc — Armourers Shop. Work normal. Received Seventy europers. | |
| | 31 | | Visited O.O. Indents (also reference ammo to American troops, Ampt. Total 500 Ibs S.A.A. Dummy Drill for D.A.D.M.C. Staff 1 Lt. Mathews Regt. 5th N. Staffs, Lts. Showard Tooke 40 Devons MOVES. 2nd Royal Dublins 710, and 2nd Royal Munsters 710 to D. 11 to Jan. 31 Stev. Intents handed in accordingly | Sunsull A.A.C. Sm Merchant Lieut A.D.B.S. 16th A.O. Div |

# WAR DIARY
## or
## INTELLIGENCE SUMMARY.
*(Erase heading not required.)*

Army Form C. 2118

| Place | Date | Hour | Summary of Events and Information | Remarks and references to Appendices |
|---|---|---|---|---|
| Second Army | June 1st | | Conferred with Quartermaster 4th American Division reference issue of Ordnance Stores to American Formations. War Normal. | |
| | 2nd | | Nothing of importance. | |
| | 3rd | | Demanded 393 Complete sets of equipment for 10½ M.G.Bn. 776 do do for 11th M.G.Bn. | |
| | | | 13 American Armourers reported 8/30 A.M. for fortnight's instruction. | |
| | | | Drew food from Base Aachen. St Omer. | |
| | | | Visited Offrs of AOD 39 Div. re issues to Americans. 1 Army Staff. | |
| | 4th | | Conference at Q Office reference method of supply of Ordnance Supplies to American Units. (Lieut McPhearson) advocated scheme on the same lines as worked in British Armies, which practically needed no alteration for the American Divisions. Lieut J.E. Metcalfe AOD returned from No 8 (British) Ext (200) Hospital. | |
| | 5th | | Instructions (2nd Army Area QS 2840) received for first Melcalfe AOD to communicate with ADOS. 16 Div. to have Present to proceed to HQ. 46 Div. for temporary duty. Past balance on impest of all correspondence handed over to McPhearson. | |

McPhearson
A.D. O.S.

# WAR DIARY or INTELLIGENCE SUMMARY

Army Form C. 2118.

D.A.D.O.S. 16TH (IRISH) DIV.
Date June 1918

| Place | Date | Hour | Summary of Events and Information | Remarks and references to Appendices |
|---|---|---|---|---|
| SAMER | 1918 June | 5" | Assumed duties of D.A.D.O.S. 16th Divn. from b-May. Ammunition for 4" American Brit. transport, now 1000 2nd Reef, 500 contains as a reserve. | |
| | " | 6" | 14317 American Rifles received. Arrangements made for exchange with British Rifles. Took Conference with Q and Ammunition Foreman Exchange of Rifle. Sent to Branch of American troops, handed in their Rifles & were to give Lt A.W. Buchanan M.G.C. for the 46th Divn. Have to send 550 for British Rifles. | |
| | " | 7" | 12366 Bayonets & Cartridges arrived for exchange. Also received & withdrew British Lewis & Vickers M.G.s from 4 American Divn. arranged for this to be done: all S.A.A. transferred to ammunition dump by Divns. Machine Guns to H.Q.s All British equipment & American Cartridges transferred by Divns. to ammn station to arrive as their troops. All American troops to be billeted at G of the 16th Divn. 80th American Division to take over the billets etc of the 16th Divn. | |
| | " | 8" | British Rifles returned by Divn. 13477 Bayonets, 13377 Rifles. Queries all Ammunition in from Divn. Below to have these rifles with regt. ammn BAR. average 15 rds per company. | |
| | " | 9" | 4" American Division left. Infantry Victor Bdes. & Trains left in Victor Trains M.G. Coy Supp. returning 96 Lewis Guns to make up 80th Divn. up to Scale. 96 L.G. 36 M.G. per Batn. 4 American Div. left behind British SAA, an amount of Cartridges (American 91. 4th Div.). Find to have Cartridges removed to their store. | |
| | " | 10" | Received instructions to send the British Rifles to Base (having wired o/s 3702 9.6.18) asked for ammn check. | |

Signature
D.N.F.S. 16" Div.

**Army Form C. 2118.**

**WAR DIARY**
or
**INTELLIGENCE SUMMARY.**
(Erase heading not required.)

D.A.D.O.S.
16TH (IRISH) DIV..
No. 111
Date June 1918

| Place | Date | Hour | Summary of Events and Information | Remarks and references to Appendices |
|---|---|---|---|---|
| SAMER | June 11th | | New form not for the 80th American Div. an arrangt with British Rifles. As I have arranged to cope with British Rifles have seen army of I Shown Corps. some trips for passage of American rifles to 80th Div are still armed with them. Very difficult to get info information from the Americans yet. Surrendered 6909 British Rifles to Calais today. Informed army & J.Gam. | |
| " | 12th | | Sent 12 Lewis Guns with Vickers M.Gs (taken from 4th Div) to J am Park. as per 1st army instructions. | |
| " | 13th | | 12 Lewis Guns exchanged with Lewis M.Gs sent to J am Park. today. Have left by the 3rd American Division. American Ordnance Officer & OM Staff station under instructions British Ordnance cook but him and pin appt number. Exchanging our American Rifles for British. | |
| " | 14th | | Receive orders from Scarf Thingo 16th Div No 5, 189, 14.6.18 that K.Q. and Coy any Unit of 76th Divsn. are to proceed to England but accommodation will support. Travelling. They will not BOULOGNE on 17.6.18. The 34th Divsn is to take over the Tainny. of the 80th American Division in SAMER area. | |
| " | 15th | | D.D.O.S. 34th Divsn. called reporting the Taking on of the 80th American Division. Arranged he should send a WO to each of Field and FA. of 34, D.O., Sub-WO & Clerk Stake over. Everythg, ie m/s and lenses not Untorcer, Lidents, Stores, Office MTan etc. | |
| " | 16th | | Left SAMER for BOULOGNE for ENGLAND. | |
| " | 18th | | Returned to BOULOGNE for Embarkation. | |

Murdoch A. Knight
DADDS 16th Div

Army Form C. 2118.

# WAR DIARY
## or
## INTELLIGENCE SUMMARY.
(Erase heading not required.)

D.A.D.O.S.
16TH (IRISH) DIV.
No. 1
Date June 1918

| Place | Date 1918 | Hour | Summary of Events and Information | Remarks and references to Appendices |
|---|---|---|---|---|
| ALDERSHOT | June 18th | | Arrived from FRANCE at Station at BOURLEY CAMP ALDERSHOT. | |
| | | 19th | Equipping was unit of the Division. An advance party which consisted of the Regs. Staff in advance of was arrived to Boulogne to be available as the unit arrived. No field store (G.1098) was made available when an advance party reported for requirements. Reference packed to the Office of War Office for Cheques, Requisitions, then taken to the Q.M. of Baths to the Field stores for drawing stores. This method worked splendidly. In case an arrival of units is seen. | |
| | | 20th | The following are the units of the 16th Division then Equipment: | |
| | | | 47th Inf. Bde.     48th Inf. Bde.     49th Inf. Bde. | |
| | | | 14th Leicestershire Regt.   22nd Northumberland Fus.   6th Inniskilling Fus. | |
| | | | 10th Welch Regt.     10th Lancs. Rifles     1st Gloucestershire Regt. | |
| | | | 9th R. Highlanders     11th R. Irish Fus.     34th London Regt. | |
| | | | 11th Hawks. (Pioneers).   No 3 Section D.A.C.   X. T.M. Battery.   Z. T.M. Battery. | |
| | | | | |
| | | | Lieutenant Colonel, D.A.D.O.S. 16th Div. | |

**WAR DIARY**
or
**INTELLIGENCE SUMMARY**
(Erase heading not required.)

Army Form C. 2118.

| Place | Date 1918 | Hour | Summary of Events and Information | Remarks and references to Appendices |
|---|---|---|---|---|
| ALDERSHOT | July 1st | | Company Donning with Tech. Stores. All stores on 91098 received. He and stores that are important & not available are a few spare | |
| | 6 | | parts for the 6" Newton T.M. Battery. These may be available in France. | |
| | 16. | | | |
| | 27. | | Orders received to proceed overseas. 47 S.F.y. Coy. go on 27 July. 4 D's and Divisional H.Q. go on 31st July. 48th Div on 1st Aug. | |
| | 28 | | Routine work. | |
| | 29 | | Routine work. | |
| | 30 | | Handed over Camp Equipment to BORDEN CAMP'S Area Commandant. Packing up of Office etc. | |
| | 31 | 12.30 am | Left ALDERSHOT arrived B.E.F. SAMER. Took over stores & ammunition Dept. to W.O. Officer in new Billet. Informed D.A.D.O.S. of arrival and all essentials of service. | |

Army Form C. 2118.

# WAR DIARY
## or
## INTELLIGENCE SUMMARY.
(Erase heading not required.)

| Place | Date | Hour | Summary of Events and Information | Remarks and references to Appendices |
|---|---|---|---|---|
| SAMER. | Aug. 1918 | 1st | Reported for duty pending arrival of D.A.D.O.S. of the Division. Took over several records of Stores from D.A.D.O.S. 39th Div. SAMER. Railhead touched by enemy aeroplanes when Railway Carriages & Wt. Mat. were damaged, nobody hurt. | |
| | | 2nd | Mr. Reichard in DESVRES late SAMER R. worked over likely men serving as Stores storemen. Engaged by Issue for well being. Down - weather very hot. Drew 4000 francs from Base clothing BOULOGNE for Imprest Account. Wheat for Soft, and Green Sort, Remittance of August required. | |
| | | 3 | Routine work. Visited Ordnance BOULOGNE. | |
| | | 4 | Conference at Q.H.Q. regarding Ordnance Shoemakers Shop. Crews & Mat. out of Shoemakers Sgts. from Divis to assist the Div. Shop. | |
| | | 5 | Routine work. 1000 Pr. Reps. for Div. Reserve ordered. | |
| | | 6 | Visited H.Q. and all units of 7 & R.F.A. Div. also +9 Inftry. All found them in good order as Ordnance Supplies. | |
| | | 7 | Visited H.Q. and units of B & 47 Inftry. Bde — all O.K. looked by Q to take over the Divisional Shoemaker Shop. Routine work. | |

Rudolf Major
D.A.D.O.S. 16 Div.

# WAR DIARY
## or
## INTELLIGENCE SUMMARY

Army Form C. 2118.

| Place | Date 1918 | Hour | Summary of Events and Information | Remarks and references to Appendices |
|---|---|---|---|---|
| SAMER. | Aug. 8th | | Visited No 1 Gun Park, repairing Lights, Dial Sights 303 for own M.G. Batn. O.C. Gun Park informed me there are arms etc. sent for M.G.'s in Cuvilliers by Army. There are badly wanted for Divn. Supply is cuvilliers by Army. Sealing Showering G.S.O.1 in letter. The matter up with Army. Sealing Showering Slip with to hear from 217 Employment Coy. Some question for crutches & scissors in SAMER. — Divisional Reserve of Box Respirators (1000) arriving from Base. 9 tons of General Stores received. | |
| | 9th | | Conferred with Div. Gas Officer regarding the issue of Fleur Equip. Box Respirators. Seniors that a few Eustage Respirators should be in Dn. Reserve. Spoke to Askey Corps Chemical adviser to take the matter up. Supported Reg Supplement Sketches he added to the 9109.P.T.M. Bath TMBy. to LOWREN. Had something to attend to. I then received G.S.O.1, letter on Wire Beds. S.M.R.T. Klein Saddles the attaques & Supports Sketch, ok. | |
| | 10th | | Visits to 8th Hospl. with more Box Respirators Stores urgent organised informed by 16 Divn. (one No. 5 90. M.G. 8.12 that the Divn. is about to by XXII Corps. from Aug 12/1918. Personnel in 1st Army Reserve. Visited 47th Amulc. 48th Race Amulc. Q/15 where every Eqp. ok. Inspected Reg. Ecup. Impounder, ok. 47th has no more urgent supp. Divisional Commander (Maj Gen. A.B Ritchie CMG) Visited my Stor. Officer and Workshop and Informed himself very Satisfier with Resolve. Lee him a print of me in Ordnance Supplier. 3th Chevrolet arrived & received | |

# WAR DIARY
## or
## INTELLIGENCE SUMMARY.

Army Form C. 2118.

| Place | Date | Hour | Summary of Events and Information | Remarks and references to Appendices |
|---|---|---|---|---|
| SAMER | Aug 12th /18 | | A.D.O.S. XXII Corps visited me today. Inspected Stores, Workshops, Officers. Informed satisfaction. Says Warwick mounting Medium Trench Mortars. They say are have 9 soft metal and consequently dry seals stamped and always in need of repair. Suggestion to fit flat Kent they send so request of trench mortar. | |
| " | 13th | | Visited N.D.O.S. 1st Army. Also No1 Scrap Park & felt Supply Store C. (Ltt. Howen & Scrap C.) 34 of each for M.G. Hotchkiss guns received. Dead stove required. Stores from Road take a considerable time Trucks seemed to sit & clamp on the way. | |
| " | 14th | | Cycles &c arrive - urgently required. Routine work. Visited Salvage Dump. Look over several items for repair. | |
| " | 15th | | Routine work. | |
| " | 16th | | Warning order 16th Div. No 238 received for the durning of [?] horses into the line. Engineerien work in Armourers Shop Stores, Repair shop in commence. Visited by the A.I.A. who inspected Armourers shop, made no comments except accommodation for shop too forced. | |
| " | 17th | | Purged run knotted again sigld. Lemmermo clamonds for 3" Stores. A.D.O.S. 4" Army are united clamoncels to collect scrap park stores when we go into the Line. Clearing them to come from SAM I.O.D. | |

# WAR DIARY
## or
## INTELLIGENCE SUMMARY.

*(Erase heading not required.)*

Army Form C. 2118.

Instructions regarding War Diaries and Intelligence Summaries are contained in F.S. Regs., Part II. and the Staff Manual respectively. Title pages will be prepared in manuscript.

| Place | Date | Hour | Summary of Events and Information | Remarks and references to Appendices |
|---|---|---|---|---|
| SAMER | Aug. 18 1916 | | R.T.O. SAMER unable to send to S.S. Wagons but 1 B.S. lorry in & O.H.M.S. lorry without ambulance from Army. Ordered them over to Telephone 500 hops Rispenson demanded. Wired Dnec STIS air park SAMER Railhead. | |
| MONCHY CAYEUX | " 19. | | Wired Corps Base Cverque & new Railhead. Known situation Q. 16 " Dec. 19 Refer to Chief Cccl. Y Corps re S.A.A. & lift lorries to proceed from SAMER to BARLIN on 22 Aug. To help Div. H.Q. Take men. I am proceed myself to MONCHY CAYEUX with Div. H.Q. with Adv. H.Q. | |
| " | 20 | | Visited Gun Park & tried to purchase agricul. agricul. cars as required. Also Remounts and Tramway now available, also Railway Circulation for B-Slide, arranged to take them as Lorries. General demanded "Starratt" type Circulation for Exchange thus available. | |
| " | 21. | | Informed S.R.O.1 1st Army & A.D.O.S. 1st Corps creation of Office moving also Interragent movements. Visited Office of D.A.D.O.S. 1st Div. from whom we are taking over and found Lot to be. Wired up Office & Stores, also Commencer & Got Issuing staff. | |
| " | 22 | | Corps Randall with Lorries, Stores & Staff arrived at BARLIN & reached new Stores at 6 p.m. immediately started to settle. Returns signed. Dump S.C.C. | |

# WAR DIARY or INTELLIGENCE SUMMARY

Army Form C. 2118.

| Place | Date | Hour | Summary of Events and Information | Remarks and references to Appendices |
|---|---|---|---|---|
| BARLIN | Aug. 23 | | Visited by D.D.O.S. 1st Army and A.D.O.S. 1st Corps. Both devoted Sto for Armour Shop. machinery, stores &c. Obtained Euchanol & delivered stores to units. Demanded A.A. Reg. 26 fr Divn Sers - 8pm Bath. Lotion for Divn 78. | |
| " | 24 | | Visited 1st Corps Salvage Dump. was Two Wagons in respect of rifles for armoured section. | |
| " | 25 | | Visited No 1. Mobile Workshop. Exchanged Air Cylinders. Visited No 1. Officers Clolu. Dept. Visited Main Corps Salvage Dept. | |
| " | 26 | | Visited 148 Bde H.Q. also Q.M. Stor. 11th Hants and 18th Scottish Rifles. A.D.O.S. 1st Div. Called several workshops that Chamarys in Cookers not to take suggested that if they were re-lined for took or not used to option when in the wards. | |
| " | 27 | | A.D.O.S. 1st Corps inspected Stores &c. Visited Gun Park No 1 and started SD A.A. repr. work. regnd. Enquiring for Pole remounting for Vickers M.G. (MA) 1 Pm. how 3 ready for water. The ammunition asked for arrived for these from A.D.O.S. | |
| " | 28 | | Visited A.D.O.S. 1st Corps and C.O. 1st Corps Tractors. Yet firm Mag Boff Export arrived to inspect shoemakers shops in the Division. Inspected Armoured Shop & Shops of 18th Scottish Rifles. Received orders to raise down M.G. to 4.7. 74.5" Lefts Rifle up to scale "G." affected by write immediately no Gun Park No 1. | |

Army Form C. 2118.

# WAR DIARY
## or
## INTELLIGENCE SUMMARY.
*(Erase heading not required.)*

Instructions regarding War Diaries and Intelligence Summaries are contained in F.S. Regs., Part II. and the Staff Manual respectively. Title pages will be prepared in manuscript.

| Place | Date | Hour | Summary of Events and Information | Remarks and references to Appendices |
|---|---|---|---|---|
| BARLIN | Aug 29 | | Took Lt. Turner A.T.N. Boot Experts to inspect the regenerated Boots Shop of the Division. He expressed satisfaction. Inspected O.C. Shoe Repair Battalions in the Division. Drew 72 Drum M.S. (to scale "9") from Gun Park and issued at 2 p.m. to Coy. | |
| | 30. | | Lt. Turner left for S.M.S.D.S. 15th Division. Surplus stores from S.N. Sect. this Division to Base. Base sent supplies to replace it. S.D. coys. etc. Stores repaired nvmbered by an enormous rush today. Drew Drum 3. Rifles 126. Buzzers 31. Electric torches 9. Slow prunes 5. | |
| | 31. | | Rushed work awaited S.O.S. under cover arrived from Base. (Calonne VI.) | |

Murray Thayer
D.V.A.D.S.
16th Div.

Vol 32

# WAR DIARY or INTELLIGENCE SUMMARY

Army Form C. 2118.

| Place | Date 1918 | Hour | Summary of Events and Information | Remarks and references to Appendices |
|---|---|---|---|---|
| BARLIN | Sept. 1st | | Visited Gun Park No.1 & Mater outstanding stores that are enquired required. Two artificers and one fitter (artif.) reported for instruction in Lewis Gun. Routine work. | |
| | 2nd | | Fire Drill Order. Reported Armourers Shop Lewis Gun w.1. Refs. 10 Bugles 9, training peace ajovea, artificers are-agoing insitriicon. For L. Thomas Hd/D. | |
| | 3rd | | D.A.D.O.S. 6th Corps. Routine work. | |
| | 4th | | Receiving artif'rs (M.Corps Wire 9657 d/5 of 1hm.) 24 Lewis Guns & 6 complete 22 Northumbyland Fus. and 18th Scottish Rifles to complete. Near from Gun Park, I signed. Proceeded to CALAIS to examine Soaps as used in Army from the Base, and Divisionl property repairing it. Bought 1000 prs boots and material for the Divisionl Laundry also phones & 500 min rings, hand needles & Canvas for boats & the Carriers. Reported Lewis Guns 1 Brigade 3, Rifles 51, Automatic Rifles 6 th, returned 1 French Meunathve Thermal 4 of these are bay & cannot to 16 Dn. M.G. Batn. Have no circulation with them. | |
| | 5th | | Returned from CALAIS, had I hard the Lewis Range made, as orders & purchase. Routine work. | |
| | 6th | | 12 Lewis Gins shipped. Munitions 5th Royal Irish Letter Fus. 3 Grove Munitions shipped arrival. 3 bicycles replaced. Sw Coveh. SAUNDERS WO. 16th Dn. Artillery arrived with Seath. Visited Q.M. 17th Royal Irish Dn. allin nice. | |
| | 7th | | 16th Dn. Artillery reported the Division from I am allowed 84 & head 147 b Bry. Brigades R.T.M. in the Line. Setting M.T. Coy, 142 Coy, A.S.C. MT Supple Coluth Divisional Artillery. Serth out BERLIN. | |

**Army Form C. 2118.**

# WAR DIARY
## or
## INTELLIGENCE SUMMARY.
*(Erase heading not required.)*

| Place | Date | Hour | Summary of Events and Information | Remarks and references to Appendices |
|---|---|---|---|---|
| BARLIN | Sept. 1918 | 8th | 2 NCO's and men finished Lewis Gun Instructional Course & found that all our Carriers of machine gun sparing section Lewis Gun Transports. No 7/6192 S/Sgt. ASKEW. W. No 7/1083. Sgt. MCTAGGART. D. No 07255. F/S. Ewen. HOSE. L. E. 12 Lewis Guns received, shipped stores & range. 3 Officers obtained. Visited A.O.S. 1st Corps regarding Lewis Gunnery. Started for G. Newton T.M. There are continuing making & appeal & spare discs light to made in advance Workshops & sub-marine being not of action. A.D.O.S. has seen the Corps A.D.O.S. on the subject. Visited No. 1 Gun Park. Important stores such as R.H. sights still not available. Endeavour to air exchange at 1st Army Mobile Workshops. |  |
|  |  | 9th | 11 (Canal) Lewis Guns overhauled & tested at Range. 341.5 sec Officer Equipment instructors in Armourer shop & Lewis from 1st Welsh Regt. under took. |  |
|  |  | 10th | Armourer Shop fully overworked. Arrange for Armourers who have been long in rest of the A.S.C. to move to new Armouries. 30 rifles overhauled. Services received. 8 Bicycles received to replace unsaveable to sent. Visited A.M. 11th Hant. C.P. also order. |  |
|  |  | 11th | Routine Work. Armourer Sorts Shop full of work. |  |
|  |  | 12th | Visited Corps Salvage Dump. General wear for AFO for the Inspect Return T. part unit in the Division. Inspected the |  |

# WAR DIARY
or
## INTELLIGENCE SUMMARY.
(Erase heading not required.)

| Place | Date | Hour | Summary of Events and Information | Remarks and references to Appendices |
|---|---|---|---|---|
| BARLIN | Sept. 1918 | 12th | Q.M. Stores, Shoemakers Shops & the following, and found them very satisfactory. 18th Gloucesters, 16th Lancs, 34th Londons, 5th Lewis's, 18th Welsh, 22nd Lond. 7th, 16th Div. M.G. Batt. Same limits of Divison with the matters inspected in G.R.O. 4784 and no get finds at large. Opinion seems to think stores not be Officers was still in| |
| | | 13th | Visited by the A.D.A. No 1 Henry Notice-Workshop. Supervises his satisfaction of the Running Shop, Method of work. Som men for future Economy. Visited No1 Clothing Dept. This dept keep as per the line Course, a great inconvenience to Officers. I'd take no Officer going to mile this work, Urgent requirements have to be brought by any means when lorry for a car to go to his dept. (sen) the demonstration of Carrying Lewis guns a Lindow G.S. at NOEUX-LES-MINES by the 35th Divison. This method does away with to Chiels, and so gives all the Men the Guns and Buffer gages are Parts Carr. Through team is Chiels. But the guns in the Buffer have to free in further Kens on horses of countershaft in Lewis Gruen Mules enter between 5 transports to Ken. Innes And Sy 1st Corps. Mem. 36 Oct. of Photography +24 guns of Mules amy with him refers to HQ. 4 & 9 Regh. Plc. | |
| | | 14th | Visited Res. BARLIN Bakhund Dark men. | |
| | | 15th | Routine work. | |
| | | 16th | Routine work. | |

# WAR DIARY or INTELLIGENCE SUMMARY

Army Form C. 2118.

| Place | Date | Hour | Summary of Events and Information | Remarks and references to Appendices |
|---|---|---|---|---|
| BARLIN | Sept. 17 1915 | | Routine work. A.C.P. of Gen. used by the Enemy in the forward area of this sector. | |
| | 18 | | Visited Selsoop Group Carpr. Allcutt, in charge for stores for heavy park of heavy guns. I saw Vickers Stripper overheaters & also 8 Trojans - have new pattern system runner. | |
| | 19 | | 7 Vickers guns overhauled & taken on charge. I Corps to Kinchenerser from 1st Army & V Army at 12 noon to-day. Issued 16"BH N°S 6015/11 Y19. 9.15. | |
| | 20 | | Visited A.D.O.S. 55 Division with view of taking over his Offices Notes etc. When 16"A warn were arranged to take over as i.e. Details. | |
| | 21 | | Visited OD. N°1 Clothing Depot to purchase scarf, fur offices in the field. Received order to purchase 500 Buckles for new wristlets of cope to Lewis Guns. (Auth. Q.O.C. 16"A.W. T/2. 7.81.) Purchased 109 Very cartridges & obtain. | |
| | 22 | | Routine work. Received 43 Bales of Blankets for winter service. | |
| | 23 | | heavy today. 6 HOWCHIN and taken over premises of A.D.O.S. 55 "D"ovision. Good accommodation but appearance & furnishings bad. Will be bad in rainy weathers on account of soft ground. | |

Army Form C. 2118.

# WAR DIARY
## or
## INTELLIGENCE SUMMARY.
(Erase heading not required.)

Instructions regarding War Diaries and Intelligence Summaries are contained in F. S. Regs., Part II. and the Staff Manual respectively. Title pages will be prepared in manuscript.

D: A. D. O. S.
No. .........
DATE Sept 1st 1916
16TH DIVISION

| Place | Date 1916 | Hour | Summary of Events and Information | Remarks and references to Appendices |
|---|---|---|---|---|
| HOUCHIN | Sept. | 24 | Fines up new arranged Depot. Visitor by A.D.O.S. I Corps. Pack Mule arranged. Change date from leave as a guest D.O.S. who will visit me on Sept. 26. | |
| | | 25. | Routine Work. | |
| | | 26. | Visited by D.D.O.S. I Army and A.D.O.S. I Corps. Seemed very satisfied & inspected Office Stores &c. Also Travelling and Office Reserve. | |
| | | 27. | Handed over duty to Lieut. RANDELL during my absence on leave. Handed over Cash from Imprest Account 66.5.0½d. Also 190 hrs proceeds of payments for Boot making &c. Proceeded on Leave to U.K. today. | |
| | | 28. | Routine work in absence. Armourer overhauling Lewis Guns – Bootmakers very busy. | |
| | | 29. | Routine work in absence. Armourer overhauling 12 Lewis Guns – Bootmakers – Bootmakers also very busy. | |
| | | 30 | Routine work in absence. Armourer overhauled 12 Lewis Guns – Bootmakers still busy. | |

2353 Wt. W2544/1454 700,000 5/15 D. D. & L. A.D.S.S./Forms/C. 2118.

# WAR DIARY or INTELLIGENCE SUMMARY

Army Form C. 2118.

*(Erase heading not required.)*

*Instructions regarding War Diaries and Intelligence Summaries are contained in F.S. Regs., Part II. and the Staff Manual respectively. Title pages will be prepared in manuscript.*

D.A.D.O.S. No. 7  DATE 0ct 1917  16TH DIVISION

Vol 34

| Place | Date | Hour | Summary of Events and Information | Remarks and references to Appendices |
|---|---|---|---|---|
| Houchin | 1917 Oct 1 | — | Div Oin Ordnance Stores received him salvad. The 18 pdr Gun Carriage demanded for C.147 Bat (condemned for firing). Armourers repaired 10 Lewis Guns and 2 Vickers Guns. Shoemakers Solid heeled 26 pairs of Boots. Shoe work Normal. | |
| -do- | 2 | — | One 18 pdr Gun Carriage drawn from Ordnance No 1 Gun Park handed over to the D.G.M. Do 1 Workshop to assembly before issue to another. Armourers repaired 9 Lewis Guns & repaired 6 Bicycles. Shoemakers repaired 26 pairs of Boots. Shoe work Normal. | |
| -do- | 3 | — | 1500 Rnds SAA received from Park. Armourers repaired 9 Lewis Guns & 10 Bicycles. Shoemakers repaired 23 pairs of Boots. | |
| -do- | 4 | — | Four MITRAILLEUSES and One German machine Gun returned by 16 Div MG Bn (Inf. wanted) sent them to 1st Corps Troops. Armourers repaired 12 Lewis Guns and 6 Bicycles. Shoemakers repaired 24 pairs of Boots. Shoe work Normal. | |
| -do- | 5 | — | 1100 Rnds SAA received from Park sent them delivered direct to Artillery Units who were hurrying it up. It was very difficult to locate owing to advance move during this day. 5 ant Demand stores received also for its Artillery Units, what at heavy retarded in attempts for filling, watched Kewin Guns & Bicycles by Cyclists of 96 Div Repaired. 3 Bicycles. Shoemakers Shoe work Normal. | |

# WAR DIARY or INTELLIGENCE SUMMARY

Army Form C. 2118.

*D.A.D.O.S. No. ... Date ... 16TH DIVISION*

| Place | Date 1916 | Hour | Summary of Events and Information | Remarks and references to Appendices |
|---|---|---|---|---|
| HOUCHIN | Aug 6th | | Work Normal. Armourers & shoemakers repairing 6 Lewis guns & various small repairs. 21 pr shoemakers repaired. | |
| | 7th | | Work Much as usual. Armourers rebored 20 rifles & 2 receivers, repaired 22 guns & 17 pistols. Shoemakers repaired 28 boots. | |
| | 8th | | Work Normal. Armourers & shoemakers repaired 22 guns & 27 boots. | |
| | 9 | | Routine. Armourers McVickers & two Lewis Gun repaired also 40 Rifles. | |
| | 10 | | Routine - Armourers inspected the whole of the Rifles of 48th R Irfty Bde. | |
| Sailly Labourse | 11 | | Dined from firing line to SAILLY LABOURSE. Generally firing up shops, stores etc | |
| | 12 | | Routine - Armourers overhauled 12 Lewis Guns & 5 Revolvers. Shoemakers repaired 26 prs of boots. | |

**WAR DIARY**
or
**INTELLIGENCE SUMMARY.**
(Erase heading not required.)

Army Form C. 2118.

| Place | Date | Hour | Summary of Events and Information | Remarks and references to Appendices |
|---|---|---|---|---|
| SAILLY LABOURSE | 13 | | Work Normal. Armourer repaired 12 Lewis Guns & Rifles. - Bootmakers repairing 19 prs of Boots. - Major J.C. Medcalf returned off leave. Handed over Imprest account etc to Major D. | |
| | 14 | | Returned from leave & resumed 12 Lewis Guns overhauled & repaired. 6 Rifles repaired. | [signature] Randall Capt. |
| | 15 | | 11 Lewis Guns overhauled & repaired. Also mounts, spares, pannier & barrel cover repaired. Purchased 117 mittens & carriers for S.W. Notman Rovers. — General repairs. Artz. A.D.O.S. 1st Corps. | |
| | 16 | | Conferred with A.A.D.O.S. regarding more of Armourer Sergeant's way to Knowhere. Difficulty over the LA 18 A.S.B.E. & Wheel Shrink & Iron etc hire for a day or so. Dineen will inform us when & come on. 12 Lewis Guns repaired & overhauled. 30 Rifles repaired. 7 Cycles repaired. | |

Army Form C. 2118.

# WAR DIARY
## or
## INTELLIGENCE SUMMARY.
*(Erase heading not required.)*

Instructions regarding War Diaries and Intelligence Summaries are contained in F.S. Regs., Part II. and the Staff Manual respectively. Title pages will be prepared in manuscript.

| Place | Date 1917 | Hour | Summary of Events and Information | Remarks and references to Appendices |
|---|---|---|---|---|
| SAILLY LABOURSE | Oct 17th | | Wrote himself, arrived Billy also generally of S.A. Clothing. Going to town have, 20 feet creeper & cases for moment. Received in at GUINCHY. Arrangement for moved their bathing to BILLY. Asked for Cov. 2 Gun Room repaired winchester over 1000 magazine L.G. allotted & inspected. Sent to OD Gunchy No.1. Army & civilian sloppers seen from Boot Factory. | |
| | 18th | | Received orders from Bn H.Q. to move to BILLY. Wrote Billy at 7 p.m. with 3 trumpet lorries. 1 lorry shut to remain to take up finding. Head for return in time for morning. Remained Entire during the night. Bought newts code & winchester chips. | |
| BILLY | 19th | | Moved off at 1 p.m. to PHALEMPIN for good of Spec Stores. Spoke APM G regarding winter clothing who desired to hang a to trunk to help being unable to receive it filled to tip when arrived onward & kitchens and possessed. | |
| PHALEMPIN | 20 | | Moved at 12 p.m. to TEMPLEUVE. First Convoy over before Railhead (LABASSEE). Sent returned at aim with three there ste Victor One Store of 2nd Leicestershire Regt. 34th Leicester Regt. No train. All OR so repine overcoat. Store hired lorries for 100 pairs boots also blankets. | |

2353 Wt.W2544/1454 700,000 5/15 D. D. & L. A.D.S.S./Forms/C. 2118.

**WAR DIARY**
or
**INTELLIGENCE SUMMARY**

Army Form C. 2118.

D.A.D.O.S.
16TH DIVISION

| Place | Date | Hour | Summary of Events and Information | Remarks and references to Appendices |
|---|---|---|---|---|
| TEMPLEUVE | 21st | | Sent Corp to PHALEMPIN where I found a large stock of German stores & tunics & shorts. Decided to turn some of these over to troops for future wear. Selected TEMPLEUVE to make a dump as position is now similar. As promised to British but all my feelings & receipts of loans upon the D.W. and Regimental Boots & shoes, so we all be to be traced. | |
| | 22nd | | Sent for some new German tunics & tops. Made my Hd arrangements. Visited 5th Duke Royal Irish Fus. winter everything satisfactory. | |
| | 23rd | | Sent Corp to SAILLY LABOURSE & lines up remainder of Box Resp.(Reserve) Boots (retained) all etc. also all Shoemakers & 2 armourers. Railhead now MARQUILLERS. Boots Meetings had been arranged etc. Asst. ADOS I Corps wired asking here but did not come. | |
| | 24th | | ADOS wired his Divisional Conference at Corps H.Q. to consider general question, such as the conversion of unforms during present circumstances. He had authority & wished to report on the use of Ordnance Boots urgency of Dec period. Discussed Packed Boots which were sent to Corps during & unable to receive orders to issue them, and also reported by RAOS that 5th Corps Cape were & Mint them. | |
| | 25th | | A.D.O.S. I Corps visited here today. Lecture & lecture that German machine & &c & Rifles, & be found in TEMPLEUVE - to be returned to R.A.O.G. | |

# WAR DIARY or INTELLIGENCE SUMMARY

Army Form C. 2118.

(Erase heading not required.)

| Place | Date | Hour | Summary of Events and Information | Remarks and references to Appendices |
|---|---|---|---|---|
| TEMPLEUVE | 26th | | Returned German M.G. Rifles & Matchcoat. Reported in town to A.D.S.&T. Corps. Shoemakers shop working hard, with plenty of repairs on & long machinery. | |
| | 27th | | Went to SAILLY LABOURSE & arranged for our winter clothing or kit. Railway Van stationed. All alright. & CARVIN dump all putrid. Denied Matchcoat, Soap &c urgently needed. Asked Div HQ to send supplies. Received remainder of Winter Clothes (Jerkins, Gloves &c) for at present. Built supply stand. Weather very seasonal. Sent to M'S Gun Park for wheels. | |
| | 28th | | Returned advance store Dump & Matchcoat. Asked Div HQ if I were to accept all stores from Base now. Told so by A.D.O.S. reinforcements & to accept and expect stores etc. | |
| | 29th | | Sent all divis. & Carvin & received before Winter Cloth. None so far returned at present. | |
| | 30th | | Visited all units in 48th Infy. Bde. and 47th Infy. Bde., all gun shoe in order, anyhow deficit in our establishment awaiting after a big advance. I have counted & watched to provide a good boots, clothing, trousers or shirtage at the hint of the advance, and however to equip etc. | |
| | 31st | | Ammunition shop brought from SAILLY LABOURSE & TEMPLEUVE, found good accommodation in an old Smithy shop. | |

Murray F. Myles
A.D.D.S. 16th D.U.

**Army Form C. 2118.**

**WAR DIARY**
or
**INTELLIGENCE SUMMARY.**
(Erase heading not required.)

Instructions regarding War Diaries and Intelligence Summaries are contained in F.S. Regs., Part II. and the Staff Manual respectively. Title pages will be prepared in manuscript.

*Stamp: D.A.D.O.S. No. 7, Date Nov 1918, 16TH DIVISION*

| Place | Date Hour | Summary of Events and Information | Remarks and references to Appendices |
|---|---|---|---|
| TEMPLEUVE | Nov. 1st | Cleared Müllheim. Took Normal. A.D.O.S. informs us that 29th Inf. Bde. cannot accept winter clothing at present. | |
| | 2nd | A.D.O.S. I Corps visits Advanced Sec. here today. Did not review. Collected 11 German Machine Guns found in billets in TEMPLEUVE. Examined same in Summary Sheet and dispatched to Base. Corps informed. | |
| | 3rd | Lt.Col. CHESTER, D.A.D.O.S. I Corps called & interviewed Lt.Col. ROBERTSON A.D.O.S. re duties of A.D.O.S. I Corps. General Müllheim details who is taking one stone. | |
| | 4th | Work Normal. Unit, unit also believe stores etc. | |
| | 5th | No.45 Wheel arrived. Where others urgently needed. A.D.O.S. I Corps enacted. Expressed satisfaction. | |
| | 6th | Cleared Müllheim. Clothing General Stores. Wired Base for Coy accept. all stars etc. Sub. Conductor. NASH. T. ROE & Sub Cond. SANDERS. C R.A.O.C. have awarded MILITARY MEDAL under Auth. I Corps Circular order No. 3165 of 4.11.18. | |
| | 7th | Normal. | |
| | 8th | Cleared Müllheim. Returned Brummer Stores to Base. | |
| | 9th | Being Orders & Move. Cleared Müllheim Clothing etc. Nothing known from Base. | |
| TAINTIGNIES | 10th | Move to TAINTIGNIES. Cleared in the journey, including Brummer and distribution stop. Good accommodation in billets. Phone. | |
| | 11th | Cleared Müllheim at Pute de Poste (LILLE) etc. soap, printing gear. Glorious sight the News of Armistice. Taken over quietly without by the Troops. | |

# WAR DIARY
## or
## INTELLIGENCE SUMMARY.

Army Form C. 2118.

| Place | Date | Hour | Summary of Events and Information | Remarks and references to Appendices |
|---|---|---|---|---|
| TAINTIGNES | Nov 12 | | Work normal. Much clearing point work. Workshops have plenty of work. | |
| | 13 | | Work normal. A.D.O.S. I Corps visited while here inspecting units. | |
| | 14 | | Work normal. | |
| | 15 | | Received warning order to move. Sent some stores on to TEMPLEUVE & Div Stores to remain with. Pack men today. | |
| MARTINSART | 16 | | Moved to MARTINSART. Cleared down the shop. Mr Tony ran into another at NUMES. Had to do left. Dev. truck to officers' mess for repairs. I Corps instruc. order No 3204 of 13.11.18 Challenge the return of army stores held in charge or Northern Stores. Have no reason to move unit, but Q.M. Sur on subject. to M. I Corps troops informer me out of his unit written to return such stores an Lewis M/guns. Whilst out returning M/G. | |
| | 17 | | Wrote I Corps to obtain authority for the issue of 2" blankets. | |
| | 18 | | Auth returning knob, stow, not now required, such as Anti-gas clothing, Pte. letter, Rangefinders, French Stoves etc. A.D.O.S. I Corps called. Took him to see M.M. & M.g. 16" Div + after visit. Mob. Stoves were permitted to be retained. Wired Base for 1200 Rectangular enamel 404/(9 B/) mated 16.10.18. | |
| | 19 | | Visited units. 47th Fr Reg. & Lt. Parks Rec. 49 "up" Rec inncessary all Brigades. Z.D.Q's enough. Z.D's "sub" working sew all Q.M's. | |
| | 20 | | Returned M.O. Stores Deut. to Base. Work normal. | |
| | 21 | | Blankets arrived. Work normal. | |

# WAR DIARY
## or
## INTELLIGENCE SUMMARY.

*(Erase heading not required.)*

Army Form C. 2118.

| Place | Date | Hour | Summary of Events and Information | Remarks and references to Appendices |
|---|---|---|---|---|
| MARTINSART | 1918 Nov. 22 | | Wired for Blore, Wollen (120) and Jerkins. Office Stores to closed at 7.30 p.m. | |
| | 23 | | Cpn. & 2 N.C.Os. desired half Saturday & Sunday when Office was open at 11am. Sharton Sleep. Clear Railhead (FRETIN) Bennett's C.Ro authorised. Most Stores supplied for R.E. Present. Return of Most. Stores | |
| | 24 | | Half day. Clear Railhead of Escorts Stores. Benetts also Fixed. Taken Kit for car for 26 ault | |
| | 25 | | Clear Railhead. General Stores, clothing, Rice & urgently required. Wire Base to hasten | |
| | 26 | | Visit G. Beauvoir. 2.2 Entrenchment Tw. 48° D.L. R.Q. Visit Railhead (FRETIN). Enclose at AVELIN to find accommodation for office storage. & an satisfactory. | |
| | 27 | | Clear Railhead. General Stores. Informed A.A.Q.M.G 16 Div. that accommodation found in AVELIN & that all accommodation allotted to me in AVELIN to remain at present. Quarter Master obtained permission to return present quarters until further accommodation is found. | |
| | 28 | | New Railhead from to-day TEMPLEUVE. Clear Railhead. General Stores & some clothing. A.V. H.Q. move to AVELIN | |
| AVELIN | 29 | | Clear Railhead. Clothing. Actual kerchis &c. Went to AVELIN to arrange quarter &c. | |
| | 30 | | Moved to AVELIN. Pack men. Fixed up Stores. Ammunition & Box makers staff present. 2nd Lt J. RANDELL A.D.C. reporting took up for Uk on leave. Office. | |

Tuesday K. Major D.A.D.O.S. 16 Division.

# WAR DIARY or INTELLIGENCE SUMMARY

**Army Form C. 2118.**

D.A.D.O.S. 16TH DIVISION

Vol 36

| Place | Date 1918. | Hour | Summary of Events and Information | Remarks and references to Appendices |
|---|---|---|---|---|
| AVELIN. | December 1st | | Half day allowed the men, but none of Personnel had leave all day. Cleared Railhead. Dumped 14 Trg of war rifles. Issued Peters, Kings, Pelisses & Hampers for Divisn. | |
| | 2 | | Usual inspection & Conference. | |
| | 3 | | Arranged programme of inspection & Overhaul of all the tractors, Lorries & Cycles in the Division. Kriss 12 Moderns Guns & 49th Batt. No 6 Sanitary Section, No 77, 100, 116, 174, 178 Labour Corps, 822 Coml Parks Coy returned true 3 days per day. Started Dec 4th. Sergt A/Sgt MUNN & SQC | |
| | 4 | | hay come go straight to Railhead Party Int. Who ordered them to come back by another route which take them 20 min. When extra 5 MM 16th Div. to obtain passes so that can return the same way | |
| | | | 9 pm. Ambulance Inspection of Mps. Clothing &c. work normal. | |
| | 5 | | Cleared Railhead. Kerosene &c. | |
| | 6 | | Cleared Railhead. Kerosene Clothing &c. Extras for Scots against the stores running off. HR. Worked hygienic I Corps APM informs me put in Lorries to go against the arrival from Railhead | |
| | 7 | | Half day. Sent Lorry load of Stores to 156 Field Coy R.E. at ATH. | |
| | 8 | | ADOS & Capt Collens back normal. | |
| | 9 | | Visited AR & Units 28, 47, and 48th duty Coys. Seem satisfactory, the 3rd R. Irish Fus. urgently needed for boots repair, but not back in wash. Immediate lunch to get an O in & indicate overwear (Kilt Pouches) a letter Canadian Corps in officer should inspect Boot Room, Pigeons & repair before took tram 9 am for Par SBOs & Command, Officer in the Proper HQ 100 seven late 13th Batt Gordons Bell Schon Park Section, Reach turn from 8.12.18. | |

# WAR DIARY or INTELLIGENCE SUMMARY

Army Form C. 2118.

**Place:** AVELIN
**Date:** December 1918

| Date | Hour | Summary of Events and Information | Remarks |
|---|---|---|---|
| Dec 10 | | Steamed 3" Vauxhall. Trucks are coming up in bad state. D.C. | |
| 11 | | Truck with 7 Ton General Stores here 3 days over due | |
| | | Above truck to hand today. Work normal. | |
| 12 | | Work normal | |
| 13 | | 4 Truck with Prisoners still on trail | |
| 14 | | 800 Tub washing 3½ gall. arrived. Asked O for distribution. Pamph. published from issue. A.S.M. Kayser left for Leave. | |
| 15 | | 3" Blinkers advanced (3 Trucks) 2 Juicers arrived. Europ and Portuguese. Asked Q for distribution of lamps. | |
| 16 | | 30 Stn. Sgyce arrived. 22 Tukari Coy moved here for demonstration | |
| 17 | | 12 Truck cleared at Maulhead including blankets | |
| 18 | | S.O.C. CR. waited to-day, inspected my Office. Stores, Shops etc. Expressed himself satisfied with feel to saw | |
| 19 | | Worked HQ and truck - 47 and 49 duty this also HQ. Mrs. 6 Somersets | |
| | | R Gloucesters Lt. OK. | |
| 20 | | 50 Stn. Syce arrived asked O for distribution | |
| 21 | | Cleared Railhead | |
| 22 | | do Work normal | |
| 23 | | Cleared Maulhead, Paid Men. Sgt. Sequer gone on leave. Lunenger Lorry from 50 for trip from Winter | |
| 24 | | Gave I Ton Lorry of Returned Ordnance Stores to Railhead. | |
| 25 | | Xmas day Lukari No. 77, 100. Lukari Corps moved P.S.F. Area Empr. Coy to OC I Corps troops. | |

# WAR DIARY
## or
## INTELLIGENCE SUMMARY

Army Form C. 2118.

| Place | Date | Hour | Summary of Events and Information | Remarks and references to Appendices |
|---|---|---|---|---|
| AVELIN | December 1918 | 26 | Cleared railhead. Boots, Clothing &c. | |
| | | 27 | Arrived Steeple Chase. Fine day. Sports sports. Areas of 16 Div. & 74 Div. authorised for 110 Comp. M.T. for 108, 117 Bde. horses. H.Q.M.G. visited. Stores issued. | |
| | | 28 | Issued 2 lorry loads of returned Ordnance Stores to First Enquiries still num'r'c'. 100 moved re arrangements revised to meet requirements. dumped, no room for all spit. Half dak? Pack of Conferences. | |
| | | 29 | Visited by A.D.O.S., I Corps. Work normal. | |
| | | 30 | Cleared Railhead of Henry shoes. Hangers for 45th & 58th Bdes. Div G. Loan Ten Machine Guns & Belts exchanged in Div Armouries Rep. Norton Jan 2, 1919. | |
| | | 31 | Cleared Railhead. Soap oil &c. Work normal. | |

[signature]
F.R.A.O.C. 16 Div.

Army Form C. 2118.

**WAR DIARY**
or
**INTELLIGENCE SUMMARY.**
(Erase heading not required.)

Instructions regarding War Diaries and Intelligence Summaries are contained in F.S. Regs., Part II. and the Staff Manual respectively. Title pages will be prepared in manuscript.

| Place | Date | Hour | Summary of Events and Information | Remarks and references to Appendices |
|---|---|---|---|---|
| AVELIN | JAN. 1. 1919 | | Visited all Units 1/47, 1/48, 1/49 Infs. Bdes. arranged for Q.M's to take stock of all Ordnance stores in charge, and deficiencies to be accounted for by Cmdrs. of Enquiry, or O.i/c Unit certificates to Corps etc. | |
| " | 2 | | R.A.O.S. I Corps called. Mvd. 116 Labour Coy. 500 I Corps Troops took remount. Work normal. Finished white washing main blocks & Storemen's staff | |
| " | 3 | | Half-day. I Corps wire no Ordnance store. Can be sent away for 4 days (by rail.) Trucks from Bav. on Jan. 4 & 5 only to arrive instead of 2 days as promised. The seems to be the cause since the French have our Br. Railways again. | |
| " | 4 | | | |
| " | 5 | | Half-day. Work normal. | |
| " | 6 | | Heard 178 Luton Coy & D.A.D.O.S. 11" Division were coming. Work normal. | |
| " | 7 | | Cleared Railhead. | |
| " | 8 | | Cleared Railhead & Town of General Stores. | |
| " | 9 | | Visited I. Odn. No. 1 Ord. Workshop. Arr. repair to Embargo of Rail, under I Corps programme. Visited GO. I Corps Troops. Gave for him Gums under ADOS I Corps, and received verbal instructions from him that no units to return any of their kits, equipment etc. direct. Such units [?] and stores are to report in. H.Q. 48 Bde. Visited at 22 Walkant, Inv. & Guns etc. | |
| " | 10 | | Cleared Railhead, Knee-nies, Lamps, Shells etc. | |
| " | 11 | | Half-day. Cleared Railhead. Work normal. | |
| " | 12 | | Half-day. Sunday. Work normal. | |

**Army Form C. 2118.**

# WAR DIARY
## or
## INTELLIGENCE SUMMARY.
(Erase heading not required.)

| Place | Date | Hour | Summary of Events and Information | Remarks and references to Appendices |
|---|---|---|---|---|
| AVELIN | 1919 JAN 13 | | Received I Corps instructions as to working hours for R.A.O.C. Detachment. Have try to arrange as far as possible for the Detachment to work only 44 hours per week, giving them half day on Saturdays and the whole of Sunday. Have arranged accordingly and selected NCOs and men for duty during the week but in case of an emergency, not a clearing machine. Discharged two bootmakers from Div. Boot Repair Shop for extreme laziness & misconduct — returned them to R.E. 217. Two of NCOs i/c of Shops & arranged for refreshment, tea to which they keep, and arranged for rest washing — urgent. Walk round, purchased brushes for Tailors, Disposers, Armourers Shops, & required for same. | |
| | 14 | | Work round. Armourers Shop furnished mechanics and inspectors [?] all the Lewis Guns in the Division. | |
| | 15 | | Work round. Divisional Commander has written I Corps for authority to retain (temporarily) the second pair of Boot Laces for New Entries, also asks to raise S/100 [?] for each new Laces being up to the 2nd state of the Command. Letter 15.D.N. Q.617/1/12 dated 15-1-19. | |
| | 16 | | Superior with S of 16" Div. at 10.30 a.m. Subject Demobilisation. | |
| | 17 | | Half day work normal. | |
| | 18 | | | |
| | 19 | | Corpl. RANDALL returns from leave. Clerical Pte[?] Laveloes in charge of Boot room from Pare[?] going aways. Interview ADOS I Corps to ask the Pte[?] [?] to be replaced[?] requested. | |

# WAR DIARY
## or
## INTELLIGENCE SUMMARY.
(Erase heading not required.)

Army Form C. 2118.

| Place | Date | Hour | Summary of Events and Information | Remarks and references to Appendices |
|---|---|---|---|---|
| AVELIN. | JAN. 20th 1919 | | Visited HQ 1st Army. Received return of equipment on demobilization. Also demobilization of R.A.O.C. personel. Work normal. | |
| | 21 | | Work normal. Boots sizes 5.6.7. +10 urgently required, have none up from Base. | |
| | 22 | | A.D.O.S. I Corps called. Work normal. | |
| | 23 | | Sent in returns for horses Lice. Cleaned rifles. | |
| | 24 | | Issued 600 Pullover to 108 RFA Bde. | |
| | 25 | | Work normal. No Pack Train in to-day. | |
| | 26 | | Half-day. Heavy snow. No Pack Train in. Officers Corpn at HQ Bde. | |
| | 27 | | Sunday. No work. No Pack Train but snowing again. Rations entre Guerres night. Heard to-morrow stoppe to-day. | |
| | 28 | | Pack Train arrive (2) Horseshoes. Boots (8 + 9 sizes only) Rifles and L. Brackets. J.S. stuffs in lieu for [illeg] not available in indent Bots but no Portmeses to be issued until [illeg]. A.D.O.S. I Corps called. 75.1st Very Pistol Cartridge (complete) available on HQ 1st Army. later for can to get some to our arrivals. | |
| | 29 | | I Corps wire to returned Ordnance Stores are to be sent Avelins until further notice. Work normal. | |
| | 30 | | Work normal. No Pack Train in to-day. | |
| | 31st | | Work normal. No Pack Train in to-day. | |

Sincerely Major
D.A.D.O.S. 16th Division.

# WAR DIARY
## or
## INTELLIGENCE SUMMARY

Army Form C. 2118.

| Place | Date | Hour | Summary of Events and Information | Remarks and references to Appendices |
|---|---|---|---|---|
| AVELIN | Feb 1919 | | | |
| | 1st | | Half day. Work normal. Prince of Wales visited the 16th Division. Mr Sm. HAYSON. RAOC. to be discharged. Orders were S.O.S.Q.O. 9/1/19. | 9/1/19 |
| | 2 | | Sunday. Stats closed. Work nil. | |
| | 3 | | Introduced Prince Frussen to Order J. RANDELL. RAOC. Stats as usual. Work — | |
| | 4 | | Visited ROD Faidreal FRETIN. Returned. Delivered Vans accumulating awaiting return to Base. Tel: spoke to RSOL I Corps on subject. Visited HQ. 1st Army. Saw D.D.O.S. asked that certain questions on desorganisation of RAOS should be cleared up. Wrote to RAOS hor the tools in Reserve. Charges received. Clothing etc. | S.O.S.Q.O 9/1/19 |
| | 5 | | Work normal. AROS. I Corps phoned concerning Pavecin on leave. Services, HQs. Avenir's appointment. 3 Bootmakers in the Div. Bootmakers Shop to be designated Divisional Foreman. Application to DDOS 27 Infantry Coy for replacements. | |
| | 6 | | Look over duties of DADOS. Major F.C. Medcalfe. Left for Paris on the evening of Feb. 1st. Major midwife left for leave. Only 16 Div No. 907/70 d/3/2/18 - 8 tons general Stores received from Boyne. Stats normal. Weather frosty. Work in Shops | |
| | 7 | | Sent me army to VALENCIENNES for clothing Immunities wished by APT ASVC 13th Corps as being anything to the Div. requirements of No 4. 18th Divnl. Stores still is awaiting of Bits I Quinbys at Abonchend. See S.R.O. 1020 7/2. Weather still frosty. | |

2353. Wt. W2514/1454. HP29000 5/15. D.P.&L. D.S.S./F6405/g 2118.

**WAR DIARY**
or
**INTELLIGENCE SUMMARY.**
(Erase heading not required.)

Army Form C. 2118.

Instructions regarding War Diaries and Intelligence Summaries are contained in F.S. Regs., Part II. and the Staff Manual respectively. Title pages will be prepared in manuscript.

| Place | Date | Hour | Summary of Events and Information | Remarks and references to Appendices |
|---|---|---|---|---|
| AVELIN | 8 | — | Weather still very frosty and large quantity of hoar frost being used. Work in shops rather normal. | |
| | 9 | | Sunday - Closed | |
| | 10 | | Nothing unusual occurred. Still very frosty - D.R.O. considering all work & clothing due out to units so it was thought proper to discontinue where it could be reduced. Result: Issues received nearly 50%. Stores and Office work normal. | |
| | 11 | | 4 ton General Stores received from Rnes. Weather still frosty. Work Normal | |
| | 12 | | Nothing unusual occurred - Work Normal | |
| | 13 | | A.D.O.S. 1st Corps visited shops - appeared satisfied with everything. Weather still frosty. Work Normal. | |
| | 14 | | 1 ton set in. Work Normal. | |
| | 15 | | 4 ton General Stores received from Rnes. & just managed to clean "Still thawing" | |
| | 16 | | 1 ton Stores received from Rnes thru Presenting Chief 16th operation - with lorries before thaw. 16th Divn now promised to do all its own Transport to & from Rnes. Rubbish now overhauled during slack items to help with service refits. Clothing received from Rnes supplies to units. | |

# WAR DIARY
## or
## INTELLIGENCE SUMMARY.

*(Erase heading not required.)*

Army Form C. 2118.

| Place | Date | Hour | Summary of Events and Information | Remarks and references to Appendices |
|---|---|---|---|---|
| AVELIN | 17 | — | Normal. Have no further comment | |
| " | 18 | — | Received wire from 10th Corps ordering 2/Lt P. Riley RAMC to be demobilized. Asked Division for instructions. Received 5 tons gen stores from RMS. | |
| " | 19 | — | Normal. | |
| " | 20 | — | 2/Lt P. Riley RAMC sent to concentration for demobilization. Notified Corps — asked for another man to replace. Recd 1 ton General Stores from RMS. | |
| " | 21 | — | Normal. Work Normal. | |
| " | 22 | — | Normal | |
| " | 23 | — | Stores forwarded on removal as from OO91. Lorries 24/2/19. Work normal. | |
| " | 24 | — | Recd 1 15/5 tr B.177, 1 tr A.180, 1 tr B.108, 2 tr A.177, 1.3 tr C.177. Also + tons stores + tons been stored. | |
| " | 25 | — | Attended Conference at 1st Corps in connection with internments. Clearing Stationed. Sent 30 tons of old stores to Rome | |
| " | 26 | — | Sent 20 tons of old stores to Concentration Camp for demobilization | |

# WAR DIARY
## or
## INTELLIGENCE SUMMARY.

Army Form C. 2118.

| Place | Date | Hour | Summary of Events and Information | Remarks and references to Appendices |
|---|---|---|---|---|
| AVELIN | February 27 | | Work Normal | |
| " | 28 | | Visited 47th Bn. Hqrs to see 16 men allotted for advance duties at Calais. Work Normal. | |

Samuel ? Maj.
DADMS

www.ingramcontent.com/pod-product-compliance
Lightning Source LLC
Chambersburg PA
CBHW081405160426
43193CB00013B/2111